4 WAY STREET

Also by Dave Zimmer

Crosby, Stills & Nash: The Biography (with photographs by Henry Diltz)

4 WAY STREET

THE CROSBY, STILLS, NASH & YOUNG READER

Edited by Dave Zimmer

Da Capo Press
A Member of the Perseus Books Group

List of credits/permissions for all pieces can be found on page 365.

Copyright © 2004 by Dave Zimmer

Cataloging-in-Publication data for this book is available from the Library of Congress

First Da Capo Press edition 2004
ISBN 0-306-81277-0

Published by Da Capo Press
A Member of the Perseus Books Group
http://www.dacapopress.com

Da Capo Press books are available at special discounts for bulk purchases in the U.S. by corporations, institutions, and other organizations. For more information, please contact the Special Markets Department at the Perseus Books Group, 11 Cambridge Center, Cambridge, MA 02142, or call (800) 255-1514 or (617) 252-5298, or e-mail specialmarkets@perseusbooks.com.

1 2 3 4 5 6 7 8 9—08 07 06 05 04

CONTENTS

⤔ CONTENTS ⤕

INTRODUCTION

The story of Crosby, Stills, Nash & Young is a complex and compelling tale filled with drama and magic, tragedy and recovery, frustration and triumph, resulting in an ongoing musical legacy that has endured into the twenty-first century. Musical frontiersmen who forged new ground in 1969 with a signature sound filled with soaring squalls of vocal harmony, ringing tiers of resonant guitars and vibrant stands of personal lyrics and songs that have stood the test of time, these musicians embodied the spirit of Woodstock Nation and thirty-three years later provided comfort to a shaken country, post-September 11, with their extensive Tour of America.

While often labeled a supergroup, CSNY did not come together as a promotional vehicle for disparate superstars—though, of course, David Crosby in the Byrds, Graham Nash in the Hollies, and Stephen Stills and Neil Young in Buffalo Springfield had each previously achieved degrees of success. Instead, CSN, then CSNY, came together like a band of brothers based on equal parts proximity, trust and fate in a climate of freedom, experimentation and discovery. In the beginning, the creation of this "aggregate of friends" evolved out of the freewheeling musical combustion that pulsed through living rooms, backyards and recording studios in Los Angeles in 1968 and 1969.

What happened to CSNY over the course of the ensuing 30-plus years has been told and retold many times, in newspaper and magazine articles as well as in parts of books. As a fan and later as a journalist doing research for my book, *Crosby, Stills & Nash: The Biography*, I collected original copies of many of these printed pieces, which have been stored in plastic tubs in my attic ever since.

The germination of the idea for this book began several years ago, when I realized that many of the best writings on CSNY were no longer available in print form—at least not available to most people who did not have a library-like collection of books and publications like me and my long-time friend Scott Oxman, who has maintained his personal CSNY Archives for more than 30 years. While a number of the articles have been scanned and posted on various sites on the Internet, the selections were often scattershot. Stephen Stills once mentioned to me that he would love to one day see a book that included all of the different points of view presented by the many writers who had written about CSNY over the years. Well, Stephen, many of them have now been collected together and are presented in this book.

Early on in the process of putting the CSNY Reader together, it became apparent that I would not be able to include every piece that I truly valued among the more than one hundred that were in "the first cut" and the roughly fifty that made what I thought might be "the final cut." Subsequently, I was forced to make some hard choices, whittling down the collection further with the help of my friend and editor Ben Schafer. This Reader, then, is like a selection of distinctive voices. While not the full choir, I hope the works included here are enjoyed as a rare blend.

The chance to collect and feature such a wide spectrum of writers and points of view between these covers has been a privilege. I felt my role as editor was akin to being a director, a travel guide—choosing the routes, setting the stage, then getting out of the way as the stories unfold. I am truly honored to be able to present some of the best work by such gifted writers, including Ben Fong-Torres, Cameron Crowe, Ellen Sander, Roy Carr, Peter Knobler, Ritchie Yorke, Lenny Kaye, Joel Selvin, Vicki Wickham, Gary Graff and all of the others. Their distinctive styles and viewpoints that emerged during conversational interviews and candid impressions form a colorful quilt—stitched together by the thread of CSNY. As you will read, different writers take different approaches, and elicit unique responses from Mssrs. Crosby, Stills, Nash and Young while offering special insights and personal descriptions of the dynamics of the combination.

From the start, I was intent on reducing the repetition of band history as much as possible—though different perspectives and cross-currents are presented—creating a narrative flow that I hope feels like a cohesive book. While some solo, duo, and trio ventures are covered in the course of these pages, it is the CSNY "mothership" that leads the way. During the final selection process, I focused on the pieces that contributed most significantly to an understanding of CSNY and what is special and unique about these four musicians—their artistry, their intelligence, their personalities and the forces that drive them together.

In the end, the primary goal of this book was to create living and breathing word pictures of Crosby, Stills, Nash & Young that capture moments in time—reaching back to 1968/1969 and moving through CSNY's 2002 Tour of America. To me, the beauty of collected works such as this is that many of the opinions, observations and reactions are reported in the period in which they occurred rather than as reflections—which can often be colored and reshaped by the passage of time.

Critics and fans alike have sometimes focused on how much time and opportunity for creation CSNY has wasted over the years. But the reality is that CSNY has never been about the pursuit of quantity. In countless interviews, the musicians themselves have articulated what forces and emotions are at work when they join together, noting the inherent differences between CSN and CSNY projects. The legacy of the latter is based on a remarkably small number of live performances (full-fledged tours in 1969, 1970, 1974, 2000 and 2002) and recordings—three studio albums: *Déjà Vu* (1970), *American Dream* (1988) and *Looking Forward* (1999); one official live album: *4 Way Street* (1971); one premature retrospective album: *So Far* (1974); and several tracks on the box set *CSN* (1991) as well as various soundtracks and compilation albums.

In some ways, though, while CSNY has not always lived up to public and personal expectations, the mercurial, fragile nature of the combination has contributed to its allure. The group could be there one moment, gone the next. Consequently, we have learned to savor the music while we can, because it could all be over in an instant.

CSNY, then, is not about flat expanses of consistency, repetition and production. It is about peaks, valleys and, yes, canyons. Appropriately enough, it is a particular canyon in Los Angeles where this collection of stories begins.

—Dave Zimmer

"At Large"
Excerpt from *Trips: Rock Life in the Sixties*

BY ELLEN SANDER
Charles Scribner's Sons
1973

During the late '60s, the vibrant music scene in Los Angeles was ripe with blossoming talent—particularly a loose community of musicians who were "at large" in Laurel Canyon since leaving behind their previous bands. Writer/poet Ellen Sander was one journalist who was there. In this excerpt from her 1973 book *Trips: Rock Life in the Sixties*, Sander provided an intimate, first-hand insight into what it was like to hang out and be at the elbow of everything that was happening before and after David Crosby and Stephen Stills first blended voices with Graham Nash and the CSN sound was born. Sander further covered the trio's formative phase, the recording of the first CSN album, and the addition of Neil Young for the creation of CSNY.

Joni Mitchell, David Crosby and Eric Clapton trade songs in Cass Elliot's backyard. Laurel Canyon. February 1968. Photo: Henry Diltz

Laurel Canyon was very mellow. Groups had broken up over 1967–68, the past year. Everyone was wondering what was next, a little worried, but grooving nonetheless on the time between. Days were permeated with a gentle sense of waiting, summer blew up the hills, past the painted mailboxes and decorated VW buses, and musicians were floating about. Cass Elliot's dune buggy (with a racing stripe) was parked outside David Crosby's house in Beverly Glen and she was inside visiting, sitting on a huge unmade bed with David and her old man, Jim Hendricks. They all looked forlorn. The Mamas and the Papas had broken up and Cass wasn't working. Since leaving the Byrds, Crosby had produced Joni Mitchell's first album and the Jefferson Airplane were recording "Triad." He would survive on what those two projects would bring in, but he wasn't playing and he wasn't happy about it. He had been trying to put a solo album together but just couldn't find the right producer. "Cass," he implored, "somewhere on one of the tracks on the tape in your head you must be thinking of a producer for me." Cass took another hit and continued talking about something else.

    Litter spread outward from the bed onto the floor. Clothing, blankets, boots, laundry, luggage, and some guitars filled the small room. Crosby was living in the downstairs apartment of the house, having rented the upstairs to B. Mitchell Reed for a few months, to save money. He picked up one of the guitars and sang some new songs, "Guinnevere" and "Long Time Gone" among them. He sang with his eyes closed, mustache drooping, red hair folding around his face.

The days were long and lazy, ivy-tangled hills and houses sat quietly as summer went by. The sun glittered on swimming pools pulling one day into the next with shameless ease. It was a time of endings and beginnings.

Joni Mitchell, newly come to Laurel Canyon, was decorating her cottage with antiques, colored glass, and small carved creatures. Her opening at the Troubadour had been triumphant, her career just about to crest, her music unleashing all the changes of every girl who ever hurt from having loved too much. "She's a love gangster," said Stephen Stills. "Every man within fifty feet falls in love with her."

Stills was playing some tapes for producer Barry Friedman down the canyon, some sessions done just for fun with Buddy Miles. Eric Clapton was running around the canyon with an advance pressing of the Band's *Music From Big Pink*, playing it for everyone, helping establish it as a musician's music.

Judy Collins was rehearsing her band at Cass Elliot's house, out by the pool. Everything else was going on at Peter Tork's pool.

Peter Tork had quit the Monkees and was growing a beard. When they were first casting for the television series the production company had auditioned someone recommended to them as a highly promising youngster, Stephen Stills. They liked his music but his teeth were wrong, and they didn't feel he had the wholesome, American boy teen appeal they wanted so they asked him if he had a friend. Stills recommended Peter Torkelson, who got the part and shortened his name to Tork. The series was successful. Stills went on to join the Buffalo Springfield, one of the most infectious and beloved bands to come out of Los Angeles in the mid-Sixties.

Tork became quite rich and bought an estate in Laurel Canyon behind a sentry gate that was always open and where crowds of the pop elite and the obligatory hangers-on would come all summer long and swim nude. All day long Tork was host to music people and supported a houseful of resident freeloaders. It was almost as if he were apologetic of his bogus group's huge success and afraid of being alone. It must have been hard being a Monkee at a time when rock and roll was just beginning to be taken seriously.

In time, with the money running out, Tork assembled his own group with his girlfriend, a singer, and a bass player. On the day people were coming to audition the group at his home a few friends showed up to swim. Peter cautioned them that the company men were coming and please don't freak them out by screwing on the jungle gym or anything. The guests laughed, talked about the fuck flicks made there the summer before at the pool, threw off their clothes, and jumped into the water. They took a quick dip, then ran upstairs into the sauna, afterward bathing together in a huge bathtub. Tork was desperately trying to impress the agents downstairs, whose attention was diverted to the naked nubiles who scampered about the house with the boys. Finally the band started to make music and the musicians there sympathized with Tork. "OK, everyone, let's put our clothes on, go downstairs, and show the agent people which parts to boogie to."

Somehow it didn't work. The company men went away unimpressed and the band fell through sometime later. Peter Tork began to collect $75 a week unemployment, his only income. His accountant called him frantically a few days before the telephone was shut off. "You can't support eleven people in your financial shape!" he insisted. Peter listened until the accountant was through and told him to pay the bills and let him worry about it. Some months later the money was all gone. Peter told the accountant to tell the creditors to do what they usually did when people had no more money and he moved from his estate to the downstairs apartment in David Crosby's house with his pregnant girlfriend. It was over, that was all; it was a great ride and it had ended for the time being. He accepted it completely. Stephen Stills, with a new group forming, bought the Laurel Canyon estate, shut the sentry gate, scrupulously screened visitors, and later entertained the Rolling Stones there.

Sunset Strip was a mess in the summer of 1968. Cops had moved in on it and rousted packs of kids each night. A big billboard of Lenny Bruce looked somberly over the scene.

The Mamas and the Papas had once recorded a song called "Twelve Thirty," about having once lived in New York, coming to California, and living openly and freely. Neil Young had moved to Topanga Canyon, far away from the center of L.A. "It's beautiful," he enthused. It was secluded, his house was on a hill overlooking a pasture with horses. "There are about eight girls who go around, keeping house, cooking food, and making love to everyone." Groupies and groups in pop mecca, all living out their fantasies.

• • •

Hungry, insatiable crowds were devouring concerts. Chicago had set everyone running scared and pieces of the scene were falling around our heads. We were ducking, dodging, running fierce and furiously. The leaders of this country never confronted how badly we were being torn apart until too late. The nation's children were seceding from the union and forming their own, something new and unafraid, not without its own flaws. The leaders of the new culture refused to face its insufficiencies just as carelessly as the leaders of the old. The difference between the two faded, it became a matter of which one was more fun. It was not as if there were a certain portion of revolutionary youth that had violent intentions and another portion that was pacifist; it was that each and every one of us teetered on that edge, releasing all our anxiety and energy into one another. Songs got braver. Groups got bolder. Enthusiasm was fired by response. We got higher and more finely sensed. The tide seemed unstemmable and rising. We could only push so far, they could only push so far back. It was clear that whatever it was that was happening would come to a head again and again in different and more outrageous ways until something, somewhere changed.

In the wake of Chicago, David Crosby and Stephen Stills were moping around in Crosby's Los Angeles home one morning as summer was drawing to an inconclusive end, reflecting on the urgency and at the same time the idiocy of revolution.

"I don't think a violent revolution is what we're going to have here," said David. "I think it's going to go down in a way it's never gone down before. There's going to be some of that, the spades are going to give it and they're going to get it. That's probably what will happen to the cities."

"If you don't believe it," said Stephen, "go hang out with some of those little old ladies with blue hair that elected Lyndon Johnson. The right wing is

Crosby, Stills & Nash singing on the back step at art director Gary Burden's house. Hollywood. 1969. Photo: Henry Diltz

a lot stronger than the left wing and that's where the trouble is going to come from. It's a fact. And when it starts to come down, boy, I'm going fishing!"

"I'm just trying to stay alive," retorted Crosby. "Nobody's come along and sold me a political bill of goods. I'm not playing parlor revolution, that is not a game. Those idiots are endangering us all, the best they can do is to take some of the heat off *me*."

"It's not a game!" glowered Stephen, jumping to his feet, grabbing Crosby's rifle, which was sitting in the corner of the room. "It's not a game but that's how they're playing it and it's *dangerous*, just as dangerous as having this gun in your room!"

"Of course," agreed Crosby, "if we get into that we're beat, they've got us totally covered. They've been doing it for years and they know how to slaughter."

And later, one stony night in his Beverly Glen house, Crosby sat hanging out with Carl Gottlieb, of the Committee, discussing a medal Joni Mitchell had given Crosby "for conspicuous nudity in the face of the enemy." They were improvising on the possible history of the porcelain medal for the benefit of the household and everyone was giggling at his own clever repartee.

"In this house, even bullshit is an art," I yocked.

Crosby grinned on me and squinted his eyes. "Everything is an art," he said, "and it's *all* bullshit."

David still had no gig together. Stephen had been sitting around since the Buffalo Springfield broke up, staring at the side of a mountain. They had been hanging in and hanging out with one another, jamming, singing, trying out new songs. Graham Nash, having left the Hollies, came to Los Angeles from England. It was simply the place to be in that quivering of time when everyone was in between groups and trying not to think about it while the days got imperceptibly shorter and shadows of insecurity crept up the canyon wall.

One afternoon Crosby and Stills were at Cass Elliot's house, sitting on the floor and singing. John Sebastian was there too, and some other friends and Nash dropped by. Crosby and Stills were wailing, into their songs so heavily they were unaware of where they were. They harmonized, trading off lead parts by instinct, their voices twining like longtime lovers together, sure and rhythmically. Nash followed the song in his head for a few moments and then opened up his throat and laid a high harmony over the top of them, skimming the sound, peaking the energy, completing the soul of the song. Something in the room changed the moment he did that, it was like a split second of destiny come to pass, after which none of them, or their music, would ever be the same. In the months that followed they did little more than sing together; there was nothing more gratifying for any of them to do.

7

In every other respect those boys were a mess. Crosby had never really gotten over Joni Mitchell, who had jilted him for Leonard Cohen, who had jilted her. Stills was sensing that his desperately involved affair with Judy Collins was coming to a real end. He spent half his time agonizing over it, the rest of it trying to convince her to marry him. To keep his sanity, he sang his hungry heart out. Graham Nash was falling in love with Joni Mitchell; she was falling in love with him. And quite perceptibly Crosby, Stills and Nash were falling in love with one another. Their sound sent everyone within earshot into rapture.

As winter bore down they went east to Sag Harbor, a small whaling town near the tip of Long Island, and lived there with John Sebastian, polishing their music. Session bassist Harvey Brooks was called in briefly to play bass with them but, according to Crosby, he was too good. He put Stephen Stills uptight and was dropped. Brooks didn't even know he was dropped until the day he went to pick up some tickets to join the boys in London and was informed that there were no tickets left for him.

Egos were high and flying. The sound got tighter and tighter. Recording together was going to be a problem contractually because they were all signed to different companies. A manager worked it out so that Atlantic traded a then new group, Poco, to Columbia for Graham Nash's release so they could all record for Atlantic, and it was set. They would make a record soon but for the time being they went to London to rehearse and hang out some more. A friend of long standing, Dallas Taylor, would be the drummer.

Contracts took all winter to work out, huge amounts of money changed hands. Came the first glimmerings of spring, it was time to make an album.

By the time Crosby, Stills & Nash were halfway through making their first album, it had been raining for forty days and forty nights in Los Angeles. The town was uptight, people were cabin-bound, and nothing was happening in the clubs. News of the new association of the three musicians was around but nobody saw hide nor hair of them during that time. They were locked up in closed recording sessions almost every night. On a rare night off they hung out together with a very few friends, piecing their voices together, conspiring on the technicalities and metaphysics of making a beautiful album.

Crosby's house in Beverly Glen was glowing. Inside it was all redwood, candles, and incense and they were watching TV. It was a rerun of an old Pete Seeger program featuring the then deceased Mississippi John Hurt and the three were watching intently, rocking softly to the late old man's music. The program ended and they each tried to pick out Hurt's peculiar style of double-thumbing the guitar. Stills got close and started to sing "You Got to Walk That Lonesome Valley," culminating in a self parody so perfect it might have been intentional. At twenty-four, Stills already qualified as a veteran of the American music scene. He'd been on the road since he was fifteen, his first job was as a stable boy at a racetrack down south. He craved success, money, and stardom so hard you could feel it in his voice, but he came on like a stone hick whenever he lightened up. His presence was a studied forbiddingness, he said little, smiled less, dropped perfectly uproarious one-liners when they were least expected.

Star Trek was interrupted by a visit from Jim Dickson, who came to play the original Byrds demonstration tapes for David, to get his permission to issue them as a record (the record that eventually became *Preflyte*). They sounded like a bunch of guys who used to be the Everly Brothers and wanted to be the Beatles. "Mr. Tambourine Man" swarmed out of the speakers, its euphoria filling the room, plunging everyone into nostalgia, a remembrance of innocence, a promise of experience, a paean of joy. David Crosby looked at the listings on the tape box and alerted Graham Nash. "Wait'll you hear the *next* one!" And the next one was a song that reeked of phrasings embarrassingly derivative of the Hollies, but nowhere near as good. "Wot, did you listen to oos?" exploded Nash, slapping his forehead and laughing. "Sure," said Crosby with an overly casual flip of his hand, "the folk process." Crosby winced as he listened closer and heard himself hit a particularly sour note. He giggled. "Sure," he said to Dickson, "go put it out; I'll be a sport if the others will."

Dickson stayed and inquired about the new group endeavor. By that time Van Dyke Parks and Paul Williams had joined the household for the evening. "Let's play the album," suggested Nash, grabbing for a guitar. Stills picked up another and began to play the opening riff of "Suite: Judy Blue Eyes." They ran through the entire album, singing and playing without a pause or a spoken word between them. When it was over the room was silent and stunned, overcome with amazement at how beautiful they sounded. They sang "Blackbird" as an encore and dickered about putting it on the album. Paul Williams had written a poem called "The Word Has New Meaning." David Crosby thought it might make a song and wanted to compose music to it. Paul wrote the words down and Graham Nash looked over his shoulder. "I know that word," said Nash, "it's the same word as, you know, 'all you need is word.'" He grinned at his own cleverness. David Crosby raised his eyes and shook his head softly. "Graham," he said quietly, "you are so stone beautiful I can hardly believe it."

The following evening they were at Wally Heider's studio on Cahuenga Boulevard, piecing together tracks for the album. The engineer, Bill Halverson, a beefy blond man, hunkered over the control board, locating instruments on each track of the tapes, isolating and labeling them, playing them one at a time to get a reading on each. The boys were in the studio, through a glass wall. The connecting microphones were shut off and they played and jabbered silently. They were joking around with songs, feeling out parts, and goofing on each other's riffs. A light on the panel indicated someone was at the door, a massive, soundproof door that took great strength to open. Outside stood Donovan like a scrawny scarecrow, coming to visit after taping a Smothers Brothers show. He came in and they played the tapes of material already finished. He danced around the room in delight. They all went into the studio afterward to let Halverson finish the reading; Donovan and Graham Nash played Beatles songs together.

It was time to record again. Graham Nash sat alone in the studio and played "Lady of the Island." It was perfect, that one take. Everyone was amazed. All the other songs took about thirty takes each to get right. David Crosby went into the studio to sing a second part over it. Halverson played the take Nash had just completed, opened up another track on the tape for Crosby to sing into, and rolled it. Crosby free-wheeled it, creating harmonic circles around Nash's voice. He came back in the studio and they all listened to the three parts together, one guitar and two voices. It was perfect. Halverson moved the volume controls around on the board, adjusting each part to the other and fading it gracefully at the end. Everyone watched the oscilloscope as he did it, to make sure the parts were in phase, not combating one another. The green signals formed ellipses which spun around and around, creating circular designs, winding, spreading, quivering, finally shrinking as the sound faded, compressing into a tiny agitated dot that skipped around the very center of the instrument, then disappeared. The lights were dim. Pungent smoke was heavy in the air. There was silence, heavy, meaningful silence.

The doorbell light flickered again, intruding on the almost darkness. The lights were faded up and the door answered. It was Jerry Wexler and Ahmet Ertegun. Stills, from the studio, saw Ertegun through the glass, ran through the door and gave him an enormous bear hug. They were made welcome, and in walked their faithful Indian companion, Phil Spector. They played the finished material for everyone again. "Yessir, we're working hard," said Crosby, trying to sound credible. "At two bucks a minute we can't afford to socialize. We may even bring this one in on time, Ahmet. That'll improve our reputation in the business a lot, right? Specially Stills."

Stills yocked and guffawed, the laughter hissing out in throaty spasms between his crooked front teeth. Ertegun ruffed his hair.

They hadn't yet chosen a title for the album and Jerry Wexler suggested *Music From Big Ego*. It was flatly rejected. "Guess they don't have the distance to appreciate it," mumbled Wexler, amused.

Spector, Ertegun, and Wexler left, smiling. A few moments later, with a clatter of hooves and a hearty heigh-ho guru, Donovan left and they got back to work because a more difficult task was at hand: "Long Time Gone."

The song just wouldn't hang together the way they had been playing it; it sounded overweight, clumsy, preachy, and preposterous. Crosby sang it and he sounded like Stills. It was getting to the point where they were wondering whether it should even be on the first album after all. Crosby was frustrated. Stills was impatient. Nash was concerned. The arrangement between them had been for an equal distribution of each other's songs and whose song it was, in a difference of opinion, got the last word. "Long Time Gone" was coming to a short dead end.

It was very late, they had been in the studio for nine straight hours, and had accomplished a great deal. They prepared to go home and get some sleep for the next night's sessions. Stills grumbled about putting away the guitars and stayed late. When the others left, he worked all night long and into daylight, going home on the verge of collapse. The following night the group assembled in the studio again. Stills sat at the control board and ran the tape. Out came an entirely new arrangement for "Long Time Gone" which he had single-handedly put together the night before. It was gorgeous. It churned out rhythmically, the lines meeting with the incredible force the song contained. An organ part undulated along the top of it, insinuating a siren. David was agog. He swigged a jug of wine, went into the studio, and sang in an entirely original way. As if possessed with the immensity of the music, he broke through. He was tearful at the end. "I finally found my voice," he said afterward. "Five years I've been singing and I finally found a voice of my own. Every time I had a lead vocal part with the Byrds I choked up because I was so scared. But these two loved me enough to let me find my own voice."

He thanked and complimented Stills on the arrangement for the song. "You make me ashamed of myself," he said, with no small measure of admiration, and even more affection. Stills, who always had trouble accepting open praise from anyone, had his eyes down, and when he raised them the expression on his face said plainly and silently: *I arranged your song better than you could have in a thousand years. And don't you forget it.*

Crosby didn't respond in kind but it wasn't lost on him. The time for *real* ego clashes was yet to come. They loved and fought like a family. They made up to make music and money together. None of them singly had the same kind of weight that they had together.

Joni Mitchell, who was working on her own album at the time, dropped in later that night with a big box of homemade cookies. She played some of her new songs for the group. One of them was a song for Nash, whom she'd nicknamed "Willie." She sat at the piano and sang, "I will be his lady all my life…." Nash leaned over the piano, enchanted, and went misty. Crosby watched from across the room, the utter heartbreak on his face unnoticed by either one of them, they were so wrapped up in each other.

11

Crosby, Stills, Nash & Young, with Dallas Taylor and Greg Reeves, at Stills' house. Los Angeles. August 1969. Photo: Henry Diltz

Shortly the group started recording again, doing the last vocal over-dubbings on another song. It worked out so beautifully it even surprised them. Everyone was excited, happy, enthusiastic, tired, and hungry.

A break was called. The road manager, Chris, had brought some wine, cheese, fresh fruit, and deli. Everyone dug in. Joni and Graham were off getting silly with one another. Stills muttered something about getting back to work. Crosby slumped on the couch, cuddling a bottle of wine. He closed his eyes and his mouth curled into a smile behind his mustache. "I've never had so much fun making an album in my entire life!"

In the interim between the time the album was released and their first tour, they had to find a bassist and a keyboard player. Stills got hold of Bruce Palmer from the old Buffalo Springfield. Palmer tried, but couldn't cut it. "It got low," reported Crosby. "We were trying to tell him he wasn't making it and he was insisting 'Yes, I am.' It was really hard to do." A bassist appeared, a very young black boy from Motown who played with them on the first tour only. Stills politicked very hard to get Neil Young into the group over Crosby's and Nash's angry protest. Neil Young was still intent on making it as a single artist but he hadn't broken out yet. By that time Stills was the power in the group and he wielded it with a heavy hand. They broke up, re-formed again. Young was in.

The original group was Crosby, Stills & Nash. The deal was that they were financial partners in the group. They wanted a bass player and keyboard man to tour with them for salary, earning good money but considerably less than the group members, who would get percentages of whatever they brought in, which by that time, they knew, would be in the area of seven figures. Halverson got a small percentage of album receipts, but one that amounted to a great deal of cash. They finally, under protest, gave Dallas Taylor some kind of minute percentage also. Greed was setting in. But when Neil Young joined the group, he joined not only as a keyboard man but as a writer and an additional superstar, giving the group more weight. He was cut in for a considerable percent. Their concert price skyrocketed, promoters revolted but gave it to them, having to raise their ticket prices. Dallas Taylor so resented Neil Young's getting a bigger piece that he would mess him up on stage. Young hit the roof when it happened once too often to be accidental and insisted he'd never play on the same stage with Taylor again. Taylor had to leave the group.

They never got a better drummer. They broke up and re-formed again and again. Finally Graham Nash, who by that time had parted company with Joni Mitchell, became involved with Stephen Stills' new girlfriend. Stills, whose heart was much too vulnerable, said he was splitting for good. That time Ahmet Ertegun believed him and was quite upset about it. "That group is gone." He shook his head mournfully. "The only way they'll get back together again is for the others to go to Stills and ask him to come back and they'd never do it, they're too proud and they're too hurt."

"Why don't you just get another bass player," suggested a well-connected friend. "I know of one just as famous, talented, even as crazy as Stills and I bet he's looking for a new band himself."

Ertegun, without a trace of suspicion, brightened and bit. "Who?"

The friend grinned triumphantly. "Paul McCartney."

Ertegun, without missing a beat, replied, "That's a tremendous idea, tremendous! I wonder how much Apple would give me for the other three?"

• • •

CROSBY, STILLS, NASH, YOUNG, TAYLOR AND REEVES

BY BEN FONG-TORRES
Rolling Stone
December 27, 1969

Rolling Stone magazine, founded by Jann Wenner in San Francisco in 1967, supported CSNY fully in its pages in the early days. Ben Fong-Torres, one of the magazine's editors and primary feature writers, had an acute understanding of what CSNY was going after and achieving. In this article, he got inside the machinations of the band off stage, on the boards and in the studio—where the musicians were recording tracks for what would become CSNY's *Déjà Vu* album. Fong-Torres also picked up on the powerful impact the group was having on its audience.

Taylor and Reeves with CSNY. Laurel Canyon. 1969. Photo: Henry Diltz

ehind them, a crew is setting up the curtains that'll hide their electric gear until their acoustic "wooden music" is finished. The curtains are black; there'll be no light show behind Crosby, Stills, Nash & Young. It's Thursday, 5 p.m., rehearsal time at the Winterland Auditorium in San Francisco. Four hours before showtime, a guard is already stationed at the old Ice Capades auditorium's doors, brusquely challenging all visitors. Outside, in brisk autumn weather, a line has already begun, a sidewalk full of hair and rimless glasses and leather and boutique colors. These people know Crosby, Stills, Nash & Young won't go on until 11:30, maybe midnight. No matter. They'll grab good places, on the hardwood floor at the foot of the stage. And they'll wait.

Dallas Taylor, the drummer, is moving along the foot of the stage now, out of view from Stephen Stills, who's on the stage testing out the piano. Taylor is edging toward Stills, a mischievous smile splitting his wide face. Suddenly Taylor springs, with a shout, up behind Stills, his right hand now a pistol, and kills him. Stills stiffens, falls off his seat, and plunges straight into David Crosby and his guitar, causing a crashing cacophony.

Across the floor, in the first row, Graham Nash is stirred alert by the noise. He's trying to put together the order of tunes they'll do that night. He calls out to Taylor, who's scampered off to stage center by now: "Hey, man— not around *axes*, man! Not when you're near an *axe!*" Taylor nods, but he knows that any minute now, Stills will have to come back and kill him.

More puttering around the stage, and suddenly it happens. Stills pantomimes the biting of the ring off a hand grenade, waits three seconds, and stuffs it into Dallas' mouth. Taylor dies beautifully, jumping out of his skin at the "explosion," then falling six feet down off the stage, tumbling, landing on his back.

Nash looks up again. No guitars in the way this time. He smiles, shakes his thin, rectangular head, and goes back to work on his list.

Crosby, Stills & Nash coasted up the charts effortlessly this summer behind Blind Faith, Creedence Clearwater Revival, and Blood, Sweat and Tears. Then their single, "Marrakesh Express," hit the Top Twenty, then "Suite: Judy Blue Eyes." Then *Crosby, Stills & Nash* surged up again, past Blind Faith and the others.

And here's Graham Nash, sitting atop a softly vibrating bed in Steve Stills' motel room in San Francisco. "We didn't have a *band* with just the three of us," he is saying.

Crosby, Stills & Nash was Crosby and Nash and Stills, and Stills on organ, and Stills on bass, and Stills on lead guitar and overdubs of additional guitar tracks.

"We could sing the LP," Nash said, "but we couldn't play it." For their concerts, he said, "we knew we'd have to represent the sound we had on the album. Now we have a whole different band."

Dallas Taylor, with the trio from the beginning—which was a year ago—has been joined in the background by Greg Reeves, a quiet, nineteen-year-old bassist right out of Motown's studios. And in the foreground—for most intents and purposes—is Neil Young.

Neil Young, composer, guitarist, singer with Buffalo Springfield, has written a couple of tunes for the next album—"Country Girl" and "Helpless," the latter including a chorus featuring the high, soaring harmonic blend of Crosby, Stills, and Nash—the blend that is perhaps the prime attraction of the group.

But mostly Young is a luxury, a utility man as well as yet another creative force. In the studios, where Stills reigns but shares the reins with opinionated co-producers Nash and Crosby, Young is a solid fourth corner. "We may shape the album," Stills says, "but Neil'll come along and give us that extra thing."

Nash choruses: "He gives us that bit of direction we may need to resolve a question. He's good at making records."

Young was brought in, says Stills, because "we wanted another life force. I always wanted another rhythm section. But instead of a keyboard man, we thought, why not a guy who could do other things—write songs, play guitar, be a brother and stuff."

Here come the life forces into the dressing room at the Winterland Auditorium. It's 1:30 a.m. Sunday now, and they've finished their third of four nights. Dimly lit in red, the room is small, attic-like, but serves as an adequate shelter. Crosby, Stills, Nash & Young—and Taylor and Reeves—want some quiet. David's voice is out, and he's slumped into an old couch, his doctor standing over him.

David had had a sore throat since midweek and that day— Saturday—had wrecked it at the Vietnam Moratorium rally in Golden Gate Park. "He got carried away a bit," Nash had explained that evening backstage. "After the first thing he yelled he realized he'd gotten carried away." By the time he'd reached the stage at Winterland, with each of the 5,000 onlookers able to shout louder than him, he knew he'd paid the price. He could talk best by nodding, smiling and crinkling his 'stache up and down. At the mike, Graham explained David's ailment, and the crowd cheered at their disabled compatriot.

Stephen, seated with an acoustic guitar on his lap, and facing David, went into "Suite," and the audience, just itching for the group to justify the adulation they'd already poured onto them, whooped it up. Slowly, surely they galloped through the number, until the verse beginning, "Chestnut brown canary, ruby-throated sparrow." And when David reached the high note (…"thrill me to the *MAR*row"), he couldn't make it, and the crowd applauded, anyway, while he grinned sheepishly and held his throat.

From that point on—what, five minutes into the set—Crosby was pretty much out of it, and the program had to be overhauled. David's usual solo, "Guinnevere," was dropped, along with a couple of duets with Nash. Young stepped in to sing a medley of Buffalo Springfield tunes, on acoustic guitar, with Stills. Later, during the electric half of the set, David came back to spend the remains of his voice on a hoarse facsimile of "Wooden Ships," and Steve substituted for him on "Long Time Gone," a song clearly Crosby's.

The audience, like the ones in New York and Los Angeles and Big Sur, cheered everything they did, of course, but Crosby, Stills, Nash & Young knew better. The night before, they had done their now-standard encore number—a brief, softly sung untitled Stills composition about freedom, once submitted to *Easy Rider*—and gone offstage and around the rim of the old ice capades rink and settled into their dressing room and lit up a snack, and those 5,000 freaks on the other side of the curtains were still stomping on the floor, in their seats high in the distant balconies, screaming for MORE! MORE!

Now, tonight, it was pretty quiet by the time they'd reached the room, and Steve Stills is looking up. "Hey, you should have been here last night," he says, clear eyes dancing. "Tonight was okay, but it was nothing. You know, we were *bored* out there."

And you know he's being straight. "Down By the River," the Neil Young composition used as the set-closer, seemed interminable, with Stills and Young trading lead guitar runs and strums as laconically as two men lobbing a medicine ball back and forth. Graham Nash, he of the high, silken voice, sang out a trade-off riff of his own and knocked Neil out for a second, but that was a second out of thirty minutes. Still, the audience went crazy.

Crosby, Stills, Nash & Young can do no wrong.

It could be the flawless harmony—tight as the Everly Brothers, soft as Simon and Garfunkel, melodic as the best of the Springfield. It could be reports, words-of-mouth about the mini-Woodstocks they'd created wherever they performed, sending out those effortless good vibes and coming off like "gentle free spirits." It could well be a mass appreciation of their aversion to the kind of hype that flooded Blind Faith, making them an instantly high-priced, out-of-reach act.

Young speaks: "See, the thing is, everybody—especially David—is a controversial character. Everybody has an opinion. Like, I like to watch David just to see what he'll do next." Crosby, of course—the Byrd who was canned because he wanted to speak and live as well as sing his political piece. He was deeply hurt when Roger McGuinn fired him, and over the months since his departure, Byrds interviews seemed to build a picture of Crosby as a huffy, moody, intolerable, hard-to-work-with sort of man.

Crosby loves Stills, Nash and Young, and these days he and Nash play cheerleaders at recording sessions, conducting playback parties for visitors and heaping mountains of praise onto their colleagues. "This is the best music I've made with other people," old folkie Crosby beams. Away from the microphones, he spends his time behind and to the side of the control board, hand-cleaning future refreshments or bouncing up and down, his jacket fringes dancing to the music of the band.

"Don't ask him about Christine," someone had suggested, thinking of David's fragile shell, so badly cracked when his lady of three years was killed in a bus collision on a road near his Novato home. David had been spun nearly out of his mind; the group cancelled what would have been a wonderful stay at the Winterland with close friend John Sebastian on the bill with them, and David took to the waters, to a schooner, to escape. He and Graham went to England to stew and unwind some more, and when he returned, he dove into the task of keeping himself busy, keeping up the happy front—so

David Crosby. 1969. Photo: Henry Diltz

that even his close friends would say don't ask about Christine. But David, knowing he can't, doesn't try to suppress the memories.

"Man, you *know* how hard it is to find a good woman, a woman who's just right—who's with you on every single level. Every step of the way it was right." And Crosby's looking straight at you. "But you know," he says, "at least you know that it *can* happen."

And David knows that, just as he is not alone in his joy over his music, he is not alone in his sorrow over lost love.

Stills lost Judy Collins and let his broken heart dictate the words: "Listen to me baby—Help me, I'm dyin'…It's my *heart* that's a-sufferin', it's a–dyin'…That's what I have to lose…"

Graham recently parted from his lady of the island, Joni Mitchell, and bassman Reeves "had a slump," as Stills puts it, over a chick. Both Dallas and Neil are married, Neil to a lovely girl with Judy Collins-eyes named Susan.

"We've canceled a lot of studio time because of woman troubles," Nash says matter-of-factly. "Women are the most important thing in the world next to music."

Lament Over Lost Love provided the theme—if anyone ever listened to the words—of the first CSN LP. But where "Suite: Judy Blue Eyes" opened and paced that album, a song called "Carry On," written by Stills, will set the tone for the second:

> *Rejoice!*
> *Rejoice!*
> *We have no choice!*

Stills, for what it's worth, is apolitical. In that song, written when the war was still largely confined to Sunset Strip, he wrote of pickets proclaiming nothing stronger than "Hooray for our side." In the song he wrote for *Easy Rider*, he encapsulated the movie:

> *Find the cost of freedom*
> *Buried in the ground*
> *Mother Earth will swallow you*
> *Lay your body down.*

—But it was a synopsis, rather than any analysis.

And at the Vietnam Moratorium rally at Golden Gate Park, he pounced on the piano to pound out a searing, machine-gun-paced version of "For What It's Worth"—but only after shouting to the 125,000 marchers: "Politics is bullshit! Richard Nixon is bullshit! Spiro Agnew is bullshit! Our music *isn't* bullshit!"

Stephen Stills. 1969. Photo: Henry Diltz

As Neil put it: "Steve's trip comes to its head when he sings."

Stills is the one most intensely involved in the group's music. Onstage he bounces from acoustic guitar to piano to organ to electric lead. In the studio he directs most of the sixteen-track traffic, writing and singing the most songs, overdubbing the most tracks, staying the longest time. On several occasions, working on the second LP, he put in sixteen-hour days at Wally Heider's studios, located on the fringe of San Francisco's greasy Tenderloin district. He stayed at a motel a few blocks away. It was like he was on call to the burgeoning music, constantly in labor, in his head.

"We—Dallas and Bill [Halverson, their engineer] and I—spent last night till six doing *this*," he said one evening at Heider's, holding up a stack of one-inch tapes, "Drunk out of my head playing the piano," a backing track for one of the tunes on the new album. "That's what you can do when you've had a gold record." Beaming like a newsboy who's just won a trip to Disneyland and gets a day off school.

In the studios, Stills is a man of restrained excitement, of quiet pride, of nonstop devotion to the task of making records. "Steve's whole thing right now is the group," Young says. "It'd be impossible to have everybody into it as much as him. It'd be complete bedlam."

In the studios, Young, who so often clashed with Stills in the illuminating but frustrating Springfield days, generally stands back with his scowling demeanor, big-eyed, glowering stares shining out between messy black curtains of hair. He seems content in the shadows, thrashing his guitar mercilessly, like a country bluesman possessed. Young is a satisfied man—secure with his own band, Crazy Horse, on Reprise Records, as well as this insane, perfect gig with this superb, if not "super," group.

While Young and Reeves work out their backing for Young's "Country Girl," Stills hovers over engineer Halverson, and, with Nash, act as unofficial conductors. Nash picks out the slightest flaws in tuning, pacing, whatever—and relays his thoughts to Stills. Then the group works it out, a team considering each member's errors as remorselessly as a mistake in mathematics. It's a stop-go-stop-go process, of course, but somehow a song flows, maintaining its vitality and spontaneity, through the constant self-interruptions.

Neil, the fourth corner, is wandering off from the control room following a playback on the track he and Reeves have just done. "What we've got to do is listen with an eye to simplicity," he says. "Think how we can make it bigger by simplifying it."

Steve Stills was the leader of Buffalo Springfield, but Neil Young stood out the most—tallest, darkest, fringiest, flashiest, writer of some of their best songs ("Nowadays Clancy Can't Even Sing," "Expecting to Fly," "Flying on the Ground Is Wrong"). And he was the most desultory and uppity, quitting

Graham Nash. 1969. Photo: Henry Diltz

the band twice before they folded, saying he never wanted to be in a group anyway, just like you wouldn't have Dick Nixon to kick around anymore.

But this is different. Young is in two groups, right, but, as he explains, "Before I joined Crosby, Stills & Nash, I made it clear to both sides that I belong to myself."

First, there was Crazy Horse, who'd backed him up on his excellent second LP, *Everybody Knows This Is Nowhere*, and who're working with him now on his third album. They're also setting up a concert tour beginning in February, with Neil, of course, in the lead.

"I didn't want Crazy Horse to die just as we were getting it together," he says. Crazy Horse is important to Neil as a counterbalance to the tight, structured kind of music Crosby, Stills, Nash & Young put out. "Crazy Horse is funkier, simpler, more down to the roots." Young has production control with Crazy Horse. "I dig a lot of bass and drums, man. To my mind, the bass drum should hit you in the stomach. Listen to *Nowhere* at the same volume as *Crosby, Stills & Nash* and you'll know what I mean."

Neil will do Don Gibson's country classic, "Oh Lonesome Me," on the LP with Crazy Horse. He couldn't hope to do that kind of thing with CSNY. "But then, see, I have another side to me, and it's technically too far advanced for Crazy Horse—so the other band plays that. They complement each other inside me."

Young is contracted to Reprise and has a "temporary contract" with Atlantic, the remains of his five-year pact as a Buffalo Springfield. Hassles are few since both companies are under the Warner Bros. umbrella. Neil works out his tour schedules so that both bands know when they can have him.

With Crosby, Stills & Nash, Young sings lead on his numbers—with the three others building waves of smooth harmony behind his high, hard-edged voice. He does very little harmony singing himself. "I don't consider myself to be a background singer."

Away from either band, in what he calls his own scene, Young is getting into the movies—writing a song for *Strawberry Statement* and doing the score—with Crazy Horse—for *Landlord*, "a racial comedy about a white guy who buys a tenement house in Brooklyn and kicks out the floor to build a New York City-type townhouse out of it and gets into all kinds of shit…voodoo fights and things—with the neighbors. I think one of the stars is Pearl Bailey."

Young is also getting into filmmaking, beginning with a brand-new Beaulieux Super 8, which he coos over like a newborn baby. He and Susan (who he met last year at a Topanga Canyon cafe she ran) are planning to move slowly toward "the big time," when they'll blow their scored films up to 16mm and have showings at the Topanga Community House, where the local women's club usually meets.

Neil Young. 1969. Photo: Henry Diltz

Neil, married for a year now, plans to stay at his redwood, hillside Topanga Canyon house, their home since August 1968. He's even building a sixteen-track recording studio under the house.

Crosby has settled into a ranch in Novato, in north Marin County, and Stills is looking for a house in Marin County. Reeves lives about ninety miles north of San Francisco, in Guerneville. If Young moves, he says, it'll be to either Big Sur, on the Pacific Coast, or back to Canada.

Whatever the specific moves, there is a migration, of spirit, at least, to San Francisco. Stills and Crosby are close friends of Jefferson Airplane and the Grateful Dead family. Stills joined the Dead at the Winterland at one of Bill Graham's San Francisco Band nights and he and Garcia got it off for four or five numbers. And Jerry, in return, is now an unofficial member of CSNY. Garcia dropped by a session at Heider's one night and ended up playing steel pedal guitar on Nash's light, once only slightly country tune, "Teach Your Children."

"We just sat down and fiddled awhile," Stills said, "and we got an incredible take. The opening lick will just curl your whiskers."

Jerry Garcia and Neil Young, and young mojo man Greg Reeves, cool half-black/half-Indian bassist, and Clear Light Dallas Taylor, all in addition to Crosby, Stills & Nash. If the first LP was a milestone, this new one should be an event.

The first LP hid the words, lovingly intertwined harmonies and impeccable instrumentation shading out most attempts at verbal communication. David's song of political strife and personal anguish, written after the Robert Kennedy assassination, came out of the speakers like a celebration, an orgy of joyous voices. So did Stills' "Suite." How can you cry when you sound like a sparrow?

The words are on a separate sheet and you can read the poetry of Crosby's "Guinnevere" (which he now has difficulty singing, remembering Christine) and the unrhymed agony of Stills' two paeans, any time.

Back when the LP was being recorded, Stills, the construction engineer, had said, with tongue only slightly in cheek, that all he wanted to do was produce "the best album of the year." He and his friends put out one of the best, certainly, and they all had a right to float through the spring months, as they did, waiting for the LP's release. Now, Nash says, "Our main complaint on that LP was that it sounded so constructed. This will change with Dallas and Greg, and with Neil and me branching out more." Still, "it's all one man's opinion, whatever's said. So we have three one-man's and that's it."

Next time around, Nash says, it'll be the same as before: "Our main thing is to set some kind of a mood; our only rule when it comes to choosing our music is to pick something that gets us off."

At this point, Crosby, Stills, Nash & Young are coasting. Their next album is pre-sold gold, judging by their success across all fields of music—

Top Forty, "underground" and "middle of the road" (their LP even reached Number Thirty-five on *Billboard's* Soul chart). Their concerts, stage-managed by Chip Monck Industries, are near-perfect, the group relaxed in subdued light, making love with their soft, bluesy, acoustic music, slapping palms, soul style, after a particularly well-executed number, then charging on with a full load of amps and speakers, then collapsing in a circular embrace at the end of it all.

And their heads are straight. Stills, aglow with recognition as some sort of musical genius after those two years with Buffalo Springfield ("a sheer case of frustration," he calls them), won't play huge arenas where sound is sacrificed for a bigger gate. "And we won't have any ball-busting one-night tours. So you make your million dollars in thirty days instead of fifteen, right?"

Money, and lots of it—right. But not so fast that the music, or the mind, is sacrificed. "The important thing," Graham Nash says, "is to make people happy."

"The good thing," Stills says, "is to do a concert and instead of giving them one big flash, leaving them with flash after flash, and people come up and say—softly—'Thank you...thank you, man.'"

CROSBY, STILLS, NASH & YOUNG: FLYING FREELY

BY LENNY KAYE
Circus
March 1970

Writer/guitarist/author Lenny Kaye was obviously taken with the musical chemistry that CSNY created together in the group's early stages. The power of the music led the way and Kaye's take on it and the musicians themselves was free of cynicism. Kaye was a published feature writer before he became a fixture as a guitarist with the Patti Smith Group. Most of the quotes that are scattered throughout were drawn from interviews conducted by writer Ritchie Yorke during CSNY band rehearsals in 1969 and later packaged as "A Rap with CSNY."

Nash, Stills, Crosby and Young during an acoustic set at Campus Stadium, University of California, Santa Barbara. November 9, 1969. Photo: Henry Diltz

Thornton Wilder once wrote a book called *The Bridge at San Luis Rey*, where he followed back the lives of the victims of a bridge collapse, to find out just what it was in their personal histories which made them cross a certain point at a certain time.

Crosby, Stills, Nash & Young are like that: four paths that came together because of a fate-like series of circumstances with each moving at his own speed and pace, entering the wave just at the particular point when he could best handle it. Call it magic if you will, or a weird kind of luck, but everything that happened to the group in its formative phase came like clockwork, working like a jigsaw puzzle, each piece falling neatly into place.

Take Neil Young, for instance. Throughout the cutting and eventual release of the first album, he remained apart from the group, content to work on his solo LPs with Crazy Horse, a Los Angeles band. And then: "Their first album was a very successful album," says Young. "Stephen played organ, bass and guitar on it, and anyone knows that Stephen can't play organ, bass and guitar on stage all at once, and sing too, so they had to get somebody else as an instrumentalist, and I was the only one they could get at the time." Take also Dallas Taylor and Greg Reeves, who now comprise the electric rhythm

33

section of bass and drums. They also seemed to arrive just at the time when they were due, as punctual as if a time clock awaited them. Taylor, formerly one of the Clear Light drummers, had been with Crosby, Stills & Nash since the first album, in a more or less official capacity. (If you look hard, that dim face behind the screen door on the back cover belongs to him.) Reeves, a 19-year-old ex-Motown bassist, arrived when it was about time for them to go on the road. Appropriately, they call him the "missing link," the final, magical chunk that fell in precisely when necessary. "All of a sudden," explains Steve, "Bruce [Palmer, the Springfield bass player who had previously been slated to go on the road with them] wasn't there and Greg was..."

But if all Crosby, Stills, Nash, Young, Taylor and Reeves had going for them was a sort of destiny-ridden luck, we might be able to end our story here, wishing them a fond bye-bye as they moved straight toward the now classic Kamikaze plunge we've seen so many times before. Somewhere along the line, though, the script was changed. All well-experienced, seasoned musicians, they realized the pit-falls that were to be strewn in their path and conscientiously set out to avoid them, one after another, each as they came up in turn.

For one, they didn't make the mistake of rushing their first album. Say what you will about *Crosby, Stills & Nash* being a record lacking in spontaneity, a pretty thing with little else but perfection to recommend it. It is a fact, though, that it has stayed together over these many months, kept up its relevance and not become a disc which could easily be filed between Critters and Cyrkle, left there slumbering, forgotten for weeks on end. As time passed, it seemed to have the capacity of gradually becoming more of a friend, with things not apparent in those first hurried listenings coming slowly to light. And can you deny that it has been a joy to hear "Suite: Judy Blue Eyes" programmed on your local AM station? One of the powers of that first album was that it encompassed an incredible variety of styles and fields. At one and the same time, it made a name for itself on the Top 40 listings, the underground stations, the easy listening charts, and even, by some weird stroke, made it up to number 35 on *Billboard's* Soul Survey. Not bad for a little ol' first effort.

Their new release, *Déjà Vu*, clears up any of the clouds left over from the first album, not only beautiful on a musical level, but fine, alive, a bit looser as well. Credit Neil Young, if you're looking for a source, for it is easy to see that it is he who has brought a much-needed immediacy to the group's sound. Credit also the solid feel of the bottom as laid down by Messrs. Taylor and Reeves, for in their new-found roles, they've given a roundness to Crosby, Stills, et al that adds the final touch to an already near-perfected band.

In any consideration of the group's sound, however, you have to turn your attention to the principals in the group: Crosby, Stills & Nash themselves. Regardless of the general excellence of the newer additions, it is they

CSNY jam during the electric set at Balboa Stadium concert, San Diego. December 21, 1969. Photo: Henry Diltz

who have constructed the harmonic blend which takes the music into those special realms, who work with that special alchemical hand that turns everything they touch into pieces of gold. Stills is probably the major force in the studio, overseeing production, spending long days and nights among vast arrays of electronic instruments, finding the exact way in which the sound can best be preserved. Along with Nash, whose trilling vocal flights still remain as strong as they were in the days of the Hollies, and Crosby, almost abashed and sentimental, the three have created a form which is easily the end of decade version of that mid-'60s genre known as folk-rock. When it works, and it usually always does, there are few who can come close to matching the purity of the blend.

In live performance also, Crosby, Stills, Nash & Young seemed to veer away from the dangerous edges of superstardom. Rejecting the approach of Blind Faith, who immediately began playing for huge, stadium-sized crowds where it was not so much the music, but the spectacle that was important, CSNY seemed to lean toward the smaller-sized halls, the Fillmores, the large clubs, places which could better handle their basically unassuming music. It was a good move. In one swift stroke, they made themselves more accessible to their audiences, up close, where you could almost reach out and touch them. Instead of seeing these little specks somewhere off in the distance, Crosby, Stills, Nash & Young were right up there,

35

letting you be a part of the music and the group. You could sit there and watch it flow off the stage, letting it come down and settle, covering everything in a big wide swath of good feeling.

The group's live performance has served to keep them going, gaining rather than steadily losing fans. This is not a collection of individuals who use a theatre as a place in which to wage war against each other. Instead, there is a bond between each member, a deep friendship and love that makes itself apparent even as early as the first few songs. Everyone seems geared toward helping the other make the best music imaginable, stepping back, letting each have his say in turn. All are very much aware of the whole in which they are dealing: it's not David Crosby who you see on stage; it is the Crosby of Crosby, Stills, Nash & Young. And the same holds true of the other five.

It's easy to see that they all genuinely enjoy themselves on stage, not just up there to play a job and make a little bit of spending money. A typical performance is not a tight, theatrical, closely choreographed affair. During the first half, they sit alone on stools, all acoustic guitars and voices, with just a dark curtain behind them and a lot of lights. A nice, friendly sort of gathering. They sing for a while, interchanging lead parts as the occasion demands, joined by one, then another, sometimes just sitting back and talking in a casual way. Graham Nash will tell a little joke, and the others will crack up, laughing with and to the audience. They work on the principle of the slow build-up: instead of one big rush, they go for a collection of little highs, moving slowly so that the crowd is able to rise with them, level by level, piece by joyous piece. David sings a beautiful "Guinnevere," Stills does "Suite," they all play a bit with "Wooden Ships." The audience responds; it's a good start.

After a while, those dark curtains open, revealing a full complement of huge amplifiers, stark and omnipresent. Dallas and Greg take their places; Neil Young, who had made spot appearances throughout the acoustic portions, comes out again. They tune up, check and look at each other for a bit, then plow into the heavier (well...) material. You can clearly feel Young's influence at work here. When they hit "Down by the River," stretching it long and languorous, using it to bring things to a final peak, you can watch them lock in and hit their stride. Stills and Young are trading guitar riffs, measure after measure, each one building firmly on the last. Surely, precisely, it rises to the climax...and almost on cue, the bubble bursts, waves of vibrations splashing out over everybody in the place, coating them, making them ready to go back and face a sometimes-hostile world.

Graham Nash said it: "When we get out on stage, in front of all those people...why, I think we can do a lot of good." And you turn to look at the smiling faces that stick around after the group leaves the stage, people walking about, just feeling nice inside, and you can only nod and say yes, because you believe him.

But for Crosby, Stills, Nash & Young, it doesn't end there. No group can make peaceful music when it is in a state of war; no group can hope to function on any level if its pieces are pulling in several directions at once. The true secret to CSNY's success, beyond the albums, beyond the stage appearances, beyond the music itself, it the fact that they all love one another. Even if there was no band, they might be friends, and if they couldn't be friends, they might as well be brothers.

"We're a family," says Crosby, "and it gets stronger every day."

Part of the answer lies in the fact that Crosby, Stills, Nash & Young all respect where each member of the group is at, and are resilient enough to realize just how far each one can go at a certain time. Of all the major four in CSNY, this applies most to Neil Young. On an outer level, he is probably the most volatile, given to dark impulses and quick flashes of mood. And of all, he is the one most concerned with his independent status. "I consider myself more of a writer than a guitar player, but in this band, I'm more of a guitar player." For this reason, he has kept up his ties with Crazy Horse, the Los Angeles group with which he recorded two solo LPs, and is now currently working on a third. In an interview with *Rolling Stone*, he noted that "Crazy Horse is funkier, simpler, more down to the roots...But then," he continues, "I have another side to me, and it's too technically advanced for Crazy Horse; so the other band plays that. They complement each other inside me."

It all becomes a process of accommodation. Difference, and not similarities, give a group its special individual flavor. CSNY is a living testment that a band can function and make music based on difference, providing always that a driving spirit is there first, just to add that much-needed shove in the right direction. Crosby, Stills, Nash & Young takes everybody into account, works around that, and then creates a music not of compromise, but rather of integration. It is a process which requires a kind of internal deferment, the ability to listen to what each member has to say, and then cares about it also. "I tend to be a little conservative," says Stills, "a little less running off the deep end. David is the other way...you have to slow him down sometimes; he tends to get carried away. But I really believe him when he tells me something, and I have respect for what he says. And," he added, "he is also one of my dearest friends."

Friends. In a word, that might sum up the way Crosby, Stills, Nash, Young, Taylor and Reeves work. It pinpoints the source and direction of their art, the magic way in which they are able to put it over. And because they are so diverse musically, because they can encompass so many fields and bring them into each of their songs, they have literally nowhere to go but all the way.

Let's let David Crosby end this, talking about a Group, a collection of individuals who have come together in a single, near-priceless thing that has a lot of names: one, in fact, for each of its parts:

"I think we can explore our kinds of music almost endlessly. There is no limit in anybody's head to what we can do or try...and with that kind of attitude, plus the amount of talent these cats have...I just can't see any boundaries in sight. They might be there, but I can't see them."

He's very right. All the barriers are down now. Wooden Ships, you can go on home to port.

DAVID CROSBY:
THE *ROLLING STONE* INTERVIEW

BY BEN FONG-TORRES
Rolling Stone
July 23, 1970

David Crosby engaged in a series of free-form interview sessions with *Rolling Stone's* Ben Fong-Torres in 1970. Stephen Stills sat in and added a few comments early on. Croz flowed from topic to topic with ease, eagerness and interest. Little wonder that he eventually wrote a song ("Anything at All") in which he referred to himself as "The World's Most Opinionated Man." Discussion of CSNY darted in and out of this fascinating interview, and the group's powerful presence could be felt throughout.

David Crosby. 1970. Photo: Henry Diltz

*I*n *his third year as a Byrd, David Crosby was kicked out of the band. There were a number of reasons, none of them made public, but several of them easy enough to guess. Crosby, rhythm guitarist, singer and composer, was continually at odds with Roger McGuinn, acknowledged leader of the group. While McGuinn steered the band's uneasy course from "folk-rock" through space-rock to country, Crosby, equally energetic, equally opinionated, equally brilliant, kept tampering with the wheel. Crosby worked out and executed the intricate harmonies for the group's three-part vocal lines, but he went beyond "folk-rock" early in the game. He wrote "Mind Gardens," "Eight Miles High," "Everybody's Been Burned," "Why," and "What's Happening?!?!" He called Byrd music "folk, bossa nova, jazz, Afro."*

Away from music, but still on stage, Crosby insisted on speaking out on politics, and he did it articulately and abrasively. At the Monterey Pop Festival in June, 1967, he delivered a rap challenging the credibility of the Warren Report. Four months later, he was no longer a Byrd.

Crosby was an easy interview; he'd become a friend through past meetings for different stories. He said he'd found a journalist he thought he could trust. I'd found a musician/spokesman I knew I could believe. When the tape machine wasn't running, we spent time on the deck of The Mayan, *docked*

41

at Marina del Rey, and talked about London, about women, and about trips he had made in the waters and the winds while he planed and sanded down hatch doors and revarnished various pieces of the boat's woodwork. Downstairs, whenever we talked, friends would invariably gather to listen. At dinner at Stephen Stills' house in Laurel Canyon, he made pitches for the rest of the band to support campaigns being waged by Jess Unruh, Jane Fonda and Dr. Benjamin Spock. He taunted and debated Stephen and Graham about "Yo-Yo Lennon," and about the impossibility of carving out a perfect male-female relationship. But he conceded that Yo-Yo and John might have one worked out.

A few weeks later, Nixon and the National Guard in Ohio did their numbers, and Crosby, Stills, Nash & Young fell apart, and David called up to tell about it, to say he thought it'd be together again soon. Days later, Neil Young had written "Ohio," and Crosby's prediction had come true; the band was back on the road. We met again and talked some more, over breakfast at a restaurant in Hollywood, after the waitress had finished hounding him for concert tickets for her kids—promising an incredible blow job in the restroom ("And I've got false teeth," she said).

He spoke, not too specifically or certainly, about the band, and it sounded like maybe Crosby, Stills, Nash & Young might be staying together just long enough to save their legal necks on the concert tour. Young and Stills were at it again. Broken arrows.

But in the spring of 1970, Crosby, the catalyst, sounded very certain: "The music has been so good," he said, "that as far as I can see, we'll do one tour and one LP a year for the next ten years. Steve and Neil were fuckin' hugging and shaking hands after shows. And if me and Willie and the others can get those two cats up and keep 'em up... Well, we can work it out." And meanwhile, he and Nash will do a joint LP this summer, and Stills will have a solo album out, and CSNY have six Fillmore sets recorded for a possible live album this fall, and so David Crosby has a lot to talk about, indeed.

You were talking, when we first met, about what you hoped Crosby, Stills & Nash would be. And you were saying something about what a joy it was to be able to not have to just sing three-part harmony, to be able to find your voice. You were hinting at limitations as a Byrd and the whole range of things you went through as a Byrd.

Man, there's limitations inherent in anything, I suppose. The thing you gotta do in a group is fill whatever needs to be filled that you can fill and try not to be too specific about it. No, the limitations worked out usually in the areas of there being nobody else to sing harmony.

The way we did the first three Byrds albums, I guess, was Gene and McGuinn would sing the melody together and then I would sing the harmony parts and then finally we got Christopher to start singin' and along about then Gene dropped out. Then we got to singin' parts more. But for most of it, it wound up bein' me singin' harmony because I could sing that high and I could stay in tune, and that's about it. And also I really love singin' harmony and I love thinkin' up weird ones, and they used to enjoy the weird ones. So I wound up never singin' lead. Now, I'm not a great lead singer. But there are songs that I like to sing; and then they could all sing it. So...he used to want to, and it used to be a matter of habit within the group to try and keep everybody in roles, you know what I mean? When we started out makin' groups the first time around, we thought it was sorta like *Hard Day's Night*, and we thought everybody had to have a role.

It got to be a matter of habit that I would do that and this would be that and that...and it's hard to break habit, man. Habit's even harder to break than some kind of deliberate plot, 'cause it's not maliciousness on anybody's part. There wasn't anybody in that group trying to hold me back. There was no real maliciousness in that group until right near the end, y'know? Along around "Eight Miles High" and Monterey Pop Festival, y'know? They used to get uptight that I was playin' with Stephen and Buffalo Springfield. They got uptight behind Monterey, me sayin' that shit about Kennedy and the Warren Report.

What exactly did you say?

"Who killed the President?" basically. It was a standard introduction. We used to do it—you saw us do it a hundred times. We used to do it every single time we did "He Was a Friend of Mine." The introduction for a year solid was: "We'd like to do a song about this guy who was a friend of ours. And just by way of mentionin' it, he was shot down in the street. And as a matter of strict fact he was shot down in the street by a very professional kind of outfit. Don't it make you sort of wonder? The Warren Report ain't the truth, that's plain to anybody. And it happened in your country. Don't you wonder why? Don't you wonder?"

And then we would sing the song. Now, admittedly that's a little extreme for an artist to get into those areas at all. Got no right talkin' about that. But I was pissed about it, and I'm still pissed about it! I guess I overstepped my bounds as an artist. By rights I shouldn't get into that area at all. I'm sure no political genius. I don't fuckin' know what to do. I sure am sure I was tellin' the truth. But I sure am sure that it didn't fuckin' do no good. I mean he isn't alive, he's dead, and nobody still knows why. Or how or who. And everybody's guessin' and everybody's scared. So I guess it didn't do a hell of a lot of good for me to mouth off.

You say "overstepping your bounds." It sounds like at first, the whole band was with you. They knew just what you were saying.

They all believed the same thing, but I don't think any of them would've said it…well, they didn't say it.

Did they feel it was improper for Monterey?

Probably. Maybe they thought the focus was there. I know that everybody was conscious of the cameras because it was the first time anybody was filmin' rock and roll, y'know. We were all very camera-shy. I was camera-shy to an extreme degree.

Steve Stills: Being convinced that you were ugly.

Crosby: Well, there are mirrors in this world. For god's sake, man. I mean, Lord. The truth hurts!

So you're up to Monterey and the uptightness begins. Was Stephen really a big part of it?

Stephen has been a big part of my life, man, for the last three years. The cat came over to my house and played one evening with me, and it was very clear to me that he was a stoned goddamn genius. And I don't know whether anybody else knew it then, but I was firmly convinced of it. He plays rings around everybody. Everybody! He plays everything better than anybody. So, I wanted to hang out with him.

How'd you meet him?

How the fuck'd I meet you, man? I guess I came and heard you.

Stills: You guys paid us $125 for our first gig.

Crosby: First gig? Were you paid on those Byrds concerts?

Stills: Yes, you…

Crosby: No wonder you guys were really loose. I wondered why you were loose. [The Byrds' producer, Jim] Dickson didn't tell us that. That's groovy. You sang really good. You put me uptight, as a matter of fact. I felt competitive.

Stills: I know. We watched. We laughed a lot.

Crosby: Oh, you mean guys. Kicked our plug out, too…I caught you, bastard! Yeah, so, but they were good, man. That was early Springfield. I didn't really know what he was, man, until he came over to my house one time and we played acoustic guitars. And then I knew what he was. I wanted to obviously do some of that, 'cause it's groovy. Like, I don't know, we like music, we like a lot of music.

At that point, see, my band was turned off to playing. Everybody goes through that stage some time or another, I guess. Right then they were all really turned off to playing. I mean Roger would stop in the middle of a song to look at his watch and see how much more time he had to do in the set. And I'm not kidding you, he'll tell you it's the truth. He's seen him do it. Maybe you haven't seen him do it. I've *seen* him do it.

Stills: I watched Chris, though, right in the middle of a song stop playing and turn around and take a draw on a cigarette and then start playing about six bars later. Seven and a half.

Crosby: Twenty to one it was one of my songs.

Stills: As a matter of fact, it was.

Crosby: Okay, so now, anyway, it got to be to a point where one time I was tryin' to sing a song where my energy level was so dissimilar from theirs that Christopher turned around to me and said, "Ah, the David Crosby Show." And it pissed me off so hard that I got frozen up like they were. I mean there was a real disparity between how we wanted to get it on in music.

Now I saw this cat, man, I mean he loves to play. He will play 25 hours a day. Now, didn't I just want to hang out with somebody that loved to play? I love to play, man. And, fuck, we would get it on. We would have a good time playin'. And I was fuckin' starved for that. I mean I was going on a stage, man, with a band that was a burn. It was like goin' out and selling parsley on the street and havin' to meet the people the next day. Byrd-shit! It wasn't the Byrds; it was the fucking canaries.

It *was* a burn, but it didn't start out to be, so it really was a turn-off to watch it go that way, you know? So I had a very negative scene on one hand that was rapidly turning into a worse and worse psychodrama because I had made a terrible mistake and led everybody into a cat who was taking us to the cleaners. Manager cat. Pure poison. Ruined a lot of people and I led them all in. The only thing that I can also say is that I tried to lead them all back out again.

How did he ruin people?

Stole their money. He was a very direct fellow. Wasn't subtle or anything. He would steal. That was his trip. Anyway, so I had an immensely bad scene on one side, and then I had Stephen on the other side; Springfield was falling apart, too. Neither Stephen nor I could wash the taste of bein' in a bad group out of our minds. For us, you gotta remember, those two groups—and they were not bad groups—for us they were intensely painful psychodramas at the time. A mismatching of purposes, of motivations. Everybody was windin' up doin' it for different reasons. Well, Stephen and I hung out, and hung out, and we made some demo tapes and I played 'em for Atlantic and Atlantic said, "Sure, kid, I'll buy that." And I was shoppin' around. Capitol offered me a better deal. I was gonna sign with Capitol as a single. And when Graham came to the United States...

And a twinkle lights up your eye...

Yes indeed. At that point it started to get good. Now Graham Nash— this is gonna sound like a hype—Graham Nash is one of the most highly evolved people on the planet. He is my teacher and he's certainly the finest cat I know. Excuse me for usin' that word, because I know a lot of really fine cats. He is just an incredible human being! And don't just trust me. Ask anybody

45

that knows him and they will tell you that he is just one of the major joys in their life. And he started bringing my spirits up.

We started singing together and one night we were at Joni Mitchell's— Ah, there's a story. Cass was there. Stephen was there, me, and Willie [Graham Nash], just us five hangin' out. You know how it is this night, I mean this time of night, so we were singin' as you would imagine. We sang a lot. What happened was we started singin' a country song of Stephen's called "Helplessly Hoping." And I had already worked out the third harmony. Stephen and I started singin' it, Willie looked at the rafters for about ten seconds, listened, and started singin' the other part like he'd been singin' it all his life.

That's how Willie does things. And the feeling of that, man, was like havin' somebody give you head all of a sudden in a sound sleep. It was like waking up on acid. I couldn't begin to tell you how that was. That was a heavy flash, 'cause that's a nice thing. You know it was. Especially if you're a harmony singer and you love singin' harmony. And I am and I do and it got me off. So that's what we were doing.

That time in Chinatown when you were having dinner, you made a comparison between yourself, and your relationship to McGuinn, and the roles adopted in the movie by Dennis Hopper and Peter Fonda, in *Easy Rider*.

Yeah, well, Dennis and Peter used to watch us a lot. Peter's been a good friend for years, and Dennis, too, for that matter, although I don't know him as well as I know Peter. I wouldn't say that Dennis had me down exactly. He did grow a pretty good mustache, I'll say that for him. And, as a matter of strict fact, although it's a really technical detail, he got the knife right, too. Peter's a sailor, too. Dennis—I really dig Dennis. He's outrageous. I went to a wedding party the other day and he's still outrageous. Michelle Phillips in a girl scout uniform. No underwear. God knows I love her…

How about the relationship between Fonda and Hopper in the movie and the relationship between you and McGuinn?

It was frequently that. Brash extrovert that I am, and that I was even more, then. Energy source. And McGuinn, a laid-back, highly complex, good multi-evaluating, highly-trained brain.

And optimistic?

Probably not as much as that praise would have gotten everybody to believe, but certainly intelligent about planning the odds. I think he used me as an ice-breaker more than he used his optimism. I'm naturally going and already moving. Easy enough to slide in and then try and get me to go which way he wanted. McGuinn's really a good one for trying to figure out the least effort way to accomplish something. Me, too, for that matter.

So how did it come to be that you left the Byrds?

Roger and Chris drove up in a pair of Porsches and said that I was crazy, impossible to work with, an egomaniac—all of which is partly true, I'm sure, sometimes—that I sang shitty, wrote terrible songs, made horrible sounds, and that they would do much better without me. Now, I'm sure that in the heat of the moment they probably exaggerated what they thought. But that's what they said. I took it rather much to heart. I just say, "OK. Kinda wasteful, but OK." But it was a drag.

In later interviews, McGuinn would say that the Byrds missed your musicianship and the kind of music you contributed. And later on he said different things again.

Well, I don't know. I wish he'd said it at the time...Say, it's OK. Rog's doin' fine.

Compared to the Byrds, does this band offer you something closer to total freedom?

This isn't total freedom, no, of course not. I have to—not only am I not free to just express myself, but that can't even be my main concern. Not if I really want this to be a healthy group, which I really do, 'cause I really love it. And I love the cats and they can really play. That's nice. They all also really get off playing. They're doing it for the right reason, thank god. It's really part of it. Why you do it really affects the flavor, man. And I do it 'cause it gets me off, every time, man, that I get stoned and put on a guitar and somebody points me at a microphone, I have—I can't say every time—99 times out of a hundred—I have as good a time as most people do balling. And wouldn't you want to do that? And wouldn't anybody want to do all they could? I want to do it all *I* can, 'cause it gets me off. I love it.

I mean—you know, I did it—all I can say is that I've done it for every single reason I've been able to find. I've done it for money and I've done it for the glory and I've done it for the chicks and I've done it 'cause I was 19 years old and I thought I was Woody Guthrie on the road, man, and it was hip to sling my guitar over my shoulder. I've done it 'cause of every reason I've ever heard of, and doin' it cause it's fun really is an absolutely out of hand good trip.

Neil Young wrote a song about Kent State. He surprised everybody.

Yeah. He said, "I don't know. I never wrote anything like this before, but..." There it is. I watched him do it. We were at...Actually we were up in Chicago. We all came back and it was really crazy and really a drag. I couldn't get mad at anybody, make myself feel righteous, so I split. We went up to Pescadero, and I watched him do it. It wasn't like he set out as a project to write a protest song. It's a folk song. I'll admit that, it is definitely a folk song. But he didn't set out to write it, man. It's just what came out of havin' Huntley-Brinkley for breakfast. I mean that's really what happens. We've all stopped even watching the TV news, but you read the headlines on the papers going by on the streets.

He didn't seek out his subject matter, it's what forced its way into his consciousness, when he had defended his consciousness against it and tried strongly to keep his head in personal good trips all the time. But it's very hard to ignore that Kent State thing. They were down there, man, ready to do it. You can see them, they're all kneeling there, they're all in the kneeling position and they got their slings tight and they're ready to shoot. And there's this kid, this long-haired kid standing there with a flag wavin' it...I mean, I cannot be a man, and be a human, and ignore that, I don't think. I don't *think* I can. And I'm not political. I don't dig politics. I don't think politics is a workable system any more. I think they gotta invent something better. And man, it's really right down to there. It's really not happening for me to live in a country where they gun people down in the streets just for that, for saying they don't dig it that way. You can't do that. President Nixon, you can't do that!

How did Graham and Stephen react to the song?

They said, "Well, how soon can we record it?" And there was no question in anybody's mind. We all felt the same way about it. As a matter of fact, as soon as we played it to Stephen and Graham we just all went to the studio and recorded it. We cut the whole record, both sides, in one night, and finished it the next day. We went in, we played it like that. Those extra words on the end: "Why?" "Why?" "How many?" "How many more?"...you know, that? That wasn't even part of the song, that was just what happened when we got to the end. It was all one live take, man, of cats just reacting to our world, that's all. I don't see any holy word or panacea or answer in what we did, we're just people. We live here, too, and they just kicked us in the face.

Do you think it'll just keep getting worse?

Well, now, the way I see it, the seeds of the better are already here. There's the new ways for people to relate to each other and live with each other and grow up. A whole new society inherent in the way that young people are relating to each other now. And communicating with each other on levels that squares never achieve, man, it's that simple. They do not communicate with each other that well.

The shared experience of people who've been high together, the multiplicity of levels that they can relate on and do relate or is not frequently found in straight people. It's a new way, OK? It's only a matter of degree and not really kind, but it's really quite a change in degree of communication. I mean you and I relate to each other on an awful lot of levels. You're reading my skin temperature, my tension, my stance, my position in the room, my tone, inflection, pitch, attack, rise, fall, tension, my blink-blink, my respiration rate, my heart rate, and in the middle of all of those you're copying me telepathically, and I know it. Empathically, anyway, for sure. If you're not doing that then it's different. I see people doing that, man. I see people relating to each other in ways that haven't happened before for people. There are huge numbers of them doin' it. I see, for me, quite plainly a new humanity, I mean a bunch of people who are concerned with being human. I also think that I can see that it's going to get worse before it gets better.

It's something like we have only this one plot of ground, y'know, and we've built a house on it and it's an old frame house and we didn't use redwood. And it's rotten. And we have propped it and shored it and buttressed it and sky-hooked it and everything we can think of to keep it up, man. And I don't think it's happening. I think at least we're gonna have to kind of bust it up for the lumber. And I don't dig it, man, because I don't dig destruction, man. I'm a builder. I've always been a builder.

But I'm afraid that's what's gonna happen, man. I'm afraid that's what has to happen. I told that to Albert Grossman last night and he got so angry with me he wouldn't talk to me any more. I played "Ohio" for him last night and he got angry. He said, "What are you tryin' to do?" And I said, "Well, actually, if you really want to know, I'm not really trying to do anything. But I think we're gonna help tear it apart a little bit." And he said, "Well, man, you're just children, and you don't understand what's going on." Went into that kind of rap, and I said, "Albert, you're comin' on hip all the time, but in truth you're just another old man who's really got all his marbles in this system. And the real truth of it is, man, I just scared you. You don't want that system to go. You got every fuckin' egg in one basket, Jack. If they burn the bank you're screwed, Albert."

And he got really scared. If they burn the bank I've still got my two hands, and I ain't scared of it. I've done it, a lot. I've caught my own fish and ripped their own stomachs out, and cleaned them, and cooked them. And done the same for the animals. It isn't as if I don't dig civilization, I do, and I don't want to blow it. But I do want to blow this political system. I had a long talk, man, with the head of the Democratic party in California. Like, there's a cat who's got a lot more information than me.

Jess Unruh.

Right. He's firmly convinced that if we don't change something radically, soon, that it's gonna come apart at the scams, too.

When did you talk to Unruh?

He came down to the boat. He wants us to help. I kind of dig it that he's at least willing to go out and talk to longhairs, because quite frankly he's a very shrewd politician, and he must know that he doesn't have to cater to us at all. We have absolutely no choice in this election but to support him.

But it's a gamble for him to alienate more of the moderate voters by associating with longhairs.

Yeah, that's what I felt, too. I thought it was kind of brave for him to do it.

Maybe he's trying to envelop you so that there's no third party formed to maybe take a large chunk of votes from him.

Maybe so. He's up against pretty heavy odds, y'know. He's up against California oil money and the original power bloc of this state. And they're after his ass. And they've got idiots—just full-out clowns, front men—like Yorty, and they've got truly dangerous people like Reagan.

What's Reagan's importance in terms of what he's done to the state or to people, to the youth movement—what has been his contribution?

Crystallization. The more pressure you put on coal the sooner it turns into diamonds. I mean the cat has polarized the entire minority so that it isn't a minority any more. It's a majority of minorities. He's got the intelligentsia and the blacks and the "kids" and the "hippies" and he's got everybody, man, sort of universally aligned against him because he has sort of gone physically insane right in front of us and threatened our freedom, and our right to breathe, move, think…

You wrote "Long Time Gone" and "Almost Cut My Hair" right after Robert Kennedy was shot. What exactly did he mean to you?

See, I didn't know him, I never talked to him. I believed in him because he said that he wanted to change stuff. And I believed also that in my probably naive conception of politics he had not made so many deals that he was unable to change course at all, which is the case in Johnson and Nixon both. They're cats, politicians, who've made their deal. Years ago. They've sold out to the special interests and controlling powers in this country in order to gain power. Now I thought Bobby Kennedy was one more opportunity to have a leader who had not made those deals.

You believed that, even knowing who his father was and what that family meant in terms of seeking political power?

I can't defend the father or the family. The cat was young. Right, wrong, or indifferent, he was interested in change. He still had balls. He still had the willingness to change and grow, you know? And he had the willingness for this country to change and grow…I think. Who knows what he could have done, man. I mean we didn't ever get a chance to find out about him, right?

We found out what kind of reaction there could be to that kind of person…

We found out that he—in actual fact, man, the way I figure it is, I was right. He was very close to getting that much power. And he was also not signed, in a sense, to a company. Now Ronald Reagan is a bought and paid-for man. And there's no question in anybody's mind that looks at it, really. I mean, when the oil interests are performing ecological crime on a mass scale, that certainly is no less offensive to the human race as a long-range thing than Buchenwald or the worst examples of human depravity. OK? Any of that is not worse than what the oil companies are doing, particularly in California.

Multiple mass murder of living beings and for nothing. For nothing, man. For bread, for money, dig? Well, now, I was quoted the tax figures on those platforms off Santa Barbara, and if the tax figures they quoted me are correct then the government ain't gonna shut them down. 'Cause they pull in a lot of bread out of there.

Now, that same bread, man, not only comes in in taxes from the oil companies, but it comes in in contributions. And I'm not just saying the oil companies, but in California they happen to be a controlling interest. And he very definitely is totally sold out to those people, y'know. Otherwise he wouldn't keep instructing them to let him have more and more new licenses to go out and do it more and more. The federals, too.

The point is that the problems we're up against, and those include environmental crime, race crime, political, total, obnoxious corruption, and international crime, which is war—all of those problems, man, relate to a power structure that is running this country.

We got a whole bunch of people who clearly identify that, and they say, "OK. Now we're gonna just shake this power structure by the roots." Right? I laugh at 'em. I laugh at the SDS and I laugh at those fucking parlor-pink revolutionary kids going around saying, "I'm a revolutionary by trade." Bullfucking pukie. They haven't any idea what it is, man. They should go watch a newsreel of the last three days of Budapest, and think it over. Asshole kids. They don't know what they are up against, man. You can't convince this power structure to change its course. It's inextricably—a curious word—inextricably involved in its course. I'm trying to explain to people that it isn't the President, it isn't Congress, it isn't the governors. It seems like it, but as far as I can tell, it's an interlocking whole socioeconomic systems group. And they're all interlocking...There's this guy who makes the transistors for the guy who makes the radios for the guy who makes the planes for the guy who makes the wars for the guy who mines the tungsten and the transistor.

It's all interlocking, man, and I don't see how they're going to change the course. I had to think up a phrase to describe it. We have "societal inertia." And we're moving—Look, man, I'll just bring it down to the basest of terms that made it clear to me: How are you gonna get 'em to close the gas stations, what are you gonna do with the pumps? That's inertia. How are you gonna convince Chevy, Ford, Volkswagen, Cadillac, Honda to all take four, ten, twelve years of profit loss re-tooling to another power source? The men who run those companies do not own them. They are there only as long as they win. They cannot make that decision. It's not that they won't. They can't. They've got to show a profit every year or they'll get another man. That's the truth. Environment be screwed. That's how those companies are run.

That's not the only place. The oil companies are not the major criminals in this world; they are amongst the major criminals, and that example of inertia is not the only one. I'm talking about the 5,000 or so people who run

51

the world. I would like to see these fucking SDS revolutionary bullshit kids come up with a list of those cats' names and addresses. Then they'll convince me that they're serious. OK? As long as they fucking stand around on the steps and shout and yell, and wait for the cops to come in an bash 'em on the head so they can look heavy: "I got hit by a pig." Far out. You probably kicked him, y'know? And I don't like the police at all, man. I'm not making bones about it. I just am really sick of the revolutionary kids, man. I'm really sick of the talk and I'm really sick of the kids I see at the rallies and stuff. Hey, they're jokes. Fuckin' revolution, man. They forget that they already ate revolution alive. That's not happening, man. It's not happening even with AR-16s.

It ain't even happening for the Panthers. And I don't blame them. The Panthers feel, and quite rightly so, that they're in a kind of Warsaw ghetto situation. I don't blame them for buying guns, not even a little, man. I ain't aligning myself with anybody, but I sure don't blame them. Boy, I sure don't—*uh*-uh. It's hard to make 'em forget how many people voted for Wallace. It isn't like they didn't do it or anything, they did, you know. Hard to make them forget that. So, to get back to interlocking systems and what we're up against, the reason I feel hopeless is because I have no way to communicate with those men, those nameless cats, man. I mean we only know the names of a handful, and they're the loan-shark, robber baron, last remaining few or another generation of billionaires: Hughes, Getty, Hunt, Kaiser, he's still one, Ford, Rockefeller.

I mean you know a few of them. Who are the other guys? And what do they care about? Does J. Paul Getty like seagulls? Does H.L. Hunt care about pelicans? I don't know how to make the point, but I'm struggling with it. I don't think that they're bein' realistic when they judge this power structure that they're up against. I think they attack its lowest and best-defended levels.

I looked at it ten years ago and came to, on less data, the same conclusion and decided that the only thing to do, the only crack left, was that they didn't really consider time—being sort of blind and being sort of in love with the fact that they were on top and in power. They would figure that…Well, most of those cats, man, always make the mistake of thinking they wanted more. It looked like it'd make it a thousand years. It made it about 30. I figured the only thing to do was swipe their kids. I still think it's the only thing to do. By saying that, I'm not talking about kidnapping, I'm just talking about changing their value systems, which removes them from their parents' world very effectively.

And I didn't change 'em, I just offered them an alternative. On one side you got war, death, degradation, submission, guilt, fear, competition; and on the other hand you got a bunch of people lyin' out on the beach, walking around in the sun, laughin', playin' music, makin' love and gettin' high, singin', dancin', wearin' bright colors, tellin' stories, livin' pretty easy. Half a million of 'em get together and not even punch one cat out. That's pretty easy. You offer that alternative to a kid, man, and the kid ain't crazy yet. The kid ain't had time to be crazy. He can make a very clear decision about alternatives like that. I think that they've probably lost the majority of their kids by now. I don't know, frankly. I guess we'll have to wait and see.

If you knew, then it might wipe out a lot of the hopelessness you expressed.

But see, man, how can you pin down to a statistical chart the degree to which a person, or even a statistical universe of persons, have changed their value systems? There are certain key, surface symptoms of value system change that you can watch: dress, manner, hair length. These are, y'know, good indications, but they don't indicate it all.

How about rock and roll?

To a degree. I wouldn't limit it to rock and roll. The artists in every area of art in the United States have been saying what the rock and rollers are now saying, for a lot longer than we have. I mean let's not forget the writers. I mean those are the cats who've laid it out a whole lot more complexly, more heavily, more literately, more multivaluedly and more multileveledly than most of us. For the poets, I mean we can go right on back through the history of artists, man, who were willing to tell the truth about their environment and include all the environments. It ain't just us that are doin' it now. What the trick is with us is that we're mass artists, and there's never been that kind of stuff before until Gutenberg, y'know, and that didn't really happen until you get up into the electronic mass. And that's simultaneity and interaction on simultaneity and numbers of a very wide scale. It's far out, man. That's the main difference.

It's a tricky thing. I could be dead wrong, man. Richard Nixon might be right, and I'm crazy enough to admit it. I just don't think so. Gotta do what you believe. I believe that all those cats are wrong. I believe what they say matters is not it. Now, I also believe everybody is underestimating the amount of inertia. I believe that that big conglomerate blob of interlocking systems, all moving down this one big socioeconomic path…I don't think it can change its course. I'm sorry.

So you can't escape. Now, how does your boat tie into this? Several times in crises—mental crises—when the Byrds fired you; when your lady Christine died—you went to the boat. So in a sense there can be an escape.

Well, try to understand. When the hassles in my head, and confusion, and pain sometimes—and everybody's got confusion and pain, I guess—there's no hiding or running, there's only working it out. That's when the boat helps, because the boat has great beauty and constancy and meaning, on a very, very close-up level. It was grace and comradeship. And all of those things get to your head.

It also keeps you very busy…

Yeah, but it's on extremely high levels that it works on you. It's not just the mechanics of keeping yourself busy. It's really, it's truly, right up to the very highest levels of it, a rearrangement of how you think. And it's helped me a lot, each time that I've had to try and put myself together and figure out what to do. I'm like everybody else, man. I walk along and stumble and crash straight to the ground, 'cause I sure don't have it figured out.

I didn't pick the boat as an escape route. When I started wantin' to sail I was eleven and a half years old and I wasn't thinking about escape. It happens that it is a good way to go elsewhere. But the reason I do it is…Well I tried a lot of different philosophies, and none of them worked. So I came down to "if I can't work out any logical, overall ethic to work by, then I've gotta just do what gets me off"—which points of consciousness were the highest ones, the peaks. And do whatever it was that got me there—a lot. I mean, God, sailing puts me in the highest kind of consciousness I have, makes the best person out of me I know how to be. It takes me to the same levels that balling does, and music does, and being high and doing both of those things does. Y'know. It's not a philosophical or a political decision at all. It's just me wanting to enjoy it.

Talking about Altamont, you compared it to "My Back Pages." Altamont attempted to re-create the spontaneity of Woodstock. What was "My Back Pages?"

It was a formula, it was a cop-out, it was a total backward shot. It was, "Oh, let's make 'Tambourine Man' again." It was a formula record, anybody could hear it. It was a piece of shit, had all the commitment and life of a four-day old mackerel.

At what point of Byrds history did that come?

A point of desperation. At a point when it was just the four of us and we were kind of uptight. And we had done an album that was good, *Younger Than Yesterday*, and we needed a single. And so we sat in a studio and tried to figure out how many different ways we could sell out, essentially. I don't think anybody thought they were doing that, but the point is we came down to making a formula record. And that's a mistake.

It's also a surprise, because you know how all the talk was about the Byrds emerging with a new musical form, taking the roots, and experimenting with raga, and blending different kinds of music…

That's what it was about. Listen, our whole thing was opening up like a can-opener. We may have been less than sophisticated, man, but we were a goddamned good fucking ice-breaker. 'Cause we were unafraid. We made mistakes, but in order to be unafraid, you have to be willing to make mistakes—publicly! At the same time, man, it was a bunch of human cats. And like one of the mistakes they could make was to cop out on their whole thing. And you can be sure, man, that in the course of a long and dreary career you make all of the mistakes there are. That's one that got me. Hey, and that's not a slur on those cats, man. They are far-reaching cats, and you know it. Roger McGuinn? Lord knows, that cat has a far out head and he's certainly one of the farthest out musicians on the scene. Before, then, now, probably always. And Chris Hillman isn't exactly a dope, either. He did some things on the bass, man, that no one up till then had anywhere near enough balls to try. "Everybody's Been Burned." Ever listen to bass on that? It's a running jazz solo, all bass, all the way through the song. Never stops. Nobody else had done that when he did that, man, not from any rock group. No Fender bass player playing that kind of shit. So, I don't know…I'm proud of those cats, but that record was a cop-out. It was a total sellout, for me.

Given the economics of survival for a band, I can see where you might say, "Well, let's do this one so that we can grow more later."

It's pretty far out to be in a band, man. The economics of survival of a band—how far out is it that in order to be an artist at all, in order to get your brush and your palette and your canvas, you must sell a million or two of them. Isn't that weird? In order for a group to really survive, man, to really cook and get it on, they gotta be some kind of success. And that means they have to sell in the marketplace, just to have fuckin' amps, and dope, and food.

Steve Stills and the rest of Springfield must've gone through shit, just thinking about the total lack of recognition that they were getting.

It wasn't that total, man. There were people around that knew what he was doing. Neil Young knew what he was doin', and he knew what Neil was doing. I knew what they were both doing. And the first time I heard 'em I went and said, "Hey, you guys are doing it!…and you gotta do that a lot!"

So they knew for themselves, but in terms of public acceptance, and support, and survival…

Public acceptance is a…yeah, and survival. In survival terms I'm sure that they paid their dues. I think everybody did. I can remember times when I played five sets on a Thursday and seven sets on Friday and Saturday in the Peppermint Tree in your fair city. When we first got there, man, there were a couple of topless chicks workin' with us, and it was hip. And Lovin' Spoonful started a few blocks away from there. Everybody pays their dues. I did four, five years of coffeehouse time before that, y'know, in North Beach.

Where do you come from? Maybe you ought to give a quick autobiographical sketch of yourself.

I was born in L.A., a movie family—my father was a filmmaker—and therefore it was an unstable family. Nice, but unstable. Moved around a lot, most of it in Santa Barbara. Went to a whole bunch of different schools and got thrown out of them. Disciplinary problem. The best one was for being, and I quote, "of dubious moral character." *Dut*-dut-dut-dummm…

What'd you do?

It was a note passed between two girls in the junior class, comparing notes, as it were, and it was not appreciated by the faculty. Listed a number of other young ladies in the same manner. It caused some scandal in the school, as a matter of strict fact.

What school was this?

Hmm...I have to search for the name. Laguna Blanca. It was high school age. I went through several high schools. Started off in a prep school. Bad place to be, no girls, but a good school. Didn't do a whole hell of a lot of anything until I started acting and singing and started doing that at coffeehouses and little theaters and stuff like that. It got me off some, so I went on doing that. Supporting myself mostly with a life of crime. I was a burglar.

What—mostly house jobs or what?

Yeah.

Where were you singing—mostly around home, too?

Right, in the coffeehouses in Santa Barbara. The first one that I ever started in was called the Noctambulist, the nightwalker. I sank by myself. Thought I was going to be an actor, took a long look at movie people and decided I didn't want to have anything to do with that much ass-kissing and copping out.

Are you saying that's among actors in general?

Pretty much anywhere. The channels into acting from the bottom are so lame, man, that I don't blame anybody for quitting. The only way to get into acting is to cross over from another field, like we do, or as we are doing, I should say, or drop into it through some other achievement or through some pipeline. It's not worth it to try and fight your way up through the studios.

What'd you say could be the rewards of an acting career?

Mmm...they're not as heavy as the rewards of a career as a filmmaker, that's basically what I'm talking about. I'm not trying to knock my medium. All I know how to do in the world right now is sing harmony pretty good and write some songs and play guitar. And I like making records with my friends. But the heaviest art form on the planet is certainly films. Let there be no question about it, it's the heaviest cross-fire on your senses that's possible with our present day technology, so far.

At that point, did you consider, say, acting and films to be more pertinent than music?

I changed my mind when I dug the people in the one and the people in the other. People in music are almost universally crazy but they're really quite a large percentage of really nice people playing music. They *are* all goony, but at least I met a whole bunch of cats that I thought were men and cats I can respect. I met a whole bunch of really nice ladies.

Who were the first music people you met?

The first were...God knows, I don't even know where I started listening to music. I started singing when I was a kid with my family. People would pull me into the coffeehouses to see and hear people. Travis Edmondson was the first folk musician that would teach me anything. And it was a good trip.

But North Beach—yeah, it was just before Sausalito. Sausalito was prime, just cream. And then, Dino Valenti, who is a great person to be on the same bill with, since he will go up every set and just sing his ass off, y'know. Unless he's on some kind of change, he will usually go up and just really do his level best to stir your brains around with a spoon. He's a very alive cat, y'know.

I was surprised to see him join a rock and roll band, after all those years. He told me he was asked to join the Byrds, at one time.

Yeah. Everybody was very surprised to see him join Quicksilver, even though he's always had that very close friendship with them. He and David Freiberg and I were dropping acid together years ago. And David and I were livin' together for just a long time. David and I and Paul Kantner, in Venice, with several others—Steven Shuster, Ginger Jackson, Sherry Snow...

What kind of a scene was that?

It was your basic little keep-your-money-in-a-bowl, share your shit...we never wanted for food, nor smoke, nor a guitar to play on, nor fresh strings, for that matter, to string up on it. We had a Volkswagen bus, in the classic manner. And we spent most of our time doin' exactly as we pleased. Which meant mostly laying around on the beach, going back, playing, goofin' off, stuff like that. Kantner's really a fine cat to live by, man, and so's David Freiberg.

Were they into the same thing you were—single folk artists?

Yeah. This was right after Sausalito. We were getting it together here after the scene up there.

In terms of the music around this time, was this during the period of the decline of folk—the hootenanny days?

"Decline of folk." There's a phrase for you.

Or over-commercialization of folk.

There's a better phrase. Folk being eaten alive by the gigantic entertainment monster. I mean the entertainment business is not music. Or theater, or culture, or filmmaking. The entertainment business is the marketplace. Let's somehow desperately struggle to remind ourselves of that fact, 'cause it's the truth, man. And the fuckers are really, really twisting us up, a lot. They are the prime reasons that people fuck up—in bands, anyway. Peripheral trips, man. Money trips, and star trips, and selling-it trips. "You want to really be a hit, this is what you gotta do," [Sings:] "So you wanna be a rock and roll star..."

Can you at all get behind a person like Albert Grossman and his ethic?

No. Now mind you, I hung out with Albert and I kinda like him. I even kind of respect him. But I would not do business with him.

What's the difference between the way he operates and what Bill Graham does?

I'm not able to discuss it. Talking about other people's business and how they work and what they think is important about it and what they apparently don't think is important about it is a pretty touchy area. Besides which, I'm no fucking businessman. I'm not really capable of assessing their true motives or what they intended to do with the money.

You're concerned to the point, though, that you want to be sure you've got a man who knows how to handle the other people so that you at least get a fair share of whatever.

Oh, yeah. But we've got a human being. We've got a cat who is like us. Well, now see, that's me patting me on the head, I guess, claiming I'm a compatible type. But the cat is—I don't know how to say it—he's our friend. Elliot Roberts is a good dude. And he is not a fair-weather friend, and he is not a bullshitter. However, he is, in his managerial capacity, capable of lying straight-faced to anyone, anytime, ever. But he's really a beautiful cat, he really has a heart and it's plain that he does. You just naturally do get to love the cat...unless you gotta write a contract with him. In which case you may just not ever want to speak to him again, 'cause he's really—he not only doesn't give away anything, he's armed robbery in a business deal.

And if he doesn't rob you blind we'll send Dave Geffen [of CMA] over; he'll take your whole company. And sell it while you're out to lunch, you know. Those two guys, man, are not kidding. And they understand what's going on and don't think it's any mistake that Elliot Roberts could step into the managing of artists business and in two years be holding a couple of million dollars worth of stuff, I mean he didn't do it by being stupid, right? And he didn't do it by just picking the right people. He made good moves. I could name a dozen. Y'know, he's really bright at it, but he's really a human being. He's a rarity.

Which brings us to the ticket prices for your concerts. One of the complaints on this tour was from people in St. Paul-Minneapolis, who were boycotting your show there because tickets were $5.50, $7.50, and $10 top.

I don't think that's the case. Didn't you tell me you had investigated it and found out that it was not the case?

No, I checked it out and found that the "plush circle" was 100 seats for $10 each and that Elliot had just called and told them to set aside 300 seats for $2 to balance it out a little. But still, the bulk of tickets will be around $5.50 to $7.50.

That's far out, 'cause Elliot told me that the last time that I checked on it that our top scaling was $6.50. If it is $7.50, I'm sorry it is, 'cause I think it's outrageous.

Well, that's the price the boycotters quoted to me. They're screaming about it.

Well, you know where it is behind promoters and the sale of groups coming to that town, see. And like (a) the promoter may be trying to pull a fullout scam on us and the agency, in which case he'll be blowin' it, heavily. Or (b) maybe our management wanted to try and get away with it this time. It might be any one of a dozen answers, I don't know.

Did you ever have to deal with Derek Taylor?

Sure, he worked for us awhile.

What specifically did he do for the Byrds? What was his contribution to developing the band as a force?

He was an excellent myth-maker. He blew us up, made us bigger than life. Turned our thing, not into something else, but I'd say he placed a lens in front of it that blew it up. Huge, it's huge.

As opposed to what is now known as "hype?"

Derek hyped us, but the thing was, see, if you're out hyping…Hyping is like, you know when your dealer says to you, "Man, say, man, I have some weed so righteous that you might just as well bang your head against the wall as smoke it." I mean now that's a hype. But whatever he says, if he delivers, that's a good hype! You go back to that cat, right? And, well, Derek Taylor used to say that it got magical and weird and shit at the Byrds, and that's a hype. Only thing as it did, sometimes.

What about the Byrds' first major success, at Ciro's on Sunset Strip? Were you ready for that at all?

Fuck, man, I was sitting there waiting an hour early! I was prepared, all right. I didn't know what it was, but I wanted it, whatever it was. If it meant money or glory and chicks, man, I really wanted it a lot.

Ciro's was the first really good gig. The first place we ever played and pleased anybody was San Francisco, at the Jack Tar Motel. There were about 200 little girls who were there for *Teen Screen*, *16*, y'know, one of those…We played three songs. They loved it. That's 'cause we got all the way through without dropping the guitars…Actually we cooked. It was the first time we ever cooked. When we came off stage we nearly thought we would fall down. It was great.

That was very early. And then Ciro's was amazing, how they handled it. The Trip, which was a little later, was not so wonderful. But, as the Trip— it was groovy. Ciro's was really outrageous. It was this great, big, over-stuffed plush Fifties rock and roll—no, it wasn't even rock and roll—it was a Fifties Las Vegas showroom that had been done "cheapy," right? And then it had gone out of business so many times…

Something I could never attest to, 'cause I didn't see the early Byrds, was the criticism that on stage the Byrds were sloppy, had an awful sound mix, never got it on, didn't care and were, in general, incredibly shoddy compared to the records. Were you?

Depended on when you heard us. There were also people—rare, but there are people, and some of them even responsible musicians, who will tell you—they heard the Byrds actually get you off. They played like angels. Oh, it was possible, it just was not all the time. Up until the time Gene left we were pretty good.

What was it that Gene Clark provided?

Focus.

As opposed to leadership?

Right. He did it well. He's an emotional projector on a huge and powerful level. If you get him on a good trip he can take everybody, anywhere in the vicinity, on a good trip. Dig it? McGuinn can't do that.

What would you call yourself in your band now? You said "energy source."

No, it's a slightly different role, frankly. Everybody in this group can communicate to the audience. We all can do it in conjunction with each other and they all can do it by themselves. It's a matter of some kind of personal honesty at some point and the ability to communicate, and the ability to love, or something like it.

Would you dig working with Jerry Garcia?

Man, I would. Now I think Jerry Garcia probably needs me like he needs a third eye. Excuse me, a fourth. He has a third. But I would be just so knocked out to play, or sing, or do any kind of music with that dude. I mean, you know I would! Hey, and he's not the only one. What about Lesh, man? Have you really considered what kind of a musician Phil Lesh is? I would like to make a record sometime with him playing classical music on an electric bass. He is certainly one of the most virtuoso string instrument players on the planet.

Somebody somewhere, sooner or later, has got to realize that the Grateful Dead is one of the best bands in the world. And I hope that it's more than just the people who occasionally see them do a really stupendous set. But they're—man, on a good night the Dead is as good as it gets. Period. I mean they can take people and make 'em just absolutely fucking boogie 'til dawn. And there's very little of that around.

You've called them a magic band, and you've said that the Airplane— and Crosby, Stills, Nash & Young—are magic bands. What's the criterion?

Magic is doin' it so well that you get it up beyond mechanical levels. Magic is making people feel good and stuff. Magic is, if you're high on psychedelics, having a great big love beast crawl out of your amplifiers and eat the audience. I don't know what it is, man. Like, they're magic. Something happens when the Dead get it on that don't happen when Percy Faith gets it on.

The Dead have got an offspring band, now, y'know.

I think it's healthy. I don't think man is naturally monogamous.

You've talked about doing things with Cass and with Kantner, and there are people like Clapton and Harrison moving around with different bands. Is there gonna have to be some new deal to free artists from contracts that tie them up with specific groups and labels?

Yeah, it's gonna have to go the way I think we've gone, for most of the people. And that is that they'll be signed not as a Burrito or a Spoonful or an Airplane; they'll be signed as Michael Santana and Joseph Stalin, Admiral Nimitz, Captain Beefheart, y'know. They'll be signed as different cats, and, well now, the record companies.

I'm certain that for a mutual profit gain these companies can be convinced to allow us to cross-pollinate, particularly if it's put to them in those terms. If it's put to them as a revolutionary, "up against the wall, futhermuckers," it will no doubt fall flat smack on its nose, and they will tighten up on the contracts. Be hard-ass, for four more years. If somebody takes the trouble to convince them that it'll net 'em twice as much money over the next ten years, we'll get it Tuesday.

You mentioned that you had written a number of songs and they all seemed to fall or end up in the same strain.

The trouble is the words all come around to "Why is it like this?" They are all mostly about Christine, and with that…and they're good songs. I haven't sung 'em to anybody and I don't think I'm gonna. 'Cause they're pretty sad and they don't draw any useful conclusion. Man, if I had learned something from it yet that I could communicate to people, I would. I got no more understanding than an ant does when you pull off his legs. I mean it's just a blind smash from God. I got no rationale behind it, I got no explanation, I have no way to make sense out of it or any useful wording to communicate from it to people. And what's the point of just communicating to them that I hurt? That doesn't do any good at all.

So what's the point of blues?

The point of blues has been pretty much to communicate it and make it a shared experience, which can lighten it just enough to keep you from going crazy. I'll buy that. But who the hell needs to hear about David Crosby's bummer? It ain't true, man, it just ain't true. Nobody needs to hear about it; nobody needs to go on that trip. It was the most horrible trip of my life and nobody needs to go on it. And the songs that I wrote are some of the best that I ever wrote, as a matter of fact, and I'm still not gonna sing 'em for anybody. I'm waitin' until I got something good to sing about, some joy.

You're saying that you'd like to provide answers as well as questions.

No, I don't need any answers; I don't even think there *are* any answers. I would very much like to talk about something other than the death of my old lady. I don't think that's a good trip for anybody.

That one point you made to me, though, that time, "Well, despite it all, at least you know that it *can* happen."

Rejoice, rejoice, we have no choice.

Carry on.

Yeah. Willie and I wrote that one. Willie and I are a great combination. That's mostly because of Willie.

That trip from Florida to San Diego…You mentioned how quickly Graham learned how to take over the boat.

Typical example, man, of Willie. There he is. Steps on the boat in Fort Lauderdale, bravely, having never been on a boat before in his life, never at all, not one minute. And the cat steps on the boat and casually—Well, man, it was nine weeks, Fort Lauderdale to San Diego, and that's a little under 5,000 miles, right? And by the time we got to San Diego the cat was standing three-hour wheel watches, dependably. So intelligently that all of us looked upon it as a good time to go to sleep if it was Willie's watch, 'cause he had it covered. The cat was doing celestial navigation better than I do it. And faster.

What's celestial navigation?

Taking star sights and working out positions. The cat was doing engine maintenance on a diesel, which is machined to tolerances of about 20 times as close as a gas engine or something like that. They're hard to know what to do with, and he was doin' a lot of things that are simple really to a diesel mechanic but relatively complex for a person approaching it from the outside. He got into it, is what I'm trying to say. He got into the whole thing just so totally and so fast it was amazing. But it's typical of him.

How does Graham see you, do you think?

Well, I hope he sees me as a loyal friend. 'Cause I am, man. If I was a chick I'd marry the cat. I think he's one of the most highly evolved beings I ever encountered. That's a heavy thing to say about anybody. I don't know what he thinks of me. I don't know what any of them think of me. They don't tell me. But they play with me, you know, and I can't ask very much more than that. I frankly don't know what anybody thinks of me, 'cept a couple of close friends. I don't know what the public thinks of me. I have no idea what my public image is and I would rather not, you know. 'Cause I got my feet firmly planted in the cheeseburgers, here, man. You can't really do any grandiose numbers with the ocean. It's a bit hard to bullshit the ocean. It's not listening, you know what I mean? So it helps me keep in perspective. I don't know…I'd be curious to know what they think of me.

I'd think you would be, because that would probably help to shape or reshape your way of communicating with people.

It would no doubt help me learn some stuff, too, 'cause they're bright cats and they probably see ways that I could improve myself as a person. But the point is, all I ask of them—all I ever want to ask of them—is that they, excuse the words, love and respect me enough to want to play with me. And I don't ask them anything more than that. They don't have to approve of my politics, my sexual attitudes, which I'm sure freak them out, and…

What about your sexual attitudes freak people out?

Erk, erk. Excuse me while I eat this napkin...

Mr. Crosby...what's so strange?

Not strange, not by me...The problem is that I've explored about every avenue of sex that I've heard of, OK? The trouble is that I like 'em, most of 'em. I'm not too fond of the bathroom trips, but aside from that in the catalog of sexual history I think that there are very few things that I don't like. Which makes me, by most people's standards, a freak. There are some things that have happened to me in my life, I haven't sought them out, I wasn't trying to freak out anybody, but there were times that it happened that I was part of a triangle, right? And there was one that worked out long and really righteously, and like that changed my attitudes about a lot of things, too. That's the song, that's "Triad."

Is it a matter of when you "impose," let's say, your attitudes on other people that they freak? It's not a matter of them delving into your private life...

No. I don't try to proselytize for sex. I'm really not trying to convince anybody else to go my route at all, on anything, least of all that.

It's hard to believe that a group of friends who worked with you would be uptight about the song.

Oh, you got me on that one. All I know is that they were...At least one group of people was very uptight by that song. This band is not uptight, behind that song at all, having been through similar experienecs. At least three of the cats in the band—four of the cats, have been through that same experience.

Well, yes. They were singing "Change Partners" at the dinner table. Now, you're planning an album of your own this summer. Are you going to do more producing?

Producing; I don't know if I'll do any more producing for outside people. There're some people that I would like to help: Dead, Airplane. Not that they need much help, but I love playing with them. There's a cat that I would've liked to have produced an album for and I don't know if I'm gonna get a chance to. I'm sure somebody else will snap him up before I have time to do it: Jackson Browne. I think Jackson Browne is one of the probably ten best songwriters around, maybe. He's from Orange County, and he's a stunner. The cat just sings rings around most people, and he's got songs that'll make your hair stand on end. He's incredible. Yeah, I don't know. There's projects that I'd like to do. You heard McCartney's album, sure, right? What do you think?

Well, Paul himself had said he could achieve the same kind of momentum and excitement that he could get with a group, you know, but it misses the band sound totally, in terms of each person contributing, helping each other work up a certain pace, and drama, and leading to climaxes.

Right. I got the same feeling, and I got that same feeling off records I made by myself. I made a couple of records by myself, band records, y'know, and employed a drummer and a bass player 'cause I don't play either of those instruments, right. But I mean that kind of trip, it doesn't work. There's no bouncing off each other. There's no excitement. And it seems to me Paul fell prey to that.

When I do my own album I won't use anything except my big 12-string. You should hear Stephen's. If you want to hear a cat go in and do the "I-can-make-a-record-by-myself" trip, check out Stephen Stills, 'cause he happens to be better at it than Paul McCartney or Eric Clapton or anybody else. That's not my trip. I can't do that, man, and I don't want to put anybody on that I'm a band. I'm not.

As you said, Stills' album is a thing like "I can make a record by myself."

But he can! I remember a record that he made of "Mr. Fantasy" that nobody ever heard except a few friends. He made every noise that was on that tape. Played every instrument, sang every note. And goddamn, man, it made Traffic look like a bad second band at the Whisky. I mean it was tight shit. It was incredible, you know. He's better at it than almost anybody would suspect, even knowing how good he is, even knowing the full Captain Manyhands image, y'know.

Well, anyway, me learnin' stuff, yeah, I want to learn stuff. Every kind of instrument, every kind of project, every kind of music I can get into for the rest of my life, but it's not directly related to making an album. And I'm not waiting on the album until I'm not doing something I would rather be doing—namely Crosby, Stills, Nash and Neil Young, which I would rather do than any other musical trip I can think of.

With people like Stills, Nash and Young around, do you find yourself playing a particular role in the studio during the sessions—when it comes down to production aspects?

Yeah, we all have things that we do. Like, I would say, if anything, that Stephen and Neil are even better record makers than I am. I would say Willie is unquestionably one of the finest mixers around. I let him mix my songs, man. I mean, we work on it together, but when it comes down to the final mix, it's very frequently Graham's, y'know. My role is my role. I don't want to get tagged into it too tight, but on the most basic level I can approach it, its energy source, communication, and focus. And I don't want to get into the techniques of it too close because it's like talking about balling; you can really blow it, y'know. There's that and then there's certain kinds of harmony-thinking that nobody else does except me, that I've found, anyway. Willie don't think the same about harmonies as I do.

What kind of reaction have you run across on your second album? Is it anything close to what *Rolling Stone* said about it, which was a putdown?

No. See, the point is that for me it's not our second album; it's our first album. We're the new group. I don't know how the other people in the world feel about it, but the first album was Crosby, Stills & Nash; the second album was Crosby, Stills, Nash, Young, Taylor and Reeves, and that's from three to six, which means that it's a different group. I think anybody should know that anything Neil Young steps into is different thereafter, y'know. I don't care if it's a bathroom. It wasn't a second album. And it has stuff in it that makes me extremely proud. I figure that the third album that we put out will be maybe two or three times better.

Were you really satisfied with the record?

I wasn't. And also, I probably brought it down by sticking to my guns on one thing. I kept "Almost Cut My Hair" in there over the protestations of Stephen, who didn't want me to leave it in 'cause he thought that it was a bad vocal in the sense that it slid around and it wasn't polished, but I felt like what I meant when I sang it, and so it always put me on that trip. Now, I don't know whether that communicated through to the people out there or not. See, I don't know whether it communicated anything but just a bunch of raucous guitar and me yelling. If it did communicate, then it was right.

You've said a number of times that there were two dominant images of you that you put out. One was the "troublemaker" thing.

Fits…

You said you were the troublemaker of the Byrds. The second thing was, you said that "At one time I used to put people down." Then you said you'd stopped it.

I'm trying to outgrow it. I'm getting better at not doing it.

When was it the very worst?

At the peak of my uptight Byrd, when I thought I should have been really heavy and I knew perfectly well that my band was turning into a shuck and I was paranoid, uptight, and slightly on top of it but very uptight. I was playing a very shaky paranoid king-of-the-mountain. And at that point in my life I used to put people down regularly—everybody, anybody. It was my thing. "Aw, that stupid son-of-a-bitch doesn't know what the fuck he's talking about and I know what's really going on, that cocksucker doesn't really understand what the fuck he is—stupid cunt motherfucker." You know. And I would just rage on and on to everyone, about everything. But, of course, that has something to do with irritability, y'know. There are certain substances which we sometimes ingest through our nose, particularly, that increase one's irritability factor, and they're bad for you. There was a lot of that going on then, too. Mostly just unbalance, a lot of unbalance, man.

Was that a reaction all the Byrds had when they "ingested certain substances?"

I wouldn't limit it to the Byrds. That's a tricky and very dangerous subject to talk about, but I would say that that particular substance induces irritability and a tendency toward extreme in everybody that I've even seen take it.

How were the Byrds a shuck?

They weren't when they started. The last year that we were working together they were a shuck because we would tell people that they should come watch the Byrds play, and then the Byrds would come there and be a mechanical windup doll. They didn't play fuck.

We would get through a set, forty minutes long—just barely—of material that we had done so many times we were ready to throw up with it. We were bored, we were uptight, uncommunicative, we were on an ego trip, we were defensive...overall defensive. Y'know, after that "Eight Miles High"/*Younger Than Yesterday* period...there was no significant advance that I know of. There was also no Byrds after that that I know of. And it's a provincial attitude, but, as far as I'm concerned, there were only five Byrds, ever. Period.

Have you seen McGuinn's group recently?

Yeah. I've also listened to their records. I think they should care more about what they're doing. If they're going to use that name I think they should care more about what they're doing.

It's like McGuinn is the Byrds and the others fill in.

Yeah, that's true. The other cats are sidemen.

What do you think of Van Morrison?

We did a concert with them and I watched him work at Croyden, I think it was, one of the halls in London. And I was firmly convinced then that he was a good singer, and if he's writing those songs he's getting to be a good writer. There's other people whose writing I like more, still. But I like what he's doing.

How about Leon Russell?

Ha! Man, you go back and listen to the first Byrds album and on a couple of cuts you'll hear electric piano...Listen, Leon Russell, Hal Blaine, Larry Knechtel and those cats...

And Joe Osborne?

Osborne...have been there all along. I don't know why somebody doesn't make a list. It would take you a whole page to make up a list of the records that those cats made...starting with "Tambourine Man." That was Knechtel playing the bass. And I'm talking about *everybody's* records. Beach Boys, Raiders, everybody that ever made records in LA, man, those cats made records with them a few times. And like with us, they started out with us, and then we said "no deal" to Columbia. "We won't even finish our first album unless you let us play it." They wanted to make tracks and just use enough of us to put the flavor in so it could be quickly packaged, easily managed little material—and also wouldn't be dependent on us to put out the record. Mmmmm. Smelly.

So, those cats were good, but there were some stupendous musicians amongst the studio cats. And Leon, I guess, would be the most highly developed of all of them. He's a stoned fucking genius.

You're saying that the entire band of session men were involved in the early Byrds records.

They were all involved in "Tambourine Man," those particular guys. They were also involved at later points, when we started losing people, they would sometimes come and play. Sometimes there was another drummer— very often. The only Byrd that played on "Tambourine Man" was McGuinn.

Who decided that?

Jim Dickson. And Terry Melcher. Over our heads. I guess they thought that they could make a hit record, that way.

How often does that happen?

It doesn't happen very much anymore, but in those days the groups that did come along not only had not been playing electric music long enough to be good at it; there weren't any good electric bands. There were none. I'm including the Beatles. The first one I remember that played really good, aside from us, sometimes, which we did at Ciro's, was Spoonful...or Butter band. Spoonful and Butter band both happened about that time...

Butterfield being more polished, having worked it out in Chicago.

Heaven to fucking Betsy. Listen to Michael Bloomfield and Paul Butterfield trading fours, man. God knows it'd rip your fucking brains out, send chills up your back. Butter is the unquestioned champion of the harmonica, for all time. There isn't even anybody close. I love the way Sebastian plays. Sebastian can do stuff on a harp that Butter can't do. Sebastian's got one whole area that nobody else can play. But Butter, he used to just tear me up. Fucking incredible. We played on the same bill with him at the Trip once for two weeks. And man oh man, it was truly outrageous.

Was there a chance of Sebastian joining with Crosby, Stills & Nash before you added Neil?

I don't know how to say it. John is on his own trip. I don't think that he'll join a band again, ever. His band was an unfortunate experience for him, and it didn't work out the way it should have. And John Sebastian needs a band like a stag needs a hat rack. But he does come and hang out with us, and he does play with us whenever he wants to and, as far as I'm concerned, John Sebastian can walk onstage with us anywhere, anytime, in the middle of anything—even if we didn't know he was there—and just pick up and start playing, any instrument or microphone or anything he wants to do, he's that good. He can take off his clothes and sit down and start doing Yoga exercises and I'll just be glad that he's there. John Sebastian is a member of our group...he's definitely one of the Original Reliability Brothers. There are some of our other friends that we like having come and visit us and sing with us and shit.

Who?

Oh, it's not exactly hard to fit Cass into a harmony part, and I don't exactly mind singin' "Get Together" with Mitchell, and, for that matter, if we're singin' "Get Together," I can remember times when there was John Sebastian and Joni Mitchell and Buddy Miles and Elliot Roberts, and all of these people, all of our friends that were onstage singing. And it was a good goddamn trip, too.

Gettin' high, it's a joy, man. Let there be no mistake about it. Unfortunately, my time has gotta be devoted to my highest priority projects, which starts with tryin' to save the human race and then works its way down from there; with all the things to keep myself going, like balling, getting high, making music.

So, after all is said, how are you gonna save the human race, number one priority?

You got me. There is no answer that I know of to save us. It's just that that's my highest priority.

But through your music, if you affect the people you come in contact with in public, that's your way of saving the human race.

OK, I'll buy that. But somehow operating on that premise for the last couple of years hasn't done it, see? Somehow *Sergeant Pepper* did not stop the Vietnam War. Somehow it didn't work. Somebody isn't listening. I ain't saying stop trying; I know we're doing the right thing—to live, full on. Get it on and do it good. But the inertia we're up against, I think everybody's kind of underestimated it. I would've thought *Sergeant Pepper* could've stopped the war just by putting too many good vibes in the air for anybody to have a war around.

Now, I am doing my level best as a saboteur of values, as an aider of change, but when it comes down to blood and gore in the streets, I'm takin' off and goin' fishin'. It's nice to know that four-fifths of the planet is water and I'm gonna be able to go elsewhere when and if it gets down to street-fighting. Let the cats who are really into it do it. If they really want to.

So your guns and rifles are more of a hobby than anything else?

No. My rifles are mostly for another kind of thing. My rifles are because I plan to live all over the world, not just here in suburban America. And there's an awful lot of points in the world where a rifle is a handy little thing. It's called a lunch gun, you know. It gets you lunch or keeps you from being somebody else's. Now, in this country, a weapon is another thing. In this country my rifles might buy me a great big 20 minutes sometime. I mean, fat chance! You can't fight them on their own ground, man, you can't take on the sheriff's department or the Army. That's their game. They got it covered in spades. Totally. But like, it might buy me ten minutes, and that might be the ten minutes that I got away in.

Look, I don't want to get into it from the level that that's what I expect is happening. I think that we might end up just with "business as usual" for a long time. But, man, "It can't happen here" is number one on the list of famous last words.

GRAHAM NASH: "WE MAY FIGHT, BUT THE MUSIC WINS"

BY VICKI WICKHAM
Melody Maker
June 1970

Journalist Vicki Wickham brought a personal perspective to CSNY, based on her friendship with Graham Nash. Far from fawning, Wickham set the scene as she saw it when she encountered Nash in New York City during the band's 1970 run at the Fillmore East. CSNY was at the top of its game despite periodic squabbles and conflicts.

Neil Young, Graham Nash, David Crosby and Stephen Stills backstage before a CSNY concert. 1970. Photo: Henry Diltz

Crosby, Stills, Nash & Young finished their week-long, triumphant stint at the New York Fillmore and were joined for a huge celebration party at the theatre by the Who, and it seemed, every face in New York. Inevitably, en route to the "refreshments" Graham and I bumped into each other, which completely blew his mind as I was the fourth consecutive person to appear from his "past." We rapped and then fixed to meet the following day and both continued towards the punch-bowl.

Next day breakfast, with Graham, Neil Young, their manager, Elliot Roberts, and a friend, was time-wise closer to "lunch" and they were wading through the trade papers when I arrived. Neil was saying how much he dug Norman Greenbaum's new single "Canned Ham" and Graham was goofing Neil that as both the Brooklyn Bridge and Buddy Miles had his song "Down By the River" out as a single this week, he just might make it if he tried a bit and Neil said: "Yes, and if I got up at 8 o'clock every morning!" With that he decided to split and dropped a 20-dollar bill on the table "for breakfast." Not a bad exit!

Graham, thank heavens, is still Graham. In his denim shirt, jeans, laced boots and a short, well-worn waistcoat and a toothbrush sticking out of his shirt pocket, he's still very polite, very unpretentious but more straightforward and honest, with an incredible memory for dates, places and times, and a friend I was knocked out to see again. We rapped a lot.

About friends: "I used to get very hung up because I never knew who wanted to know me because of who I was and who wanted to know *me*, and I often put up barriers. I blocked certain people off, and now when I see them again I see I was wrong about them." Obviously the Hollies kept cropping up in the conversation, and Graham said about Allan Clarke: "I rang Clarkie from Los Angeles on his birthday, and he couldn't believe it was me, and just kept saying it was far out. And I said, 'Why is it far out, man? I remember when your birthday is. It's me, Willy, and we used to go swimming together when were five years old. I can't forget that.'"

We talked more about Allan, and Graham was very genuinely worried that Allan felt he had to put out "commercial" records rather than do material he wanted to do because, in the same way Graham had been a few years ago, he was frightened to make that break with "security."

"I hadn't heard their new record, 'From the Bottom,' and I rang and asked Allan about it, and he said he wasn't happy with the song. I have lots of songs that would be right for them, but I didn't know if I should send them."

Though there obviously were many bad times between the Hollies at the point Graham was leaving, there is no bad feeling now, and he and Allan are getting back to being close again. He said he and Tony had gone through some very rough times, but he (Tony) was the first person in England to hear "Déjà Vu."

"I played it to him and he just listened and when it finished he just took my arm and went on to talk about something else. But I knew without him saying anything he had dug it, and that really blew my mind.

"The break had to come. I was beginning to be on stage singing one song and writing another in my head. It became mechanical and that wasn't fair to me, the audience or the boys. Also because we were 'a group' when Allan or I would want to do something different everyone got scared someone would be 'out front.'

"We [the Hollies] were in Los Angeles and we took the Whisky one night to play a gig for friends and after the show Dave [Crosby], who I'd known from when he was with the Byrds, and Steve [Stills] came up to me and we started rapping. I went in the car with them, they were in the front and I was in the back and we all just suddenly said that we wanted to sing together. We went back to the pad and David and Steve played me two songs, 'Helplessly Hoping' and 'Morning,' they had learnt their two-part harmonies on, and I just heard them run through and I'd got my part on top and it sounded great. And we all thought: 'Oh no, not another group!'

"I flew back from Los Angeles to London just to do a BBC-2 TV show we were booked on and then flew right back. The Hollies thought I was mad, but I tried to explain that Dave and Steve's music made me really happy and theirs didn't. After that I just went into the office one morning and said that I had to quit. That was December 1. December 10 we did a charity Save Rave at the Palladium, and then I flew right back here and that was it."

(If the dates are wrong it's me, not Graham. He remembers exactly when, and I asked him how? He said, "They are so much a part of my life, they are indelible in my mind.")

So began Crosby, Stills & Nash. We went on to the current happenings, with, of course, CSNY. Graham explained, with a lot of honesty and logic, that "we are four individuals with huge egos, who have an incredible love/hate relationship. We know each other so well that we know exactly how to push each other's trigger. We can and do incite love or hate, and we can cool each other out.

"But we dig, respect and need each other's music. We get off on that. There's a lot of music we can only make together, that can really excite us, though we all know we could go out on our own, we need that. If our heads aren't quite together, then our music's not. That's what happened in Denver. [Denver was the start of this current tour which ended in disaster with everyone walking off, the bass player and drummer leaving and the "split rumours" started.]

"The music was rubbish and we knew it, we had to cool ourselves out before we could get back again. People who saw us then say, 'Yeah, they've split. I saw how he walked off in the middle of the show. That's it.' Well, it was it, for that time, but we had to get back together. However many fights, we always come back.

"The time before it happened, David and I went on his schooner sailing round America to cool out. When we got back and met up with Steve, he sat down and started playing us a new tune he'd written and we were excited, joined in, and it all began again.

"Tuesday night—the first night at Fillmore—Steve was drinking a bit, and instead of doing his solo number, or saying he felt like doing a second one, he did four. He was actually right 'cos the audience wanted it and he was getting off on it, but when he came off for the fifteen minute break I got mad at him and we had a huge shout-up.

"But by the time the break was over and we got back onstage and into the electric part, it was cool and then some of the music he was putting down just blew my mind. That's the way it is.

"But now we can say it all out in the open to each other and when it gets too bad, we just split and cool out until we're ready to get back.

"At Denver some kid came up to me and said, 'Please don't split up, we need you.' That really made me think, and I wondered if I wanted that kind of responsibility. If I wanted to be somebody people could look up to. Because in our music we never try to give answers, just to tell how it is so that people are aware and can take it from there. But then I thought, 'Well I'm only one of four, so it's only a quarter of the responsibility.'

"I really feel America needs me. That's probably the wrong way to express it. The blacks and the longhairs here are treated as second-class citizens. Nixon, or his administration, did an incredible thing by 'inventing' the Silent Majority and putting them on his side. I guess he figured that there were enough people in the country who didn't say anything, so if they were labeled the 'Silent Majority' they wouldn't speak out against it.

"But I'm not sure anymore that people are unaware or won't say things. Let's say we were in France now in the 18th century and I could be a pianist or something, and we'd be talking about the same feeling of unrest and saying we're not certain it could happen. But it did happen. They had a Revolution and people were wiped out. After the incident at Kent I thought there would be more bloodshed. Something has to happen. I just don't know what is going to happen.

"We wanted to play for free in the Park on Sunday, but the officials wouldn't let us. We even asked the Mayor [Lindsay], but he said no. That's incredible.

"In England we couldn't put out two singles at once, and we couldn't put out 'Ohio'—those are some very strong lyrics." Graham's song "Teach Your Children" and Neil's "Ohio" (about the recent Incident at Kent State University where four students were shot dead by State Troopers) were released in America simultaneously this week.

"Our new bass player 'Fuzzy' [Calvin Samuels] is a quiet cat but really good. Steve found him in some club up the Edgware or Harrow Road, when he was in London recording his own album. Steve rang him in London and he came right over and learnt all our material in two hours. He told me that when we played at the Albert Hall he stood at the stage door for two hours, but couldn't get in 'cos he hadn't got a ticket, so he just had to walk home. And now a few months later here he is playing with us. That really gets me.

"Wow, Greg [Reeves] was some cat. He really got spaced out coming from Motown and joining us. He also got very involved with being an Indian Witch Doctor, and would go around in feathers carrying a case of 'potions.' Going through customs if the guy would try to open the case he'd say he couldn't 'cos there were magic powders in it. It never got opened. He was really a strong cat.

"Our manager Elliot Roberts just came about. He met Neil after the Springfield split up and said that he really dug his music and started to manage him. Then he saw this chick playing in New York and thought she was out of sight, and managed her—that was Joni. He'd been friends with David for years, so it all just fell in. He looks like a really funky cat, but he's so together, both with our money and us.

"Most managers will just pamper to your needs and smooth you over, but not Elliot. When we're all spaced out, he'll come in and tell us it's a load of—and we'll think 'Wow, this cat really knows' and it makes us think. I love him.

"Dylan was in last night, and we were all trying to be so cool, but like it was *Dylan*, man. So instead of doing all the four numbers we usually do to get us into it, we just did what we individuals felt like. That's what's such a gas; there's no set, no routine or anything. We just do what we feel like. We can try out anything.

"The other night was the first time we'd played 'Blackbird' for months, but we just got on stage and did it. After all what can happen but we goof, and so we goof. I dig it being that loose; it's like playing in your living room to friends. That's what my music publishing company is called 'Living Room.' I did the 'two jumps to the left and one to the right, the same exact set night after night' bit before."

A friend of Graham's arrived. "He's a poet and way ahead of his time. He's at the Gaslight in the Village. He's an acquaintance of mine, but he's a friend. I'd like to and might record him."

We left it there. The two of them had a lot to rap about and I'd had my fair share. "Hey, come by, man, or ring me later, we haven't even started yet" was his parting shot. I will. But there's a certain warmth that covers you when you leave Graham, that totally restores any shaky faith you have in pop music or people, and makes you feel everything yet just might work out for the world when they listen to CSNY music. 'Cos like any family, CSNY are forever going to love each other, hate each other, be together, split, cool out and then go back together. Like Steve Stills' song "Carry On"…"love is coming to us all…." I can only hope the world gets the message.

AT HOME WITH STEVE STILLS

BY RITCHIE YORKE
Hit Parader
August 1971

In this 1970 article (published in the U.S. in 1971), journalist Ritchie Yorke probed into Stephen Stills' "British period," offering insights into the artist's recording process, his musical relationships with Ringo Starr, Eric Clapton and Jimi Hendrix, his political views of the moment as well as the specter of his solo career and CSNY.

Stephen Stills at Island Studios, London, England, during the recording of his first solo album. 1970. Photo: Henry Diltz

The house, 350 years old, used to belong to Ringo Starr and before that Peter Sellers, who put in a lot of money restoring it for his then wife, Britt Eckland. For Ringo, it was a sort of incentive—an expensive one—to lure him into the Sellers film, *The Magic Christian*.

Steve Stills was living there when we talked—he plans to buy it, asking price was $250,000. Thick old oak beams, leaded bay windows, iron chandelier, wine cellar, antique brick, a forest of nooks and crannies and 20 acres of beautiful landscaped garden.

A brook tumbles into several ponds which are filled with ducks, swans and geese and surrounded by willow trees and daffodils and crocus nestling in the grass. There's a river at the bottom of the garden, for Steve Stills, with his black Mercedes 600SL and his two Ferraris, his red cowboy boots and green antique velvet suit, it's a long transplant to Southern England from the sunsmog of Laurel Canyon, California.

When we talked he had just completed the 11th track for his solo album and had spent some 160 hours in the studio in company with, at various times, Ringo Starr, Eric Clapton, the late Jimi Hendrix and others.

Stills was becoming quite Anglicised, drinking tea, pale and tired from 25 nights straight in the London studio.

He talked first about how, of all people, Ringo had come to play drums on some of the sessions.

"It was real funny. I met Ringo at some discotheque and it turned out he was making a record and needed some help. In return I invited him down to my sessions to play on a couple of tracks. We set the time for 7:00 p.m. and we all rolled up about half an hour late, expecting Ringo to turn up later in the evening. But there he was, a smile on his face, telling us he'd been there since 6:45. The stuff he did was great. Besides being very good period, Ritchie is very good at playing to earphones. He just belts it out, with a beautiful sort of feeling.

"After that, I wanted him to play on all the tracks, but he thought people would think he had joined my band. So he just did a couple and we left it at that. I didn't argue with him."

And Eric Clapton? "Eric? I love him, man. Eric's my brother, man. We've kind of been through the same changes and we're both just coming out on the other side. Eric has been a tremendous help to me with this album.

"The scene with Jimi Hendrix was different. We just stayed in the studio and jammed for four or five days and I put down four or five tracks with him. The whole scene was really weird, man. I just asked the cats to come to the studio.

"We're all a big community, I figure. Wasn't it some American poet who said something like we shall hang together, or we shall hang separately? It's like I'm willing to help anybody whose music I dig, and I figure that if I do, these people will help me and that's sort of the way it's been."

Steve suddenly remembered that Atlantic had called to say the *Déjà Vu* album was over two million sales. I wondered if a lot of people would find it hard not to think of the Stills solo album as being, in fact, the follow up to *Déjà Vu*.

"No, I don't think that happened, but I've got to leave it up to everybody to decide for himself. Neil Young once said that if everybody was into

Stills' Brookfield House. Elstead, Surrey. 1970. Photo: Henry Diltz

it as much as I am, it would be total bedlam and that's true. For example, I'm very far into the Crosby, Stills, Nash & Young records. I'm always looking at it from three or four different directions, some a mile away. Graham Nash has that perspective as well.

"Getting that second album out of us was like pulling teeth. That's why it took 800 hours to produce, and why the first album took 600 hours. There was song after song that didn't make it. Others had to be worked on an awful lot. The track, 'Déjà Vu,' must have meant 100 takes in the studio.

"But 'Carry On' happened in a grand total of eight hours from conception to finished master. So you never know. But Neil Young has his solo albums with Crazy Horse, and I think Graham and David will get stuck into theirs.

"My own album was stirring up inside of me for a couple of years. I was just waiting for the right time, the right amount of songs, and the right kind of songs. Which is to say not group songs.

"I started off by going in and cutting basic rhythm tracks, then I did the piano, organ and bass, and guitars—up to 15 guitars—and the voices and finally the strings and brass. So I suppose you could call them manufactured records, but I don't look at it that way. It's the way the first CSN record was made, and it's the way I made several records with the Springfield, it's the way Leon Russell did his album which is really fine, and it's the way Paul McCartney has done his album."

You couldn't help wondering—after the velvety-harmonies and piston-tight backing tracks of *Déjà Vu*—if Stills regarded this new album as the record of his career, or just as an extension of the group. It was difficult to answer, he said after a long pause.

"Each album that I've been involved with has no real point of departure. I've just arrived at this place.

"I considered calling the album *Stephen Stills Retires*, because I thought I might just stop for a while because I'm really pooped. Trouble is if I listen to the whole album, I can't work on it anymore. I've reached the point where the only way I can get it finished is just by coming to the studio and working on only one track at a time.

"But if I try to listen to the whole thing, I can't do anymore and I have to go home." He left California for a while because he was "getting cozy and paranoid." And anyway, he said, he'd much rather "write gentle songs about the scene than standing in the streets and screaming, 'Hey dig it.'

"A lot of people may say I'm chicken but I think unless it gets more comfortable—which I don't think it will as long as people like Agnew are up there running the damn country—then I'd like to stay someplace else."

Earlier, Stills had noted that he was becoming conservative in his old age. "I don't want to maintain a status quo, or preserve the conservative element of politics. My definition is that blowing it up isn't going to work, I mean no way. I remember getting into a fight with this little chick from the Weathermen in the middle of Chicago Airport and she really annoyed me coming on with all that Revolution business. I mean I would like to take some of those people to Latin America and show them a real Revolution.

"I grew up there and I watched that stuff go down, man, and those people don't mess around. We'd end up with a bunch of kids with machine guns with a general leading them in the streets.

"The only way to do it is due process. And as long as it's long and it's hard and they ain't big enough to have the patience to wait, it's gonna be bloody. You know what it's gonna do to them because the kids don't want their land raped and they don't wanna walk down the street and feel uptight.

"We must patiently and carefully go about the process of voting these leaders out of office, man; and it can be done because it's been done time and time again. Eventually it always works. I mean, we're not in bloody Russia and yelling about how good the other police state is, is not gonna save us from this one.

"Central America is a lot like Indo-China, and all those little governments down there are a lot like Cambodia. It's pretty nasty and pretty rugged, but there's all kinds of considerations to be made.

"I'm sure the Pentagon feels that being able to get U.S. ships through the Malaya Straits is worth selling out the Indo-China peninsula. The people in the country don't know and they don't care.

"It's only because I've seen the other side in my life. If it's that uptight and that weird, let's go build a city in the middle of Saskatchewan or something. Don't wait and scream and be killed waiting for them to die off. They ain't gonna be scared off by a bunch of kids in the street, I don't care how many.

"I mean, a good rock 'n' roll band can outdraw the President any day of the week. That does scare them, and when it gets down to it, I wonder how much they can do to scare people away from rock 'n' roll bands.

"I think on July 4, when everybody gets out and hangs out in the street, they're just going to wake up and realize that their children are on their doorsteps screaming at them, because they are creating a totalitarian state. A police state, same as Germany in the late '20s and '30s. I mean, how far is it gonna go? Is it going to get to guns in the street? Why doesn't everybody just hip up and realize what the opposition is. God knows, we're smarter. But we ain't gonna change it by running around in a big mob.

"I'm a non-violent cat, but if somebody wanted to get it on with me or I would get creamed, I would get it on, man. But America isn't that up and up, it isn't that straightforward. And that's the whole trouble, man."

And then one night at the studio, when we weren't bemoaning the U.S. political situation and after jazz trumpeter Maynard Ferguson had finished dubbing horns on the exquisite track "Fishes and Scorpions," I asked Stills what he really thought of *Déjà Vu* now. "Yeah," he grinned slowly, "everybody got off their licks and their chops and got off doing it. I personally may have coasted a little bit on the production, because I knew the album was fairly close to being right on. A few things got past me that I've regretted since."

THE *SOUNDS* TALK-IN
STEPHEN STILLS AND NEIL YOUNG

BY ALLAN MCDOUGALL
AND PENNY VALENTINE
Sounds
November 21, 1970

Stephen Stills and Neil Young, the Cowboy and the Indian, together as musical compadres, yet when these interviews took place, separated by the Atlantic Ocean and most of America. By the fall of 1970, Stills was living in England, while Young was settling into his newly purchased ranch in Northern California. Allan McDougall found Young at a point where he was alone and together, involved, but separate, there, but not there—involved with the mixing of CSNY's live album, *4 Way Street*, and preparing to begin a long solo acoustic tour, during which he would preview most of the songs that would fill his 1972 album, *Harvest*. Penny Valentine visited Stills at his Tudor manor in Elstead, Surrey, and they talked about the current state of his musical career, the healing power of working with horses and why he moved to England.

Neil Young. 1970. Photo: Henry Diltz

O f the four members of Crosby, Stills, Nash & Young it's been Stephen Stills and Neil Young that have extended their work outside the band in positive terms. Both ex-members of the lamented Buffalo Springfield, they were the first to cut solo albums away from the involvement and contribution to the main CSNY body. Even within that body it could be argued that it was their musical thinking that was the main impetus to it taking off and having wings. Certainly CSNY owed a great deal to the original thinking behind Buffalo—even with the contribution of Crosby's Byrds days. Both Stills' and Young's work reflects their own personalities to the hilt. In their different styles their lyrical quality is that of an innate loneliness and often highly personalised sheer desperation. Here Neil and Stephen talk to *Sounds* about their work as individual artists. Work that has made them two of the most influential and potent forces working in the music field today.

Neil Young Interview by Allan McDougall

Neil Young has always been a bit of an enigma, but over the last twelve months he seems to have become a legend, a kind of rock and roll Greta Garbo about whom nobody ever seems to know anything, other than what they care to read into his songs.

Canadian-born Neil—he was 25 last week, November 12 (which makes him a double Scorpio)—swore he'd never join another group after the demise of Neil Young and the Squires. But after his arrival in Hollywood in '66, he found himself in the midst of the incredible Buffalo Springfield, for whom he wrote such great, before-their-time songs as "Expecting to Fly," "Mr. Soul" and "Broken Arrow." Constant fights with Stephen Stills made Young quit the group three times, the third of which coincided with the sad end of the Springfield.

Neil made two solo albums, then confused the critics by re-grouping with Stills (and Crosby and Nash), just after the release of the magic first CSN album. A man of few words—he must be the most spaced-out character in the spaced-out world of rock—Young broke his silence this week at his newly-acquired ranch near San Francisco.

Are you completely satisfied with your solo albums?

No.

Why not?

I'm never completely satisfied with anything I've ever done. How can I ever be satisfied?

Well, is there any particular track you've done which comes near to making it, to your mind?

[Pause] Aaaah, well yeah. "Oh Lonesome Me" is pretty good. I like that because everybody else seems to hate it so much.

You mixed "Oh Lonesome Me" in mono on the *After the Goldrush* album, but everything else is in stereo—how come?

Well, "Oh Lonesome Me" is a real old song. So old, that there wasn't any stereo when it was written!

Do you ever regret the breakup of the Buffalo Springfield?

No.

How about Crazy Horse—are you going to keep them together for long?

No, not at all. We're separate now. I might do some recording with them, but no tours or anything.

So what happens now—do you go on the road with just your guitars?

Yeah, but I'd also like to take my own piano and my own hall. But I guess I can't, so I'll just travel light. Pretty light.

How much influence do you have on what Crosby, Stills & Nash play?

[Pause] Well, I don't exactly know. You'd best ask them about that.

According to them, it's a four way street—a four way split.

Neil Young at Broken Arrow Ranch. 1971. Photo: Henry Diltz

A four way what?

4 Way Street, isn't that the title of the next Crosby, Stills, Nash & Young album?

Yeah, I think so. We haven't quite decided yet.

Willie Nash seems to dig that title.

Oh really? Well, that's groovy. I guess we'll call it *4 Way Street*. Willie's already finished mixing the acoustic half, and David and I are just about through mixing the electric half. We're at the point now where all we have to do is choose the songs, you know. Sounds good.

What is your relationship with Stephen Stills these days?

Aaaah, well right now we are more than five thousand miles apart from each other, with him being in London. But, well, you know, I think we're probably more solid now than we've ever been.

Yeah, I noticed on the new album you introduce him as "A real good friend of mine, although we've had our ups and downs."

[Laughs] "Ups and downs" huh? Yeah, I guess you could say that.

Your song "Ohio" was very outspokenly political, as was Stephen's "For What It's Worth" and Crosby's "Long Time Gone." Are you as paranoid as they are that when the revolution comes, the right wing is going to bust you and sling you in jail?

Uh, I don't think about that much. I don't think about revolution. Oh, I don't know—it's a waste of energy. If it happens, it happens. You know?

What do you care about most?

Oh, I care about lots of things, I care about my songs, my writing.

Are your songs autobiographical?

No, some of them are about me, but some of them are about things other than myself. Most of the songs on *After the Goldrush* are like that.

One of the strongest songs you've done is "Southern Man." Is "Southern Man" anyone in particular?

Well, that's a political thing again. It's about what's going down all the time in the South. You can dig what I mean when you listen to it, I guess.

What are your plans now?

I'm doing a lot of work on this new ranch. Working on the house, and of course, mixing the live album. I've got a lot of new songs down on tape. I'm going to play at a club in Washington, D.C. later this month. I really like the club—it holds two hundred people, and I'm doing three days there.

Any plans to come back to Britain?

Oh, sure, I'm going to do a concert at the Royal Festival Hall on February 24th, Valentine's Day. No, February 14th, I guess. How is the Royal Festival, is it good—who plays there?

Joni Mitchell's playing there next week.

Far out.

Stephen Stills Interview by Penny Valentine

It is a cold sunny afternoon and Stephen Stills, in a dark blue sweater and grey velvet trousers, stands in front of a blazing log fire in his rambling old house in Surrey. He recently bought the estate from Peter Sellers, and he now plans to live here permanently.

Of all the members of CSNY it is Stephen Stills who is the warmest and most permanent. He says he has become more "anglicised" than ever, and has already used Britain as a base to cut his first two solo albums—the first is released here next week.

How pleased are you with your first album?

I spit shined it for six months so I guess I'm pretty pleased. A lot of people will find a lot wrong with it. I think it's more of a natural extension to what I've done in the past. The second one, which I've just finished recording, will surprise more people. I used the Memphis Horns, Otis Redding's old rhythm group, because when I used Jimi Hendrix and

Stephen Stills. 1970. Photo: Henry Diltz

Clapton and guys on the first album I had so much fun I decided to use a big band. I certainly haven't got rid of everything with two albums; I'd be kidding myself if I said I did. What I'd like to do next is walk in and cut an acoustic album in two hours.

I gather you're planning to take the band out as a package show?

Well it'll be a real road show. It won't be a Delaney and Bonnie and it won't be a CSNY. It will be the biggest road show since Ray Charles hit the stage. It's something I've always wanted to do with musicians that can cut it, and not have to write arrangements down like Stan Kenton. All the guys in the Memphis Horns are prepared to take the time and effort to make it work.

Initially it'll take up most of my time I guess, but there'll still be time to work with CSNY when the occasion arises.

What about the management company you're setting up?

I don't like getting into business but sometimes you have to. I've got real mad at the ineptness of the business side lately. Nobody does it right like they go round their bum to find their elbow. I'm setting it up to get proper people who can work on their own devices. I'm not looking for a team of robots. They'll be there to look after me, and when I say me that means the whole baker's dozen that makes up the road show.

Why have you decided to settle in Britain?

I love it here. I'm so pleased to be away from California, I can't tell you. I have this house where I'll live and work and train race horses, and just a little cabin in Colorado where I can go and nobody knows and nobody cares. A lot of people may think that by spending all the money I have on this place I've done the wrong thing. That it's bourgeoise and middle class. That I could have fed starving babies all over the world instead. But that's between me, the government and my taxes. If I could spend a quarter of a million in taxes on feeding starving babies, then fine. But that money is used for planes and bombs instead, and that's between me and the government. It's not going to be solved by blowing the government up—or my house either for that matter.

All those idiots who say they've got their finger on the pulse and are the new generation may not like the idea of me living here, but they're in the wrong business. I've just played for them. I saw them in the face and I *know*. We have Abbie Hoffman and Jerry Rubin and Spiro Agnew and they can all take a jump in the lake as far as I'm concerned. That's why I'm here, because I'm sick of all that. Look, in 1964 I wrote "For What It's Worth" and that was about a revolution for the first time in a song.

I'd just come back from Latin America and I knew a revolution when I saw it. I'll be happy here. I never knew I had a good knowledge of horses till I went to the track; then I realised I knew more than I thought. Those horses will be my future.

Eventually then do you want to get out of music?

I'm hoping I can stay out by getting a balance. And those horses may stop the little creative machine in my brain from eating me up. That machine has caused me real despair in the past—it's a killer. Jimi hadn't got anything to combat it, and that's why he died. I sat on a mountain and cried for two hours when I heard he'd died.

Stephen Stills riding one of his horses, Major Change, in England. 1970.
Photo: Henry Diltz

WILL CSNY EVER RE-UNITE AND FIND TRUE HAPPINESS?

This Is David Geffen,
by Gentleman's Agreement,
Manager to the Superstars

BY ROY CARR
New Musical Express
July 29, 1972

Interviewed by U.K. journalist Roy Carr in 1972, David Geffen, at the time manager of CSNY with Elliot Roberts, provided clear insights into CSNY as a group and as individuals. His takes were candid and rang very true. While the prospects of CSNY getting back together for an album and/or tour were not immediately apparent in '72, Geffen talked about what it's like dealing with four distinctly different personalities.

Elliot Roberts, Graham Nash, David Geffen and Neil Young at Lookout Management offices. Los Angeles. 1971. Photo: Henry Diltz

*C*olonel Tom Parker was the prototype of the definitive starmaker, the first public figure to partly transform the image of the man with the straw hat and fat cigar into that of a manager who really cared about the welfare of his talented chargling.

Since then, the rock industry has spasmodically produced starmakers whose names are synonymous with the artists they guide to fame.

The late Brian Epstein and the Beatles; Andrew Loog Oldham and the Rolling Stones; Peter Grant and Led Zeppelin; Terry Knight and Grand Funk Railroad.

To this list can be added David Geffen and Elliot Roberts who, between them, have skillfully guided the careers of Crosby, Stills, Nash & Young, Joni Mitchell, Laura Nyro, America and others.

David Geffen, aged 29, admits that he has a reputation for toughness, though not in the sense of duffin'-up his clients or occasionally their critics. Geffen is a business man who won't settle for anything but the best.

99

He admits: "It isn't my job to be popular except to those people I work for. Elliot and I are hired by these people to protect them from all those people who would try and rip them off, bring them down or attack them. We are supposed to be tough and we are. It's easy to be popular in the music business, just say 'Yes' all the time."

"Managers don't make stars," he points out, "music makes stars. Managers are like baby doctors in that they help the artist to deliver. There's no such thing as instant success, and I know that more than anyone 'cause I've had to hustle hard for all my clients."

What are the major difficulties in managing such contrasting personalities as Crosby, Stills, Nash & Young?

Geffen: Oh God...Probably that Elliot [Roberts] and I don't have enough time. It's very difficult. Even though they are a group, they are also four individuals very different from each other. The only thing that they have in common is that they are musicians—and that's about it.

For instance, Graham is very laid back...an extremely quiet and modest gentleman.

Then there's Stephen who, as you know, is not particularly modest about anything.

Neil is very shy and not interested in all the big pop-star bullshit. He's content to live out on his farm near San Francisco where he has his studio, write songs or raise horses and cattle.

In fact, Neil has just finished a fantastic movie which will be out in the Fall. It's called *Journey Through the Past*. He's very talented, a totally artistic person.

Then we have David who is quite a mixer...a revolutionary type individual.

Do the four personalities clash a great deal?

I would say they clash a lot, but I would point out that they complement each other. Together they made some terrific music, and apart they also made some terrific music. But together it was something else.

So what are the prospects of the four collaborating on another album?

Well, probably three of them will, because Graham, David and Neil are still very good friends. They see each other a lot and, whenever possible, help each other with their records. No doubt they will eventually get around to making an album together.

However, I have a feeling that it's very doubtful the four of them together will record. It's possible, but doubtful.

So what's happened to make you say that?

[Pauses for some time before answering] Stephen's off on his own thing...you see, the first major break came during the last tour. I've read all kinds of interviews with Stephen in the English trades and his versions of how it all happened.

Actually, what happened was that Stephen kinda thought it was his band, while all the others thought that they were pretty equal. In order for a band to stay together, they've got to have a certain amount of unity…one for all and all for one.

Three of them felt this way but Stephen thought it was his thing. It was obvious it couldn't last like that.

Was it perhaps a feeling that there was insufficient freedom for each individual?

They'd always agreed they were all going to do separate albums while they were doing group albums.

Neil made three solo albums while still with the group; Stephen was in the midst of recording his first solo album while the group was still together and both David and Graham had plans to cut their first solo efforts.

So that wasn't the reason for the break-up of the group.

There's a song on David and Graham's new album called "Frozen Smiles," which is something Graham wrote for Stephen, and is a certain indication as to why they're not together any longer.

There is a consensus of opinion in the rock press that once an act is represented by Geffen-Roberts management, they automatically become unavailable for interviews. Would you comment on this?

Well, let's put it this way. We're very protective about our clients…we don't believe in hype. When you say they become unavailable to the press, you've got to realize that there are managers who push their clients into doing all kinds of things.

Like they encourage them to make lots of tours, make lots of records and give lots of interviews. We don't. It's our belief that an artist should make as many records as they are comfortable with—like one album a year—keep the quality high and the frequency low.

An artist shouldn't work too much, because the more you're on the road the less you're able to be in touch with yourself. We're more interested in an artist remaining creative than in generating huge fortunes of money.

Don't you feel an artist owes a certain amount of press coverage to the people who've bought their records?

As you well know, a lot of the trouble is that many interviews come out in a different context to how an artist meant it to sound.

I agree, but surely you can pick writers whose integrity and approach you respect.

It's not always the case that we don't want an artist to do an interview. The fact is, a lot of our artists are very quiet or shy. For instance, Neil Young is extremely shy…he's an introverted person, very sensitive.

Isn't it possible for an artist to cut himself off to the point where it becomes harmful to his career?

Yes, I think that's quite possible. In order for an artist to write things that are vital, you have to be part of what's going on.

Brian Wilson locked himself away in his house for so long he ended up just writing songs about vegetables. Yes, it can be very dangerous.

Don't you feel that due to Neil Young's image of being an acute introvert he could suddenly find himself in just that position?

I don't think that's the case with Neil. Starting in January he's going on a world tour, and he's not doing it 'cause he needs the money. As a matter of fact the tickets on this tour are going to be very low priced. In America, there will be a 5-dollar top, hopefully less than that.

Actually, what Neil wanted to do was a free concert in Hyde Park, but the way in which the tour has been routed the weather wouldn't be favourable for such a gig.

Main reason I hear for artists cutting down on tours is the numerous hassles they encounter on the road.

That's correct. You have to leave your home and spend every day travelling from one strange hotel room to another.

With Neil, it's extremely hard, because he's a very big star and therefore has no privacy. To the extent that it's hard for him to just walk in the streets without having people coming up to him taking photographs and annoying him.

At this time, his wife is pregnant and he's very protective about that, and therefore, it makes things even harder.

On the other hand, David and Graham live in San Francisco and they always seem to be around doing benefits, rallies, and things like that.

Everyone comes from a different place and therefore fulfill their needs in different ways.

How much direct influence do you and Elliot have on the musical policy of an artist?

As far as the music itself is concerned, we don't get involved. After all, they are the musicians and it would be presumptuous for us to try and tell them what to do.

How we get involved is in trying to guide their respective careers, so they have the time to write, keep their heads together...so that they don't blow it.

We're very protective in that we make sure their records and tours are handled just right and in a way that will be beneficial.

How would you react if, say, Neil Young played you the tapes of a new album and you realized that it fell below his accepted standard. Would you tell him so?

Yes, I think Neil depends on the fact that both Elliot and I are completely honest with both him and everyone else.

There's very little paranoia between our clients and ourselves, because we've always been very honest with them.

We have no contracts with them. If they're not happy with us they are free to leave.

Do you mean that you have no written agreement with any artist you represent?

We have no written contracts with any of our clients. The fact that we have chosen to do this has eliminated so much paranoia and given us the opportunity to be completely honest with them.

We're not at all worried that an act is going to leave us. We do a very good job for our clients...we work very hard for them.

They've all become very successful with us, extremely wealthy and no one has beaten them or tried to take unfair advantage of them. It's very much of a family scene, we're all very close.

What was your initial reaction when you heard America?

My first reaction was: "My God, there's this group that sounds like Neil Young." I heard "A Horse with No Name" on the radio and thought: "What is that?"

How did Neil Young react?

Neil felt that here was this group imitating his sound. But that's not true; for, if you know Dewey, then you know that's what he sounds like...he sounds like Neil, but that's the only similarity.

I'll tell you, Neil doesn't feel paranoid or uptight about America. In fact, when America approached Elliot and I to manage them, we called up Neil and said: "Listen, America wants us to manage them." To which he replied: "You're kidding...how funny, so what are you going to do?"

We told Neil that if he objected we wouldn't carry the matter any further. He said he didn't object and in fact expressed a desire to meet them, to the point of inviting them up to his ranch.

As a matter of fact they met all of Crosby, Stills, Nash & Young—and all of them like America. The first thing David said to them was: "I like your records very much." America replied: "Thank you, we like your records as well," and David immediately quipped: "That's obvious." As they are older than America, Crosby, Stills, Nash & Young almost feel paternal.

There's a feeling in the industry that you've only taken on management of America in order to have control over the competitive threat they may have towards your other artists.

That's ridiculous. America's not competition for Crosby, Stills, Nash & Young. First of all, we didn't take America, they begged us to take them on.

They called us, flew to the States, moved there to be with us—because they were very unhappy with their past management. They felt so paranoid about the way in which they were being handled that they couldn't create.

They are very nice, very young and brand new. In many ways they are infants, and what they are doing now is not nearly as productive, to what they can be doing in five years.

The fact that you have no written agreements surely places you in the somewhat precarious position of possibly being left holding the baby.

That's one of the chances you take. For instance, we've already invested 100,000 dollars in the Eagles...it hasn't cost them a single penny.

There's always one thing you can count on, and that's at one point or another groups do break up. We do everything possible to keep our acts together. We try to keep them happy, healthy, protected, see that they have sufficient money and a certain amount of peace of mind, and hope that it will stay together. If a group breaks up, it breaks up.

What about the adverse criticism that greeted CSNY's "Ohio" and Neil and Graham's current single "War Song?"

"Ohio" was banned by a lot of radio stations and "War Song" has been banned by even more stations. "War Song" was recorded by Neil and Graham as a personal contribution to Senator McGovern. It was done as a magnanimous gesture. A lot of stations won't play it because they're afraid. But others are playing it.

Apart from the difficulties you can expect to encounter when putting out such records, I feel that if someone feels prone towards making a statement, then they should make their statement.

Have you encountered any direct pressure from official sources?

Absolutely none. David Crosby insists that he does, but I think it's more paranoia than anything else. I mean David has said some of the most outrageous things in concert about Nixon, but I don't think Nixon cares very much...he probably doesn't know who David Crosby is.

Do you worry when you see one of your artists—Stephen Stills for instance—doing things which you consider damaging to his career?

Absolutely. At times it becomes very hard to watch. Stephen and I have been together for many years. I'm very fond of him and wish him only the best. When I see Stephen doing things that I think are wrong...I tell him so and he doesn't listen. That's the time when we have to come to a parting of the ways.

I certainly am not going to be a part of somebody ruining their career or doing those things that I think are tragically wrong things. The only reason for staying involved in a situation like that is that you might hang on to the bread, and I don't.

Now you've set up Asylum Records, is it your intention to eventually get all your artists to place their product with you in the same way that Joni Mitchell has?

Stephen Stills at Madison Square Garden concert. New York. July 30, 1971. Photo: Henry Diltz

I'll put it this way: If they want to record for Asylum Records I would love to have them, but if they would prefer to stay with Atlantic, Reprise or Warner Brothers, then they are free to do so.

There is no obligation on anybody's part to record for Asylum...Asylum is a very good record company, and if they want to be there, great. So too are Warner Brothers, Atlantic and Reprise. We have no problems dealing with any of these labels, for I feel that the Kinney group is the finest group of record companies in the world.

Most of your artists have been extensively bootlegged. Has this affected official record sales?

No. But bootlegs affect the artist, because they are not up to the quality that these artists would like to have, and they don't get any money from them.

After all, you write for a living and if someone took your articles and reprinted them in another paper and didn't pay you, I guess you'd be pissed off. Specially if you're in the middle of a conversation somewhere and there's somebody sitting next to you there with a cassette recorder. Then you have a right to feel annoyed.

What are the major obstacles you encounter in your professional role?

Elliot and I try to avoid those things that will complicate an artist's life and work against them being creative. We also want to help young new artists...that's the thing we enjoy most.

America have been the only act that were already super-successful before we managed them. Everybody else was relatively unknown and it's been a joy to watch them grow. At the moment, we are getting the same thrill from seeing the Eagles, Jackson Browne, Jo Jo Gunne, and Judee Sill happen.

With each new act, does it become less of a personal challenge?

No, not at all, it's always hard. It's as hard to do it with Jackson Browne as it was to do it with Joni Mitchell five years ago. The trouble is that so few people want to give new things a chance, but the fun is in discovering new talent and helping them to make it.

What qualifications do you look for in an act before you will represent them?

Well, as you can imagine we get approached by a lot of successful acts because they are having managerial difficulties. The thing is that we've got to like them, because a manager-artist relationship should be a very close personal thing, and if you don't get together at this level then there's going to be no fun in doing it. As it was no longer fun with Stephen Stills.

I'd like to make one thing clear, we don't pursue artists who already have managers, because we respect a relationship that an artist has with his manager. I mean America came to us. We didn't go to them.

If an exceptionally successful act came to you for management and you didn't like their music, would you represent them? For example, let's take Grand Funk Railroad.

I wouldn't manage Grand Funk Railroad for all the money in the world. I don't like their music and there's no way that I could feel honest in trying to sell them to anybody.

Even if I liked them personally, in their particular case I certainly could not be their manager, or manager for any other act who turn me off as much as they do musically. I would feel like the world's worst hypocrite.

What are your feelings about groups who prefer to handle their own management?

I think it's very dumb for a group to handle its own business, for at some point or other it must interfere with the music. The Beatles were the greatest group in the world, four people and Brian Epstein who was part of it all.

Then sadly he dies and they hire Allen Klein and the whole thing falls apart, which has never ceased to amaze me. Obviously they must think he's a great manager. To me a manager is someone who keeps it all going.

CROSBY, STILLS, NASH & YOUNG CARRY ON

BY CAMERON CROWE
Crawdaddy
October 1974

Writer/director Cameron Crowe, a precocious teenager in 1974, was already establishing his personal brand of music journalism. In this *Crawdaddy* article, he got to the heart of CSNY's magic, turmoil and triumphs. Crowe's genuine high regard for the music and natural rapport with the artists is obvious. A perceptive interviewer and a skilled writer, Cameron was able to paint word-pictures that perfectly nailed the majesty and the fragility of CSNY.

Soundcheck before CSNY '74 tour opening concert in Seattle. July 9, 1974. Photo: Joel Bernstein

"**D**o I think CSNY will ever reform?" Stephen Stills crouched over a pool table in a room directly above Jim Guercio's Caribou Ranch studio and lined up his shot. "I don't know, man. We tried to do an album in Hawaii last summer and it fell apart. Caused everybody a lot of grief. I'd prefer not to get into the details, though. That gets into my judgments, my opinions…it wouldn't really be fair to discuss them. I showed up to play…and one day we stopped playing. I just don't know. I don't want to talk about how incredibly famous we are or how we could set the world on fire if we got back together. I want to play. I want to sing. I want to make good records. And if that doesn't happen, I'm gone." Stills paused to listen to the rough mixes of his *As I Come of Age* solo album filtering through the floorboards, then pumped the cue stick. "Nine ball, side pocket."

Stills spoke of entering "the happiest times of my life." His marriage to French singer-songwriter Veronique Sanson was about to produce a child and the new band Stills had assembled for his first post-Manassas tour was functioning flawlessly in rehearsals. It was Spring and everything was falling into place for the embattled guitarist and he flaunted that self-assurance.

"I've done it all. All of it," Stills insisted. It seemed almost a penitent's pride. "I've been the most obnoxious, arrogant superstar to walk the streets

109

of Hollywood…I'm *still* arrogant. I can be an absolute bastard. I have a bad habit of stating things pretty bluntly. I'm not known for my tact. But look, I can see that I really got carried away with myself. Being a rich man at twenty-five is sometimes difficult to deal with…you make mistakes. I've made all of 'em. But I'm thirty now and at this point it's all very funny.

"Ever since I got married, life is just a gas. This tour should be incredible. Joni Mitchell and I had a great discussion about that a couple of weeks ago. I'm basically a blues singer and blues singers are *supposed* to suffer. I almost feel guilty. I'm trying harder than I have in years. I'm determined to do the best I can. I want to be good."

On that solo tour Stephen Stills was indeed at his finest. The group was small enough to keep Stills out front and working rather than hidden behind a wall-of-sound; and efficient enough to bring out the best in him. The biggest surprise, however, came at the tour's mid-point when he boasted from the stage in Chicago that plans had just been finalized for a summer-long Crosby, Stills, Nash & Young tour. A studio album, he told the euphoric crowd, would follow in the late Fall…

Several months later, a bronzed, buoyant Stills sat in CSNY manager Elliot Roberts' Los Angeles offices and reflected on the first three weeks of rehearsals at Neil Young's Broken Arrow Ranch in La Honda, south of San Francisco. "Neil built a beautiful stage right across the road from his studio. We get out there in the sun and play for about four or five hours a day. We haven't done the old tunes in years, man, it's almost like playing them for the first time. Everybody's a better musician. And there's plenty of new songs too. We've all been writing a lot, especially Neil. It's been tons of fun and no hassles.

"It's amazing how it all came together so quickly. Elliot and Graham came and saw me, we started talking about it and figured it would be foolish not to give it another try. Neil and I got together and discussed it. We got along beautifully. I guess we're pretty much the same people, just a little older and a lot wiser. And will you look at this tan? How can you lose?!"

Considering the size of the sites (averaging 50,000-plus) and the ticket prices the group chose for the tour, there was very little to lose and, according to estimates, approximately $8 million in gross to gain. Everyone involved was defensive about the motives for the reunion in the face of this tremendous cash flow.

"It's not the money," stressed Elliot Roberts. "Listen, they'll do very well but if it was only the money we were after, the album and tour would have happened long ago." As it happens, they *had* tried that last year and it failed. "We're not capitalizing on this tour in the usual way. There will be no live album. It's not being filmed—we're not going to do any of those trips.

"There's no doubt they're going to make a lot of money. If the Beatles went out they'd make a lot of money. Bob [Dylan] made a lot of money. It's the nature of the race. But I don't think it has anything to do with why they're going out. Neil is a rich man. Stephen's got money, he's been touring. Graham has plenty of money and David isn't starving. The music's exciting for them. They realize that the four of them together are stronger than any one of them alone.

"It's a matter of attitudes," Roberts continued. "They're older and for the first time their attitude is that of professional musicians who really feel that they make incredible music. They feel that they have a commitment to play that music, that they are living up to that commitment as men." That kind of adolescent altruism seemed a little hard to believe. "It wouldn't work if just Neil and David wanted or needed to do it. It wouldn't work if Stephen and Graham and I wanted to do it. It's a combination of everybody coming to the right place in their lives at the right time."

It's a grey, rainy day in Seattle. Looking like their back cover photos on the first Buffalo Springfield album, Stephen Stills and Neil Young sit at the downtown Hilton's rooftop restaurant chattering nervously and laughing a little too loudly over their old guitar war days. After a while, Young clams up, staring silently down at the nearby Coliseum and the massing crowds. In a little over an hour, David Crosby, Graham Nash, Stephen Stills and Neil Young will find themselves opening their first tour since the 1970 roadwork that spawned *4 Way Street*.

Outside the Coliseum, gangs of ticket-hungry fans prowl for a chance to crash the sold-out show. One peach-fuzzed fourteen-year-old parades his budding machismo. "Bastards," he growls, barely out of rent-a-cop earshot. "Looks like I'm gonna have to blast off a few pig heads to get inside." Strong words from one who hadn't reached his tenth birthday when the first *Crosby, Stills & Nash* album was released in the summer of '69.

Then, CSNY represented a sophisticated harmonic oasis amid the parching acid rock of the time. Now they are the Founding Fathers, the inspiration for the current generation of prosperous L.A. country rockers. "Hey, man," Eagle Glenn Frey once said, "I bought that first album and freaked out right along with everyone else. Crosby, Stills, Nash & Young are, in essence, the Great American Supergroup." And the kids, more than the fanatical original wave of fans, seem compelled to examine the sweet-singing artifacts.

Inside, one could easily venture to say that most of the audience had never seen the band in their first period of concert activity. Most likely the majority were initiated into Crosby, Stills, Nash & Young through Neil Young. And just as a Joni Mitchell concert seems to draw an abundance of willowy, mountain-fresh blondes, the male portion of tonight's crowd is predominantly clad in patched Levi's and well-worn Pendletons, with floppy leather hats covering dishevelled hair. It will take most of them, including the reviewer from a local paper, three numbers to finally recognize Neil Young behind his electric piano sporting short, slicked hair with a strict center-part that makes him look not unlike Chatsworth Osbourne Junior III from the *Dobie Gillis Show*.

The lights dim and CSNY—augmented by Russ Kunkel on drums, Joe Lala on congas and Tim Drummond on bass—take the stage at 9:00 with a steaming "Love the One You're With." The 40-song set, which runs through virtually every favorite collective and individual effort, lasts until past 1:30. They are stronger than they were, practiced and intense. There are nine as-yet-unreleased tunes: David Crosby's "Carry Me;" Stills' "First Things First," "Bye Bye Angel," "My Favorite Changes" and "As I Come of Age;" and Young's "Traces," "Human Highway," "Love Art Blues" (for his dog, Art, the tour mascot), "Long May You Run" (for his car, a customized Southern Californian Woody) and "Pushed It Over the End." "Neil's been writing three songs a day," Stephen later confides in mock fury. "Damn it, I'm jealous."

They're well-rehearsed but loose enough so as not to streamline the original pastoral quality of their arrangements. The harsh cacophony of Stills' and Young's strident lead guitaring still injects a bristling tension to the music.

Their onstage personalities are almost intact from 1970. Unless the song demands his presence stage center, Young spends most of his time cruising the amps. His few comments are simplistic ("This is a song for my car," "This is a song for my dog," etc.) and their Henry Aldridge ambiance sends waves of uneasy chuckles through the audience unsure if Neil is looking for their laughter or not. He takes particular pride, however, in delivering the "You're all just pissing in the wind" line from "Ambulance Blues;" it is his only smile of the show.

Crosby, who looks more like Bozo the Clown every day in his purple flares and sneakers, remains the Hubert Humphrey of rock introductions. He seems self-conscious only in delivering the message: "You know, people think we're doing this for the money, but we're not. It's the music, man, the music." Graham Nash is the unobtrusive mortar that binds the other three volatile personalities into a functioning unit, and the high voice that forever winds above the others.

Only Stills appears to have undergone a major transformation. He is quieter now, more disciplined and less self-indulgent in his solo set (his howling, piano-pounding "For What It's Worth" has thankfully been retired). Still, he is fiercely intense and determined to communicate, but not at the expense of those with whom he is sharing the stage. The hostility between Stills and Young that at one time often stopped just short of onstage fisticuffs no longer hangs threateningly in the air. The same lessening of tensions since the last tour has infused the backstage atmosphere with a good deal of genuine warmth, back-slapping, hugging and verbal repartee.

At a quick post-show huddle in the dressing room, everyone is justifiably ecstatic over the performance, but expresses doubts about the potential effectiveness of a four-and-a-half hour show. It is agreed that tomorrow night in Vancouver the set will be trimmed to an airtight three hours.

They don't quite meet that deadline. The concern in Vancouver shifts suddenly to David Crosby's voice. Launching into the second verse of their fourth number, "Almost Cut My Hair," Crosby's vocals first turn reedy, then raspy, then hoarse. During the 15-minute break separating the electric segment from the acoustic set, David curses himself dejectedly. "We're basically a rock and roll band that sings harmonies over soft and electric numbers. I blew my voice out. And when I blow my voice, I blow the harmonies, which blows it for the entire band. I feel like *shit*."

Almost on the verge of tears, David trudges back out onstage for "Suite: Judy Blue Eyes." With Joni Mitchell rooting from stage left, Crosby and company just barely pull it off, and for the rest of the evening the former Byrd is deemphasized. Neil does a longer solo set, the "Carry On" jam is extended and the joyous Canadian throng finds nothing amiss. Still, Crosby is too depressed to join the small gathering back at the hotel suite of tour coordinator Barry Imhoff.

Ever the showman, Joni finds herself in the center of a picture-window panorama looking out over the Pacific. It is no accident. Eyes shut tightly and voice soaring over the gentle hum of the air-conditioner, she plays her newest songs on Stills' acoustic guitar, finishes a haunting composition ...

> *Just like the walls of Jericho*
> *I fall down, down, down...*

and lays the instrument across her lap. After a few awkward moments of silence, Stills swoons, "I wish I could think of all those *words*." Everyone breaks up. "But then again. I wish I could play with Herbie Hancock too."

"What room is *he* in?" Nash deadpans.

Stephen picks up the guitar to play "My Favorite Changes" and "Wake Up Little Susie," the latter with everyone singing along. "I really want to get into the electric guitar on stage," says Joni wistfully. "Those acoustics, with all their grey tape and wires, are so cumbersome. Neil gave me his Gretsch. I've just got to learn to get comfortable with it."

As the first sunlight glints through the grey, the suite gradually empties to allow a few hours of sleep before the afternoon flight to San Francisco. There are two days off before the weekend shows at the 75,000-seat Oakland Coliseum. For David, Graham and Neil it will be a homecoming.

Graham Nash's Haight-Ashbury home, like Nash himself, is tall, wiry and highly accommodating. There are four small floors and a cozy basement which serves as a darkroom, as well as the studio where all his recent recording work—including *Wild Tales*—was done. While the travel-weary Nash sleeps late in the top-floor bedroom, David Crosby is boisterously answering a dialless wooden phone in the downstairs living room.

Crosby has always been the CSNY mouthpiece, onstage and off. A gregarious extrovert, his rapid-fire discourse seems as much for his own enjoyment and amusement as those around him. The obvious pleasure he takes in conversation—he is a good listener as well—creates its own momentum.

"My morale," he says, "is excellent..."

"Good thing there's an 'e' instead of an 's' at the end of that 'moral'," cracks photographer-next-door-neighbor Joel Bernstein.

"Fuck you," Crosby chortles. "My morals *are* questionable, that's true, but what do you want? I'm basically—even though egotistically I'd like to think I was more complex—a pretty simple dude. There's only one thing I'm really good at and that's singing harmony and writing in groups. Being allowed to do it again after a four-year hiatus is just fucking great. Shit, I know it's what I'm supposed to be doing. If you can make a lot of people feel real good, you did something right. There's very few things in the universe you can be unequivocally right about. That's one of 'em."

"And that," one wonders, "is your main motivation?"

Crosby doesn't waste a second in answering. "When I started out being onstage, my main motivation was to get laid. When you're a teenager and you grow a set of horns, you wanna get laid. That's basically why I got started. To attract the attention of the female of the species. And, hey man, folksingers get laid a lot more than the other kids in high school. Even if you have to do it in the afternoon on the floor of the coffeehouse. I'm never gonna be good-looking enough to be something chicks would go for on a physical level. They have to be crazy enough to like me, to want to fuck me. I'm not Gregory Peck. They gotta get into the music somewhat. So either way, I got a chance. Singing folk songs, I can tell a story. And if they got a mind, I can

Graham Nash. Photo: Henry Diltz

find it. If there's somebody home in a woman, that's great. It's also rare. A lot of people are pretty vegetabled-out.

"After that, the motivation became largely winning the respect of my peers...I wanted to like me. I started to realize I had some value, that I might be good at making music. Then I went and sang coffeehouses all over the country for a long time. Later, it got to be just winning. When the Byrds were formed, we wanted to *win*. We wanted a *hit*. It wasn't the money so much, it was The Game of competing with the legendary people like the Stones, the Beatles. They were legends to us. Dylan? Naw, not so much, because we knew him. We knew he breathed, shat, sat down, fell down, ate, got drunk...He was real to us. I'd known him for a long time, from the Village, when he was singing at Gerde's with the funny hat. I had a perspective on him, it was different. But *the Beatles* and *the Stones*, man, they were bigger than life. The Beatles showed up a couple times around our recording sessions and stuff, but we were totally intimidated by them. The only one that was friendly at all was George and he was only friendly to me. That didn't make much of a bridge.

"It was achievement, attainment...the bread wasn't really that big. The Byrds never made any fucking money. I never made any money. Never. The biggest year I had with the Byrds was probably fifty grand. It was a five-way split with a bum record deal. We never made money on our records and, come to think of it, we never really were a performance draw either."

Crosby grins lopsidedly, the emblematic moustache drooping over what looks like his entire jaw. A natural-born catalyst, he has learned over the years not to take it all too seriously. "I *am* very serious about wanting to someday write a book and call it *A Thousand and One Ways for a Musician to Lose His Way and Forget what He Was Doing*. Basically it's this: There's only one special thing going on here, and that is the music. The actual magic of that moment when you make yourself and the other people *feel* something good because of those arranged sound vibrations in the air. That's the only thing going on. The poetry and the words and the emotion of that music. That's it. *Everything* else is peripheral. Not necessarily *totally* bullshit, but it's peripheral. Money, sex, glory, great reviews, respect...it's all outside. None of it has to do with the one thing: Did you make that magic or didn't you? That's my criteria. I'm not saying anybody else should adopt it—they can draw up their own set of rules—but for me, that's what's going on.

"And I personally have lost my way every single way that I can think of. I have been distracted from that criteria by everything. Money? For sure. The first taste of it I got, man, I wanted it all. I wanted Porsches, fancy clothes...I wanted it *all*. The best dope, the most expensive chicks, the most outrageous scene. I wanted houses and cars...just crap. It's all crap. Cars are a real shallow trip and houses are only good to the extent that you live in them. The only material objects that are worth a shit are instruments and tools. Sailboats are a special exception.

"The Byrds, as inexperienced kids not really knowing shit, were given a fistful of those side-tracks. And we went for them whole hog. We fell for the oldest, stupidest American piece of programming there is. The competitive ethic. All of a sudden all our time was spent in preening ourselves rather than playing. Just the fact that you can play guitar does not make you smart. It's real easy, as soon as anybody is willing to listen, to think 'Well, they're listening to me, I *must* be hot stuff. I've got to be smart.' And then you just motormouth your way into a lot of corners. I still have a tendency to do that."

In late 1967, David Crosby was booted out of the Byrds. Roger McGuinn and Chris Hillman, so the story goes, roared up Crosby's Santa Barbara driveway in matching Porsches and delivered the news in no uncertain terms. "Oh it was cold, man," David chuckles. "They said I was crazy, that I was impossible to work with ..."

"Were you?"

"To a degree, yeah, I was. I wasn't proud of myself. I didn't like myself and I didn't like what we were doing. I was a thorough prick all the time. I don't blame them for not liking me. But it was very cold. They told me I was a bad writer, that I was lousy in the band, that they didn't need me and they'd do better without me. I was very pleased to find out they were wrong." Laughter. "It made me feel great."

And what about "Mind Gardens" from the Byrds' *Younger Than Yesterday* LP? "I know, I know," Crosby interrupts. "That song of mine is supposed to be the worst song ever put on record. Actually, I know a lot of people who really love it. It's *out there*. It has no time, no meter, no rhymes...and it's sung freestyle over a lot of backwards guitar. It's entirely too strange for most people. But that's how I am. I never was pop in the first place. I've always been out on the left-hand edge of everything in this scene and I always will be. I don't want to sell the most possible records. I'm getting myself off and I will continue to do exactly that.

"My own album [*If I Could Only Remember My Name*] was the same way. It was very personal and had a lot of things on it that I'm sure a lot of people hate. The six-vocal thing that's just voices? That's got to be one of the strangest pieces of music anybody's put on *any* pop album in the last ten years. I loved it. To me, it's a high point in my whole musical career. And I don't really care what anybody thinks. Graham Nash loves it. McGuinn hates it with a passion. And you know what, I'll make another solo record and it will be even more off-the-wall than the first! And you know what else? I will love every minute of it!"

After being ejected from the Byrds, Crosby wandered to Florida. "I stopped taking drugs for a while, bought my boat and started getting healthy out in the sun. I stayed there a few months and felt real good. I walked into a local coffeehouse and there was this girl singing 'I had a king in a tenement castle.' I went *What?* Then she sang about two more songs and after I peeled myself off the back of the room I realized I had just fallen in love.

"So I got involved with [Joni] Mitchell for about six or eight months. We went back to L.A. and tried to live together. It doesn't work. She shouldn't have had an old man." David whinneys. "But uh...it helped me a lot. I had something else to put my energies into. I produced her first album and when I wasn't doing that I was hanging out with Stephen, jamming and writing songs. Stephen, of course, had just come off the bum trip of the Buffalo Springfield break-up. We had something in common."

Meanwhile, a third singer-songwriter was terminating his stay in another major group. Englishman Graham Nash, after co-authoring and performing hits like "Carrie-Anne," "Pay You Back with Interest" and "Dear Eloise" as part of the Hollies, began to break out of the strict boundaries that usually beset top-forty pop bands. "I was totally screwed over in that group,"

117

David Crosby. Photo: Henry Diltz

Graham later admits over a beef-stew lunch. "The last two years of the Hollies, I was writing more personal and introspective songs rather than those outward, three-part harmony Hollies Hits. And naturally, they wanted no part of anything that wasn't a Hollies Hit…two-minutes-and-thirty-seconds-of-right-before-the-news-dynamite. I was feeling incredibly frustrated. I mean, I considered 'Lady of the Island' and 'Right Between the Eyes' to be decent songs. But the Hollies wouldn't do them. They turned down 'Marrakesh Express' too.

"But I don't mean to say that I quit the Hollies and immediately found my niche in life. I'm totally convinced that what I'm doing now is just a phase of what I'm supposed to be doing in the long run. I don't plan to be singing 'Our House' the rest of my life."

Crosby unravels the tale. "We were at Mitchell's house in Laurel Canyon on Lookout Mountain Drive. Stephen and I were singing 'Helplessly Hoping' and all of a sudden this third voice is joining in perfectly with us. It was Graham, he had come there with Cass Elliot, and he blew us away. It wasn't more than thirty seconds of singing together before we knew exactly what we'd be doing from then on. Stephen and I, you see, had already done some demos together. We'd cut 'Long Time Gone,' 'Forty-Nine Bye Byes' and 'Guinnevere' together. The two of us knew we were putting together something very heavy. When Graham came along, there was no choice but to put the snatch on him."

"Crosby and Stephen gave me back my enthusiasm and confidence," Nash recalls. "It was almost too simple. I didn't really know David or Stephen. People were saying, 'Are you crazy? Leaving the Hollies? All that *money?!*'"

"There's always been a natural chemistry between all of us," Crosby avows. "Stephen is very much the same kind of person I am. Cocky, feisty…a real fucker with a lot of ego. I suppose we admired each other. I respect him very highly. He's a strong cat. He can fuck up monstrously, as we all know, but when he's presented properly he can destroy you with the sheer force of his personality.

"There's a reason for CSNY being as good as it is. The main one that comes to mind is the fact of having each other's material to juxtapose our tunes with. It makes everything *much* stronger. A Neil Young song sounds better after a David Crosby song than it does after another Neil Young song. Technically it works, emotionally it works, and in terms of balancing each other it's a hugely more workable thing. Neil, on his own, has a great deal of trouble externalizing and coming out to an audience. He'll tend to just get rigid and go inside himself. Stephen too. That's not my way, obviously. The stage is my backyard. I'm completely unintimidated by it. I love it. I can talk to eight million people without even getting a frog in my throat. But then again, I can't play guitar like Stephen or Neil."

It was Stephen's idea to add Neil Young to the group. "At first, Graham and I didn't want to do it," says David. "We knew we had something that worked and we didn't want to fuck with it. Stephen, though, knew we needed Neil for the stage shows. We couldn't cut it as just an acoustic act. We went out to Neil's house one afternoon and he played some songs for us. He played 'Helpless' and by the time he finished, we were asking him if *we* could join *his* group. He's a better poet than the rest of us put together. I hadn't known him well at all before that, now he's one of my best friends in the world. He's crazy, of course, but then again we all are."

The first CSNY effort, *Déjà Vu*, was released in Spring, 1970. According to Crosby, the album was steeped in depression. His lady,

Christine Gail Hinton, was killed in a car accident just before the group entered the studio. "Can't you tell?" he asks, surprised. "The first one was a joy, the second was painful. I was at the worst place I'd been in my whole life. I couldn't pull my weight. I would walk into the sessions and break down crying. I couldn't function. I was in love with that girl. It's funny, my love affair with Mitchell ran concurrent with our relationship at one point, but I soon realized that one really truly loved me and the other was an experience. You go out looking for princesses, man, and you ignore the little person hanging around that you've known a long time.

"I couldn't handle the fact that she was dead, that I didn't have her any-more. I went completely nuts. For a long time, two or three of my friends wouldn't even let me go to the bathroom alone. Graham followed me clear to England. Wouldn't let me be myself for any reason. My father is 74; he says in the long run the only thing that counts is whether you got any fucking friends. All the rest is bullshit. He's had 74 years to look. I'm inclined to agree with him.

"But now, I'm very much in love with a lady who was Christine's best friend. I feel good. It was just a thing, I went through it. It's passed. *Déjà Vu*, however, is a frozen piece of time. It's a totally different feeling of album. If there's anything I can supply in a musical relationship, it's feeling. I'm no vir-tuoso at anything except harmonies. None of us are virtuosos. But atmos-phere and feeling…now, they count for much more than the actual technical quality of the music. During *Déjà Vu* I felt awful. To me, it communicates. There's good art on *Déjà Vu*, but you can't put it on and feel like it's a sunny afternoon the way you can with *Crosby, Stills & Nash*."

Perhaps prophetically, *Déjà Vu* was followed by a tenuous on-again/off-again relationship that eventually resulted in Crosby, Stills, Nash & Young scattering in four separate musical directions. A double live album, pointed-ly titled *4 Way Street*, hit the racks. "I thought that record was atrocious," said Stills. "We all did." And on that note, each one initiated a solo career.

Proving a consistent moneymaker during the separation period, Stephen Stills released two solo efforts and then formed Manassas for more touring and two indifferently received additional albums.

"That initial tour," says Stills, "ate it. I wasn't ready. I was playing flat and singing sharp. These days, with rock and roll being such a big business, you've got to be good. I've always dug my albums, but onstage I couldn't cut it at first. Not until Manassas did that end of it come together."

Neil Young hit the number with *After the Gold Rush*, his third solo LP. Three more commercially successful albums, *Harvest, Time Fades Away* and *On the Beach*, followed. Neil kept a low concert profile, but when he did per-form live—as in his last cross-country tour a year ago—halls and arenas sold out strictly by word-of-mouth. The afterthought member of CSNY had become the biggest solo star. Young even made a film, *Journey Through the*

Past. Now nearly two years old, it is still unreleased—which is a good thing, if the early reviews are to be believed. "We're still doing some editing on it," Neil reported. "It's getting tighter. Chopped about nine minutes the other day. You can barely tell the difference except that it's better now."

Young's massive following cherishes his sequestered enigmatic image, as does Neil himself. At close range, perhaps deceptively, Young appears little more than a content, quiet and uncomplicated 28-year-old man. And yet Graham Nash, who considers himself one of Neil's closest friends, finds himself on the outside looking in. "Neil is Neil," Nash shrugs. "I love him."

Nash has created few commercial tidal waves with his solo works, *Songs for Beginners* and *Wild Tales*, preferring to stay with Crosby. Together they did a number of sessions, toured and quietly released a duet album. "I was happy with my solo career," Nash explains. "You've got to understand, though, that individually none of us make CSNY music. I was content on my own and with David, but there is a part of me that is a part of them. When we're not playing together, there's a musical hole in my life. That probably explains the monster rush I got from the Seattle show. When we started 'Love the One You're With' you could have knocked me over with a feather."

Like bashful school boys returning to class after playing hookey too long, the long-separated superstars first made plans and set aside time for a CSNY reunion album to be rehearsed and recorded in Hawaii, the summer of '73. After several weeks, the band fell apart once again. No one is willing to say much about what happened. "It's a four-way marriage," says Crosby, "and it doesn't work unless everybody wants to play. We weren't all into it. It doesn't matter who was and who wasn't." Last year, it seems, was a little more lunatic than this.

Inevitably, the subject of Joni Mitchell comes up. At one time or another she has been linked romantically with each member of CSNY.

Crosby is adamant. "For my tastes, she's the best singer-songwriter on the planet. Mitchell just cuts everybody...Dylan, you name it...to ribbons. She's the best."

Nash: "There's a totality about Dylan's music that Joan hasn't quite captured in hers yet. In 1964, Bob Dylan was so *unbelievable*. It kills me to think about it. Joan's doing the same thing now, but it's in a personal rather than social sense. She sees things with such utter clarity ..."

Crosby: "Dylan could write 'Chimes of Freedom' and blow your mind with his insight into the social structure, but Mitchell can write now about people, or your own heart, or your most personal feelings—and she'll drag them right out just to dangle them in front of you. She makes you look at them."

Nash: "The amazing thing is, she keeps hitting new peaks. And she *knows* she's great."

Crosby: "Take it from guys who know. She's about as modest as Mussolini. She knows."

Nash: "She does feel uncomfortable about knowing she's incredible...but not for long." The two collapse in hysterics. "When Joni was a young kid, she decided she'd learn to be a guitarist. So she went out and bought a Pete Seeger guitar instruction record. She went through the chords A, B, C, D, E...but when it came to F, it hurt her hand so badly to play it that she threw the fucking record away and tuned the guitar down so she could comfortably play an F chord. That's how she got started with her amazing tunings. To this day, out of all her songs, only three are played on regular tuning."

Crosby: "As soon as she junked that record, everyone else might as well have packed it in. They were lost in the dirt."

The discussion drifts to last year's ill-fated Byrds reunion album. Crosby winces. "I wasn't satisfied with it. None of us were. We were all way too careful with each other and the material wasn't good enough to pull it off. There was nothing real offensive on that record, it was just bland. Painfully bland. No one wanted to step on each other's toes."

"What's to keep that from happening to CSNY?"

"Everything. There's no chance of this thing turning sour. Everybody confronts everyone else, face-to-face and nose-to-nose, about everything. We're totally out front with each other. It's the only way we can function. We have arguments all the time. We have to or else we'll get trampled. Stephen doesn't mean to, but he could run right over us if we didn't balance him. He's that strong of a person. It's the same thing with Neil. Graham is too much of a gentleman, but that doesn't mean he couldn't completely upstage us all. You wouldn't even know the rest of us were there. There's no pussyfooting around going on."

If everything follows according to the schedule, Crosby, Stills, Nash & Young will begin work this month on their first studio album since *Déjà Vu*. Tentatively titled *Human Highway*, the album will be preceded by a greatest hits package to be called *So Far*. Crosby is particularly fascinated by the fact that Neil Young withdrew "Human Highway," at one time the title track of the LP he wound up calling *On the Beach*, from his own record so that it could grace the CSNY reunion album.

"That was a very strange thing for him to do," he says, shaking his head. "Neil is a very self-oriented man. He seldom acts against his own self-interest. And yet he did take that song, and a few others ["Tonight's the Night" and "New Mama"], and gave them to the group. It was a very, very heavy thing for him to do. It blew my mind. He's got a lot of songs, but those are gems. I thought that was an enormous sign of everything we were looking for in each other. Affection, respect…partnership. That's what it's all about. That's what *we're* all about. I honestly believe we're not gonna lose our way this time around."

Graham Nash nods in silent agreement. "Wish us luck."

CROSBY, STILLS, NASH, YOUNG AND BERT

BY ROY CARR
New Musical Express
August 31, 1974

U.K. journalist Roy Carr was in New York when the CSNY '74 tour rolled through the region. He offers colorful glimpses of life backstage and on stage with the musicians. Crosby and Nash were their usual gregarious selves. Young, while declining to be interviewed, had a strong presence in this piece nonetheless. The "Bert" references apparently stem from a '70s stage production, *John, Paul, George, Ringo and Bert,* by Liverpool playwright Willy Russell (subsequently the writer of such works as *Shirley Valentine, Educating Rita,* and *Blood Brothers.*) The theme of the play was about the rise and fall of "The Fab Four," culminating in a failed reunion concert. So there were parallels with CSNY—often described as the American Beatles—who, unlike their British brethren, managed to reunite successfully in 1974.

Crosby, Stills, Nash & Young at the Oakland Coliseum. July 13, 1974. Photo: John Gavrilis

A few weeks ago the innumerable record stores that fringe New York's Times Square were having great difficulty in shifting their stock of Crosby, Stills, Nash & Young solo albums, even at the all-time low cheap giveaway price of $1.98.

This week, with the aforementioned CSNY doing three gigs in town, not only have these stores hiked the price back up to around four bucks, but they've also mobilised extra copies just to keep pace with demand.

Meanwhile, just a couple of blocks across town, Atlantic Records reckon that the new CSNY compilation of Woodstockian oldies should strike gold (even platinum) within days of being shipped.

Despite the recent fluctuations in their respective solo careers, Crosby, Stills, Nash & Young are a hotter property today than they've ever been. Discounting a spot of box office anemia that caused the postponement of their gig at California's Ontario Motor Speedway, a rough estimate suggests that by the time the lads hit London (on September 14), they will have performed before one-and-a-half-million concert goers and grossed somewhere in the region of 11 million of the green and crinkly. And as yet there's no telling just how much they'll pick up by way of a bonus on reactivated record sales. In other words, they're filthy with it.

Crosby, Stills, Nash & Young at the Oakland Coliseum. July 14, 1974. Photo: John Gavrilis

For all their faults, Crosby, Stills, Nash & Young are the closest to a Beatle-type phenomenon that America ever produced. And that's taking into account the Monkees. So when, in 1970, they made public the fact that they could no longer tolerate one another, they left a void which no act has proved capable of filling. Though Neil Young remained prolific (for a time)—with Stills not too far behind—on their own, the individuals weren't able to generate the same kind of excitement as the basic four-piece unit. Therefore the news of CSNY's re-incarntion—in the wake of the recent resuscitation of the original Byrds, the Andrew Sisters, Dylan, Clapton and John, Paul, George, Ringo and Bert—marked the zenith of the current fixation with nostalgia; which, in itself, is an indictment of rock's stagnation but a real incentive for the Dave Clark Five to polish the rust off their Vox amps.

The whole shebang was vividly summed up in one brief moment when, during CSNY's appearance at Nassau Coliseum out on Long Island, Neil Young loped up to the microphone and casually enquired, "Would you like to hear a new song or an old song?"—to be greeted with the unanimous bellow of "An old song."

Young then strummed his way gently into the opening bars of "Don't Be Denied," proving that you don't have to serve 15 years on the car-wash to qualify for the comeback trail.

The group's manager, Elliot Roberts, recently felt the compulsion to state that, in his opinion, His Boys had spent the last few years "pissing in the wind." Whether or not it was this hype, which inspired the punch-line of Neil Young's "Ambulance Blues," is irrelevant. What is important is that Roberts' observation wasn't too far from the truth. Roberts—not the kind of counsellor to suffocate his clients with over protective paranoia, leaves his four musketeers conspicuously to their own devices as he sits to one side in the enormous room set aside backstage for the circus. He expresses the opinion that, in the light of the recent Presidential pussyfooting, it has been a most opportune moment for the band to extract the collective digit.

"The kids," says Roberts, "can identify with the early songs and that particular period in their life that they shared along with Crosby, Stills, Nash & Young. Now that the Nixon regime has come to a halt and things are more or less out in the open, American youth feel that they've come to the end of a very traumatic era.

"All the riots, picketing, sit-ins and student demonstrations now appear to have had some positive effect, and songs like 'Ohio' and 'Chicago'—which, at the time we all thought were just hollow voices in the wind—now take on even more meaning than before."

Over the microphones CSNY harmonise: "Tin soldiers and Nixon coming, we're finally on our own"—and in response over 18,000 kids jump to their feet to utter an almighty roar.

However, Graham Nash—who looks like he's still trying to thumb a lift back from Yasgar's Farm—refutes the theory that they're filling stadiums from coast-to-coast purely on a political ticket. "They haven't just turned out to hear us sing 'Ohio,'" he argues, while towelling down his greasy torso following an energetic game of table tennis (he plays at least 20 games each day to keep him trim). "They've come for the music that we're making together—and because I know that they respect us as a band. Yes, they do." Yet he doesn't dismiss that many of the things CSNY wrote and sang about in their back pages still carry a social consciousness. "I suppose with us being on the road the same time as the Watergate affair came to a head had made a lot of people acutely aware of what goes on in government—and, after what's just happened, the future is not completely hopeless."

Lugging a road-crew of somewhere between 60 and 80, the CSNY junket moves from gig to gig like a highly sophisticated military operation. But even five-star generals can make mistakes.

For instance, on the way to Nassau Coliseum, our motorcade came to an abrupt halt right in the middle of the 59th Street Bridge, when Neil

Young's GMC Camper—which he is using as both home and transportation for the entire tour—suddenly ran out of fuel.

This mishap held up the nose-to-bumper rush hour traffic in a humid temperature not far short of 90 degrees. Feelin' Groovy anyone? The day before, it was a flat tire.

The story is that Crosby, Stills & Nash, and later Young (though, John Sebastian was on the short list) first pooled their creative resources way back in '69 because as individuals they were sick of having to continually compromise themselves with the immature whims of workmates with over-inflated egos.

Though the collaboration looked like the epitome of the new Hippy Utopia, Crosby, Stills, Nash, Young, (Greg) Reeves and (Dallas) Taylor did hint that the thing was in no way binding, but at that time everyone was either too stoned or too involved in being part of the Woodstock generation to notice this smallprint get-out clause—that is, until they actually took up the option to go it alone.

Anyway, the irony of it all is this. Judging by first-hand quotes and eye-witness accounts of dressing room punch-ups, the very egotism (other people's) that brought Crosby, Stills, Nash & Young together was the failing of their own egotism that prevented them working together up until this very summer.

I take Nash to task over the fact. Howcum that in 1970 they stood on stage and sang "We can save the world"—yet couldn't save themselves from fragmenting in a rather embarrassing manner.

Nash, however, adamantly denies that CSNY ever "officially" disbanded. He explains: "All those people who say that we broke up are just a bunch of stupid assholes. All that actually happened was we didn't record together as a unit…though if you care to check it out, we all appeared on each other's solo projects and also showed up at each other's concerts to help out. Anyway, we've all grown up a lot since those days, we're more aware of what's going on in each other's heads."

Nash reconsiders the implications for a moment then gabbles, "Fifteen minutes from now it might all end up in a furious fist fight, but somehow I really don't think it will. After this tour there's the album to do and for all I know we might just decide to go right back on the road and do this thing all over again. And then again we might not. But one thing is certain—we'll be making music together for a long time to come."

Nash set off in search of his shirt and halts en route to speak to Neil Young. "Hey man," he blurts in his best Mancalifornian accent, "this is what this band's really all about. We're due on stage in about 20 minutes and suddenly Neil's decided to do 'Southern Man' in the show."

As if on cue (ten points to the roadies), acoustic guitars magically appear in the hands of Stills and Nash, and, with Crosby in tow, they gather around Young—who perched on a high stool inches from the bar—and quickly run through the number a couple of times.

On the subject of Young…A lot of folk in Britain find it hard to believe that the rather wasted and dishevelled person on his last solo tour was in fact Neil Young—favouring a theory that this was an incoherent imposter out to ruin the talented Canadian's reputation.

Watching the "real" Neil cruisin' backstage, laughing and joking, it's impossible to believe that this cheerful chappie is the very same who drove both ardent admirers and critics to the brink of tears and despair. Neil Young doesn't give interviews but it's not a prima donna attitude; just that in his own words, "I've really got nothin' to say." On those rare occasions he has broken his rule he says he's never been able to relate to what appeared in print—it always "reads like someone else instead of me."

Strangely enough, however, Young is obviously intrigued (and maybe envious?) as he watches the way Crosby and Nash sit around chewing the fat with the gentlemen of the press. And reminiscent of a panhandler outside a stage-door, he slowly approaches our table. "Hi," he intones—with nasal clarity. He's decked out in a white Buick service station windbreaker, neatly patched blue cords and hides behind a newly-cultivated beard and silver-lensed aviator shades. For extra protection, he sports a straw pork-pie hat. "Hi, Neil."

End of interview?

"Actually, I only showed up tonight 'cause I'm looking for girls," he jokes as he sets his sights on the hot buffet. "Hey somebody's been sleazin' on the food!" All the yummy fried chicken chips and deep fried onion rings have been devoured. "I'd sure like some food," he drones, trying to construct a sandwich from the salvage. Food for a song?

On stage, everyone seems hyper-protective when it comes to perform-ing one of Neil's songs.

At the previous evening's marathon Crosby went over to Young to draw his attention to the fact that one of his new songs was receiving a stand-ing ovation.

"Not only are we protective towards Neil," Crosby explains to me, "and show our deep concern when he's performing one of his songs, but we also show this very same attitude towards each other.

"We're not just hanging around waiting for our own solo spots. To tell you the truth," he continues, "we're all knocked out by the way everyone is trying so hard on everyone's material."

"And don't forget," adds Nash, "this is a seven-piece band, not just four lead singers."

"He's right," agrees Crosby. "Our bass player Tim Drummond and the drummer Russ Kunkel and percussionist Joe Lala are equally important to the success of every show."

Stephen Stills during a CSNY electric set. Oakland Coliseum. July 14, 1974. Photo: Bruce Hock

Back to Young, and Crosby says: "I know for a fact that Neil's real happy up there on stage. Some nights he's jumping around all over the place. If the music's getting him off like that, then that's just great—because Neil's quite a shy person. You've got to know how to bring him out of his shell."

Any fears that Neil Young might be a spent force were banished later that evening. During a workout of a new Young song, "Pushed It Over the End," both Crosby and Nash quickly cleared the decks to allow Stills—brandishing a Gibson Firebird—to demonstrate that he can be a bitch of a guitar player. Then Young squared up to him with a Gretsch White Falcon to trade guitar chores.

Neil Young during a CSNY electric set. Oakland Coliseum. July 14, 1974. From Dave Zimmer personal collection

Things got so intense that Young tucked his axe tightly into his frail frame, hunched his body and began revving up his right leg—like at any moment he was going to execute a Chuck Berry duck-walk.

"It's not as though they're playing," Crosby theorises. "It's more like they're having a conversation. I mean like it's been four years since they last held a conversation like that and they've a helluvah lot to say to one another." Stills hears that last remark, smiles and affirms.

One thing does seem very certain; Crosby, Stills & Nash are going out of their way to make certain that Young doesn't again experience what's best described as his recent artistic and personal nadir.

On the subject of Neil Young's highly controversial last solo tour, Crosby reflects: "Well, to begin with, I wasn't there to see it so I really don't know precisely what happened."

I fill him in on the sad details.

"But I do know that Neil was upset and, I guess, disillusioned a lot of people who love him. When an audience comes out of a show, they're usually laughing and talking, but as I hear it, there was this deathly silence when Neil's shows emptied out. Apparently, people were in a state of complete shock—they just didn't believe what they'd seen or heard. They'd been hurt and it showed."

During the period of Young's melancholia and what appeared to be an effort on his part to put on the worst show possible—he is reported to have said just this to a confidant—Young cut no less than three albums.

Tonight's the Night with Crazy Horse in attendance was, in Elliot Roberts' words, "a drunken rock 'n' roll album," and remains unreleased. The next, *Human Highway,* apparently didn't measure up to Young's personal expectations and was abandoned in favour of *On the Beach,* which has divided listeners into two opposing factions over its merits.

And the grapevine intimates that songs from *Human Highway* will be included on a forthcoming Young solo showcase.

Previous attempts by Crosby, Stills, Nash & Young at a reconciliation seem to have fallen down because their desire to sate personal appetites was totally out-of-balance with any need for intelligent cooperation.

A reunion in 1971 was thwarted, as was another in 1973. But the time they'd satisfied their hunger with various solo projects they were about as near as they'd ever be to sharing the same stage together for more than just one impromtu evening.

Emotionally, they all felt that they could relax a little in each other's company without things degenerating into a bar-room brawl. Crosby and Nash, however, had remained bosom pals through thick and thin: "We're the best friends we have in the whole world," they say of each other. It was really just a matter of tempering the love/hate relationship that had afflicted Stills and Young ever since their Buffalo Springfield days.

That was eventually surmounted, as was a feud that cropped up between Stills and Nash over a bit of skirt. And Crosby...oh, he just kept grinning like the amiable hippy he is as he sailed his wooden ship around the Pacific Ocean.

Today the four are tolerant of each other's quests for individuality, freedom of expression and other quirks. Hassles and shout-ups appear to have become almost non-existent, and ego-tripping a thing of the past.

Perhaps the fact that both Stills and Young have become the fathers (of boys) has given them a mutual interest and sense of maturity.

At first all are reticent about the problems that prevented them from re-grouping much earlier. Crosby and Nash admit that in part all four were to blame, but say they've grown up since 1969. "Look" says Nash, "you saw the show last night and you've been hangin' around with us backstage. I ask you, have you felt anything remotely resembling bad vibes man…well, have you?"

No.

"And you won't," adds Crosby. "You want to know why?"

Yes please.

"Well, it's simply because of this new found maturity. All four of us are eager to give the others more room to do what they do best without being shouted down."

"He's right," Nash continues, "and that's something that you just can't bloody well fake. If we did, and mind you I'm only saying it, the kids would have us sussed out.

"We've learned a helluvah lot from this tour, like being more consider-ate towards each other because we're all secure in who we really are as indi-viduals. The head space is now evenly balanced."

The way David Crosby tells it, the eventual re-grouping takes on a sto-ryline from an Archie comic—with the participants playing the roles of Archie, Betty, Jughead and Veronica.

"Basically," Crosby begins, "it was like this. I decided to take my boat (The Mayan) to Lahania on Maui (one of the Hawaiian Islands) for some div-ing and Graham decided to come-along because he thought it could be a lotta fun" (It was).

"When Stephen heard, he thought, 'Why should they have all the fun?' and so he came out to join us. Then, when Neil heard, and he thought, 'So why should all those have a good time?' and so as not to miss out he joined us. Before we knew it we were all hanging out on my boat, diving, really get-ting healthy and having a swell time.

"After a while the guitars came out and we found ourselves playing and singing each other's songs. And that's where it began to take off."

The scene then quickly shifted to Neil Young's secluded ranch at La Honda, San Francisco. But despite the fact that they laid down six new songs—two of which, "Prison Song" and "And So It Goes," appear on Nash's *Wild Tales* collection—a reunion was temporarily shelved.

Stills is once said to have joked that the first time CSNY hit the road it was for the music; the second for the chicks; and this time for the greenbacks.

A joke…but it's interesting to note that over the last year or so their individual record sales have drastically dipped to the point where—in Stills' case—he sells less than half his usual number. Young can only nudge the half-million mark, whereas his *After the Gold Rush* and *Harvest* accounted for approximately two million copies per album.

Now it has been announced that this tour will gross around 11 million dollars. And the statement appears to haunt the band wherever they go.

"Personally," says Nash, "I don't care if my solo albums only sell a dozen copies. I just want to make my music. It's not what's on the chart but what's in your heart that counts." He pauses mid-sentence. " 'ere, someone…quick a pen…that rhymes," he jokes.

However, only the week before he'd said he felt disappointed with the lack of response to his *Wild Tales* album, and that if no one heard one's album it was a painful blow to the person attempting to communicate.

On stage, however, neither Nash nor his compadres seem at all affected. On numbers like "Love the One You're With" and "Pre-Road Downs" they're as tight as a *fnurg's klitsch* at 20,000 fathoms, while the vocal harmonies on "Wooden Ships" and "Ohio" are as rich and close as the consecutive serial sets of *Happy Families*.

The intro to each song is greeted with audience jubilation most noticeably when Crosby performs "Almost Cut My Hair" and "Déjà Vu;" Stills, "Suite: Judy Blue Eyes;" Nash, "Our House" and "Teach Your Children;" and everything that Young turns his skilled hands to, though "Helpless" and "Ambulance Blues," whined in his best broken banjo string voice, won by a head.

" 'Ere, if people think we're only back for the bloody money they're mistaken," snarls Nash, who obviously finds talk of money distasteful. "We're on stage for well over three hours…sometimes four and we put everything we have into each show."

Crosby mumbles: "Some nights, we can hardly stand up when we come off stage because we're so exhausted." Back to Nash. "Now, if we were only doing it for the money we'd have toured long before this. But like I said, it didn't feel right until now."

"Listen man, nobody forces the kids to come to our shows but there they are in thousands each night we play. The thing that really impresses me," Crosby gleefully confesses, "is that they're a real straight, healthy bunch. No downer freaks or weird heavy dopers in the audience. We don't want that element at our shows.

"I must tell you this," he enthuses, "the other night we played a gig and it rained all day and the kids just stood out in that rain and waited for us. Nobody left. By the time we came on they were soaked to the skin but they stayed for another four hours and sang along on all the songs. Man, that really moved me. I almost cried."

Suddenly Neil Young, guitar in hand, wanders over.

"Hi Neil," says Crosby, "how ya doin'?"

"Oh, I'm just doin' fine."

Young sits down and begins previewing some songs he's been putting together while on the road.

136

"Hey Neil," Nash interrupts "why don't you try 'Hawaiian Sunset?'"

"Alright." And Nash reaches for another guitar. Stills makes it a four-some. As Young and Nash reach the chorus all four blend their distinctive voices into a mood that's evocative of songs on *After the Gold Rush*.

"That's great," remarks Nash, "and whenever you feel like doing it on stage, that's OK with me." Young smiles back shyly and offers, "This is another new one. I really haven't finished it yet...I'll play you what I've got."

This song's hook-line of "I feel like a train carrying a heavy load behind me" prompts Nash to work out an off-the-cuff harmony. It's right first time. Both singers grin at each other.

(Aaah.—*NME* Editor)

"There's a few other songs I wanna do from the old days," says Young; but before he gets side-tracked, Crosby intervenes with some almost father-ly advice.

"Hey Neil, don't play any dark shit numbers, you've got so many good numbers to choose from. Just play those things you really want to play and don't waste your energies on other things."

Neil looks up and starts laughing. "OK then." As quickly as they'd gathered together around the table, they disperse.

After about five minutes, Nash turns to Roberts and enquires: "Hey, where did the rest of the guys go?"

"Oh, didn't I tell you," Roberts begins, "they're on stage rehearsing with Garfunkel." As he leaves the room, Nash looks back at Roberts and, with a dead-pan expression, shouts: "You really know how to hurt someone." And he's gone.

So Hard to Make
Arrangements for Yourself
The *Rolling Stone* Interview
with Neil Young

BY CAMERON CROWE
Rolling Stone
August 14, 1975

While Neil Young had declined most interview requests since 1970, he apparently came to trust one writer: Cameron Crowe. Young's trust was well-placed and rewarded. In this broad ranging interview, Crowe, who had obviously done his homework, asked direct, insightful questions and Young responded with thoughtful candor. This still stands as the Neil Young interview against which all other published conversations with the man are measured.

Neil Young in Malibu. 1975. Photo: Henry Diltz

*N*earing 30, *Neil Young is the most enigmatic of all the superstars to emerge from Buffalo Springfield and Crosby, Stills, Nash & Young. His often cryptic studies of lonely desperation and shaky-voiced antiheroics have led many to brand him a loner and a recluse.* Harvest *was the last time that he struck the delicate balance between critical and commercial acceptance, and his subsequent albums have grown increasingly inaccessible to a mass audience.*

Young's first comprehensive interview comes at a seeming turning point in his life and career. After an amicable breakup with actress Carrie Snodgrass, he's moved from his Northern California ranch to the relative hustle and bustle of Malibu. In the words of a close friend, he seems "frisky...in an incredible mood." Young has unwound to the point where he can approach a story about his career as potentially "a lot of fun."

141

The interview was held while cruising down Sunset Boulevard in a rented red Mercedes and on the back porch of his Malibu beach house. Cooperative throughout, Young only made a single request: "Just keep one thing in mind," he said as soon as the tape recorder had been turned off for the last time. "I may remember it all differently tomorrow."

Why is it that you've finally decided to talk now? For the past five years journalists requesting Neil Young interviews were told you had nothing to say.

There's a lot I have to say. I never did interviews because they always got me in trouble. Always. They never came out right. I just don't like them. As a matter of fact, the more I didn't do them the more they wanted them; the more I said by not saying anything. But things change, you know. I feel very free now. I don't have an old lady anymore. I relate it a lot to that. I'm back living in Southern California. I feel more open than I have in a long while. I'm coming out and speaking to a lot of people. I feel like something new is happening in my life.

I'm really turned on by the new music I'm making now, back with Crazy Horse. Today, even as I'm talking, the songs are running through my head. I'm excited. I think everything I've done is valid or else I wouldn't have released it, but I do realize the last three albums have been a certain way. I know I've gotten a lot of bad publicity for them. Somehow I feel like I've surfaced out of some kind of murk. And the proof will be in my next album. *Tonight's the Night*, I would say, is the final chapter of a period I went through.

Why the murky period?

Oh, I don't know. Danny's death probably tripped it off. Danny Whitten [leader of Crazy Horse and Young's rhythm guitarist/second vocalist]. It happened right before the *Time Fades Away* tour. He was supposed to be in the group. We [Ben Keith, steel guitar; Jack Nitzche, piano; Tim Drummond, bass; Kenny Buttrey, drums; and Young] were rehearsing with him and he just couldn't cut it. He couldn't remember anything. He was too out of it. Too far gone. I had to tell him to go back to L.A. "It's not happening, man. You're not together enough." He just said, "I've got nowhere else to go, man. How am I gonna tell my friends?" And he split. That *night* the coroner called me from L.A. and told me he'd ODed. That blew my mind. Fucking blew my mind. I loved Danny. I felt responsible. And from there, I had to go right out on this huge tour of huge arenas. I was very nervous and…insecure.

Why, then, did you release a live album?

I thought it was valid. *Time Fades Away* was a very nervous album. And that's exactly where I was at on the tour. If you ever sat down and listened to all my records, there'd be a place for it in there. Not that you'd go there every time you wanted to enjoy some music, but if you're on the trip it's important. Every one of my records, to me, is like an ongoing autobiography. I can't write the same book every time. There are artists that can. They put out three or four albums every year and everything fucking sounds the same. That's great. Somebody's trying to communicate to a lot of people and give them the kind of music that they know they want to hear. That isn't my trip. My trip is to express what's on my mind. I don't expect people to listen to my music all the time. Sometimes it's too intense. If you're gonna put a record on at 11:00 in the morning, don't put on *Tonight's the Night*. Put on the Doobie Brothers.

Time Fades Away, as the follow up to Harvest, could have been a huge album...

If it had been commercial.

As it is, it's one of your least selling solo albums. Did you realize what you were sacrificing at the time?

I probably did. I imagine I could have come up with the perfect follow up album. A real winner. But it would have been something that everybody was expecting. And when it got there they would have thought that they understood what I was all about and that would have been it for me. I would have painted myself in the corner. The fact is I'm not that lone, laid-back figure with a guitar. I'm just not that way anymore. I don't want to feel like people expect me to be a certain way. Nobody expected *Time Fades Away* and I'm not sorry I put it out. I didn't need the money, I didn't need the fame. You gotta keep changing. Shirts, old ladies, whatever. I'd rather keep changing and lose a lot of people along the way. If that's the price, I'll pay it. I don't give a shit if my audience is a hundred or a hundred million. It doesn't make any difference to me. I'm convinced that what sells and what I do are two completely different things. If they meet, it's coincidence. I just appreciate the freedom to put out an album like *Tonight's the Night* if I want to.

You sound pretty drunk on that album.

I would have to say that's the most liquid album I've ever made. [*laughs*] You almost need a life preserver to get through that one. We were all leaning on the ol' cactus...and, again, I think that it's something people should hear. They should hear what the artist sounds like under all circumstances if they want to get a complete portrait. Everybody gets fucked up, man. Everybody gets fucked up sooner or later. You're just pretending if you don't let your music get just as liquid as you are when you're really high.

Is that the point of the album?

No. No. That's the means to an end. *Tonight's the Night* is like an OD letter. The whole thing is about life, dope and death. When we [Nils

Lofgren, guitars and piano, Talbot, Molina and Young] played that music we were all thinking of Danny Whitten and Bruce Berry, two close members of our unit lost to junk overdoses. The *Tonight's the Night* sessions were the first time what was left of Crazy Horse had gotten together since Danny died. It was up to us to get the strength together among us to fill the hole he left. The other OD, Bruce Berry, was CSNY's roadie for a long time. His brother Ken runs Studio Instrument Rentals, where we recorded the album. So we had a lot of vibes going for us. There was a lot of spirit in the music we made. It's funny, I remember the whole experience in black and white. We'd go down to S.I.R. about 5:00 in the afternoon and start getting high, drinking tequila and playing pool. About midnight, we'd start playing. And we played Bruce and Danny on their way all through the night. I'm not a junkie and I won't even try it out to check out what it's like…but we all got high enough, right out there on the edge where we felt wide-open to the whole mood. It was spooky. I probably *feel* this album more than anything else I've ever done.

Why did you wait until now to release *Tonight's the Night*? Isn't it almost two years old?

I never finished it. I only had nine songs, so I set the whole thing aside and did *On the Beach* instead. It took Elliot [manager Elliot Roberts] to finish *Tonight's the Night*. You see, awhile back there were some people who were gonna make a Broadway show out of the story of Bruce Berry and everything. They even had a script written. We were putting together a tape for them and in the process of listening back on the old tracks, Elliot found three even older songs that related to the trip, "Lookout Joe," "Borrowed Tune" and "Come On Baby Let's Go Downtown," a live track from when I played the Fillmore East with Crazy Horse. Danny even sings lead on that one. Elliot added those songs to the original nine and sequenced them all into a cohesive story. But I still had no plans whatsoever to release it. I already had another new album called *Homegrown* in the can. The cover was finished and everything. [*laughs*] Ah, but they'll never hear that one.

Okay. Why not?

I'll tell you the whole story. I had a playback party for *Homegrown* for me and about ten friends. We were out of our minds. We all listened to the album and *Tonight's the Night* happened to be on the same reel. So we listened to that too, just for laughs. No comparison.

So you released *Tonight's the Night*. Just like that?

Not because *Homegrown* wasn't as good. A lot of people would probably say that it's better. I know the first time I listened back on *Tonight's the Night* it was the most out-of-tune thing I'd ever heard. Everyone's off-key. I couldn't hack it. But by listening to those two albums back to back at the party, I started to see the weaknesses in *Homegrown*. I took *Tonight's the Night* because of its overall strength in performance and feeling. The theme may be a little depressing, but the general feeling is much more elevating than

Homegrown. Putting this album out is almost an experiment. I fully expect some of the most determinedly worst reviews I've ever had. I mean if anybody really wanted to let go, they could do it on this one. And undoubtedly a few people will. That's good for them, though. I like to see people make giant breakthroughs for themselves. It's good for their psyche to get it all off their chests. [*laughs*] I've seen *Tonight's the Night* draw a line everywhere it's been played. People who thought they would never dislike anything I did fall on the other side of the line. Others who thought "I can't listen to that cat. He's just too sad," or whatever…"His voice is funny." They listen another way now. I'm sure parts of *Homegrown* will surface on other albums of mine. There's some beautiful stuff that Emmylou Harris sings harmony on. I don't know. That record might be more what people would rather hear from me now, but it was just a very down album. It was the darker side to *Harvest*. A lot of the songs had to do with me breaking up with my old lady. It was a little too personal…it scared me. Plus, I had just released *On the Beach*, probably one of the most depressing records I've ever made. I don't want to get down to the point where I can't even get up. I mean there's something to going down there and looking around, but I don't know about sticking around.

You didn't come from a musical family…

Well, my father played a little ukulele. [*laughs*] It just happened. I felt it. I couldn't stop thinking about it. All of a sudden I wanted a guitar and that was it. I started playing around the Winnipeg community clubs, high school dances. I played as much as I could.

With a band?

Oh yeah, always with a band. I never tried it solo until I was 19. Eighteen or 19.

Were you writing at the time?

I started off writing instrumentals. Words came much later. My idol at the time was Hank B. Marvin, Cliff Richard's guitar player in the Shadows. He was the hero of all the guitar players around Winnipeg at the time. Randy Bachman too; he was around then, playing the same circuit. He had a great sound. Used to use a tape repeat.

When did you start singing?

I remember singing Beatles tunes…the first song I ever sang in front of people was "It Won't Be Long" and then "Money (That's What I Want)." That was in the Calvin High School cafeteria. My big moment.

How much different from the States was growing up in Canada?

Everybody in Canada wants to get to the States. At least they did then. I couldn't wait to get out of there because I knew my only chance to be heard was in the States. But I couldn't get down there without a working permit, and I didn't have one. So eventually I just came down illegally and it took until 1970 for me to get a green card. I worked illegally during all of the Buffalo Springfield and some of Crosby, Stills, Nash & Young. I didn't have any papers. I couldn't get a card because I would be replacing an American musician in the union. You had to be real well known and irreplaceable and a separate entity by yourself. So I got the card after I got that kind of stature—which you can't get without fucking being here…the whole thing is ridiculous. The only way to get in is to be here. You can't be here unless it's all right for you to be here. So fuck it. It's like "throw the witch in the water and if it drowns it wasn't a witch. If it comes up, it is a witch and then you kill it." Same logic. But we finally got it together.

Did you know Joni Mitchell in those days?

I've known Joni since I was 18. I met her in one of the coffeehouses. She was beautiful. That was my first impression. She was real frail and wispy looking. And her cheekbones were so beautifully shaped. She'd always wear light satins and silks. I remember thinking that if you blew hard enough, you could probably knock her over. She could hold up a Martin D-18 pretty well, though. What an incredible talent she is. She writes about her relationships so much more vividly than I do. I use…I guess I put more of a veil over what I'm talking about. I've written a few songs that were as stark as hers. Songs like "Pardon My Heart," "Home Fires," "Love Art Blues"…almost all of *Homegrown*. I've never released any of those. And I probably never will. I think I'd be too embarrassed to put them out. They're a little too real.

How do you look back on the whole Buffalo Springfield experience?

Great experience. Those were really good days. Great people. Everybody in that group was a fucking genius at what they did. That was a great group, man. There'll never be another Buffalo Springfield. Never. Everybody's gone such separate ways now, I don't know. If everybody showed up in one place at one time with all the amps and everything, I'd love it. But I'd sure as hell hate to have to get it together. I'd love to play with that band again, just to see if the buzz was still there.

There's a few stock Springfield myths I should ask you about. How about the old hearse story?

True. Bruce and I were tooling around L.A. in my hearse. I loved the hearse. Six people could be getting high in the front and back and nobody would be able to see in because of the curtains. The heater was great. And the tray…the tray was dynamite. You open the side door and the tray whips right out onto the sidewalk. What could be cooler than that? What a way to make your entrance. Pull up to a gig and just wheel out all your stuff on the tray. Anyway, Bruce and I were taking in California. The Promised Land. We were heading up to San Francisco. Stephen and Richie Furay, who were in town putting together a band, just happened to be driving around too. Stephen had met me before and remembered I had a hearse. As soon as he saw the Ontario plates, he knew it was me. So they stopped us. I was happy to see fucking *anybody* I knew. And it seemed very logical to us that we form a band. We picked up Dewey Martin for the drums, which was my idea, four or five days later. Stephen was really pulling for Billy Munday at the time. He'd say "Yeah, yeah, yeah. Dewey's good, but Jesus…he talks too fucking much." I was right though. Dewey was fucking good.

How much has the friction between you and Stills been beneficial over the years?

I think people really have that friction business out of hand. Stephen and I just play really good together. People can't comprehend that we both can play lead guitar in the band and not fight over it. We have total respect for musicianship and we both bring out the perfectionist in each other. We're both very intense, but that's part of our relationship. We both enjoy that. It's part of doing what we do. In that respect being at loggerheads has worked to our advantage. Stephen Stills and I have made some incredible music with each other. Especially in the Springfield. We were young. We had a lot of energy.

Why did you leave the band?

I just couldn't handle it toward the end. My nerves couldn't handle the trip. It wasn't me scheming on a solo career, it wasn't anything but my nerves. Everything started to go too fucking fast, I can tell that now. I was going crazy, you know, joining and quitting and joining again. I began to feel like I didn't have to answer or obey anyone. I needed more space. That was a big problem in my head. So I'd quit, then I'd come back 'cause it sounded so good. It was a constant problem. I just wasn't mature enough to deal with it. I was very young. We were getting the shaft from every angle and it seemed like we were trying to make it so bad and were getting nowhere. The following we had in the beginning, and those people know who they are, was a real special thing. It gave all of us, I think, the strength to do what we've done. With the *intensity* that we've been able to do it. Those few people who were there in the very beginning.

Last Springfield question. Are there, in fact, several albums of unreleased material?

I've got all of that. I've got those tapes.

Why have you sat on them for so long? What are you waiting for?

I'll wait until I hear from some of the other guys. See if anybody else has any tapes. I don't know if Richie or Dicky Davis [Springfield road manager] has anything. I've got good stuff. Great songs. "My Kind of Love," "My Angel," "Down to the Wire," "Baby Don't Scold Me." We'll see what happens.

What was your life like after the Springfield?

It was all right. I needed to get out to the sticks for a while and just relax. I headed for Topanga Canyon and got myself together. I bought a big house that overlooked the whole canyon. I eventually got out of that house because I couldn't handle all the people who kept coming up all the time. Sure was a comfortable fucking place…that was '69, about when I started living with my first wife, Susan. Beautiful woman.

Was your first solo album a love song for her?

No. Very few of my albums are love songs to anyone. Music is so big, man, it just takes up a lot of room. I've dedicated my life to my music so far. And every time I've let it slip and gotten somewhere else, it's showed. Music lasts...a lot longer than relationships do. My first album was very much a first album. I wanted to prove to myself that I could do it. And I did, thanks to the wonder of modern machinery. That first album was overdub city. It's still one of my favorites though. *Everybody Knows This Is Nowhere* is probably my best. It's my favorite one. I've always loved Crazy Horse from the first time I heard the Rockets album on White Whale, The original band we had in '69 and '70—Molina, Talbot, Whitten and me. That was *wonderful*. And it's back that way again now. Everything I've ever done with Crazy Horse has been incredible. Just for the *feeling*, if nothing else.

Why did you join CSNY, then? You were already working steadily with Crazy Horse.

Stephen. I love playing with the other guys, but playing with Stephen is special. David is an excellent rhythm guitarist and Graham sings so great...shit, I don't have to tell anybody those guys are phenomenal. I knew it would be fun. I didn't have to be out front. I could lay back. It didn't have to be me all the time. They were a big group and it was easy for me. I could still work double time with Crazy Horse. With CSNY, I was basically just an instrumentalist that sang a couple of songs with them. It was easy. And the music was great. CSNY, I think, has always been a lot bigger thing to everybody else than it is to us. People always refer to me as Neil Young of CSNY, right? It's not my main trip. It's something that I do every once in a while. I've constantly been working on my own trip all along. And now that Crazy Horse is back in shape, I'm even more self-involved.

How much of your own solo success, though, was due to CSNY?

For sure CSNY put my name out there. They gave me a lot of publicity. But, in all modesty, *After the Gold Rush*, which was kind of the turning point, was a strong album. I really think it was. A lot of hard work went into it. Everything was there. The picture it painted was a strong one. *After the Gold Rush* was the spirit of Topanga Canyon. It seemed like I realized that I'd gotten somewhere. I joined CSNY and was still working a lot with Crazy Horse...I was playing all the time. And having a great time. Right after that album, I left the house. It was a good coda.

How did you cope with your first real blast of superstardom after that?

The first thing I did was a long tour of small halls. Just me and a guitar. I loved it. It was real personal. Very much a one-on-one thing with the crowd. It was later, after *Harvest*, that I hid myself away. I tried to stay away from it all. I thought the record [*Harvest*] was good, but I also knew that something else was dying. I became very reclusive. I didn't want to come out much.

Why? Were you depressed? Scared?

I think I was pretty happy. In spite of everything, I had my old lady and moved to the ranch. A lot of it was my back. I was in and out of hospitals for the two years between *After the Gold Rush* and *Harvest*. I have one weak side and all the muscles slipped on me. My discs slipped. I couldn't hold my guitar up. That's why I sat down on my whole solo tour. I couldn't move around too well, so I laid low for a long time on the ranch and just didn't have any contact, you know. I wore a brace. Crosby would come up to see how I was, we'd go for a walk and it took me 45 minutes to get to the studio, which is only 400 yards from the house. I could only stand up four hours a day. I recorded most of *Harvest* in the brace. That's a lot of the reason it's such a mellow album. I couldn't physically play an electric guitar. "Are You Ready for the Country," "Alabama" and "Words" were all done after I had the operation. The doctors were starting to talk about wheelchairs and shit, so I had some discs removed. But for the most part, I spent two years flat on my back. I had a lot of time to think about what had happened to me.

Have you ever been in analysis?

You mean have I ever been to a psychiatrist? No. [*laughs*] They're all real interested in me though. They always ask a lot of questions when I'm around them.

What do they ask?

Well, I had some seizures. They used to ask me a lot of questions about how I felt, stuff like that. I told them all the thoughts I have and the images I see if I, you know, faint or fall down or something. That's not real important though.

Do you still have seizures?

Yeah, I still do. I wish I didn't. I thought I had it licked.

Is it a physical or mental...

I don't know. Epilepsy is something nobody knows much about. It's just part of me. Part of my head, part of what's happening in there. Sometimes something in my brain triggers it off. Sometimes when I get really high it's a very psychedelic experience to have a seizure. You slip into some other world. Your body's flapping around and you're biting your tongue and batting your head on the ground but your mind is off somewhere else. The only scary thing about it is not going or being there, it's realizing you're totally comfortable in this...void. And that shocks you back into reality. It's a very disorienting experience. It's difficult to get a grip on yourself. The last time it happened, it took about an hour-and-a-half of just walking around the ranch with two of my friends to get it together.

Has it ever happened onstage?

No. Never has. I felt like it was a couple times and I've always left the stage. I get too high or something. It's just pressure from around, you know. That's why I don't like crowds too much.

What were the sessions like for *Déjà Vu*? Was it a band effort?

The band sessions on that record were "Helpless," "Woodstock" and "Almost Cut My Hair." That was Crosby, Stills, Nash & Young. All the other ones were combinations, records that were more done by one person using the other people. "Woodstock" was a *great* record at first. It was a great live record, man. Everyone played and sang at once. Stephen sang the shit out of it. The track was magic. Then, later on, they were in the studio for a long time and started nitpicking. Sure enough, Stephen erased the vocal and put another one on that wasn't nearly as incredible. They did a lot of things over again that I thought were more raw and vital sounding. But that's all personal taste. I'm only saying that because it might be interesting to some people how we put that album together. I'm happy with every one of the things I've recorded with them. They turned out really fine. I certainly don't hold any grudges.

You seem a bit defensive.

Well, everybody always concentrates on this whole thing that we fight all the time among each other. That's a load of shit. They don't know what the fuck they're talking about. It's all rumors. When the four of us are together it's real intense. When you're dealing with any four totally different people who all have ideas on how to do one thing, it gets steamy. And we love it, man. We're having a great time. People make up so much shit, though. I've read so much gossip in *Rolling Stone* alone…Ann Landers would blanch. It would surprise you. Somehow we've gotten on this social-register level and it has nothing to do with what we're trying to put out. The music press writes the weirdest shit about us. They're just wasting their fucking time.

There was a recent item published that CSNY had tried to record a new album but couldn't because you "felt someplace else."

Total bullshit. That's just somebody trying to come up with a good line and stick it in my mouth. "Yeah, that's kind of ethereal. Sounds like something Neil Young might say." And bingo…it's like they were there. We had some recording sessions, you know, and we recorded a few things. That's what happened. We went down to the Record Plant in Sausalito, rented some studio time and left with two things in the can.

What was that?

A song of David's and a song of Graham's that were great. We were really into something nice. But a lot of things were happening at the same time. Crosby's baby was about to be born. Some of us wanted to rest for a while. We'd been working very hard. Everybody has a different viewpoint and it just takes us a while to get them all together. It's a great group for that, though. I'm sure there'll come a time when we'll do something again. We really did accomplish some things at those sessions. And just because the sessions only lasted three days, people started building up bullshit stories. We all love each other, but we're into another period where we're all hot on our own projects. Stephen's on tour with his new album, Graham and David are recording and I'm into my new album with Crazy Horse. Looking back, we might have been wiser to do the album before the tour. While we were still building the energy. But there's other times to record. Atlantic still has CSNY. Whenever we record together, we do it for Ahmet, which I think is right. Ahmet Ertegun kept the Buffalo Springfield afloat for as long as it was. He's always been great. I love him. There may be a live album to come from the tour last summer too. I know there's at least 25 minutes of my songs that are definitely releasable. We've got some really good stuff in the can for that tour. There was some good playing.

Why did you travel totally separate from everyone else on that tour?

I wanted to stay totally separate from everything, except the music. It worked well. I left right after every gig with my kid, my dog and two friends. I'd be refreshed and feeling great for every show.

Why did you make a movie?

It was something that I wanted to do. The music, which has been and always will be my primary thing, just seemed to *point* that way. I wanted to express a visual picture of what I was singing about.

One critic wrote that the movie's theme was "life is pointless."

Maybe that's what the guy got out of it. I just made a feeling. It's hard to say what the movie means. I think it's a good film for a first film. I think it's a really good film. I don't think I was trying to say that life is pointless. It does lay a lot of shit on people though. It wasn't made for entertainment. I'll admit, I made it for myself. Whatever it is, that's the way I felt. I made it for me. I never even had a script.

Did the bad reviews surprise you at all?

Of course not. The film community doesn't want to see me in there. What do they want with *Journey Through the Past?* [*laughs*] It's got no plot. No point. No stars. They don't want to see that. But the next time, man, we'll get them. The next time. I've got all the equipment, all the ideas and motivation to make another picture. I've even been keeping my chops up as a cameraman by being on hire under the name of Bernard Shakey. I filmed a Hyatt House commercial not too long ago. I'm set. [*laughs*] I'm just waiting for the right time.

What about a plot?

It's real simple. Maybe it's not a plot but it's a very strong *feeling*. It's built around three or four people living together. No music. I'll never make another movie that has anything to do with me. I'll tell you that. That was the only way I could get to do the first movie. I wanted to be in a movie, so I did it. I sacrificed myself as a musician to do it.

So you don't really consider the soundtrack album an official Neil Young release?

No. There was an unfortunate sequence of events surrounding *Journey Through the Past*. The record company told me that they'd finance me doing the movie only if I gave them the soundtrack album. They took the thing [the soundtrack] and put it right out. Then they told me that they didn't want to release the movie because it wasn't...well, they wanted to group it with a bunch of other films. I wanted to get it out there on its own. So they chickened out on the movie because they thought it was weird. But they took me for the album. That's always been a ticklish subject with me. That's the only instance of discooperation and confusion that I've ever had with Warners. Somebody really missed the boat on that one. They fucked me up for sure. It's all right though. We found another distributor. It paid for itself. Even though it got banned in England, you know. They thought it was immoral. There were swearing and references to Christ that didn't set well with them.

Why did you leave the ranch?

It just got to be too big of a trip. There was too much going on the last couple of years. None of it had anything to do with music. I just had too many fucking people hanging around who don't really know me. They were parasites whether they intended to be or not. They lived off me, used my money to buy things, used my telephone to make their calls. General leeching. It hurt my feelings a lot when I reached that realization. I didn't want to believe I was being taken advantage of. I didn't like having to be boss and I don't like having to say "Get the fuck out." That's why I have different houses now. When people gather around me, I just split now. I mean my ranch is more beautiful and lasting than ever. It's strong without me. I just don't feel like it's the only place I can be and be safe anymore. I feel much stronger now.

Have you got a name for the new album?

I think I'll call it *My Old Neighborhood*. Either that or *Ride My Llama*. It's weird, I've got all these songs about Peru, the Aztecs and the Incas. Time travel stuff. We've got one song called "Marlon Brando, John Ehrlichman, Pocahontas and Me." I'm playing a lot of electric guitar and that's what I like best. Two guitars, bass and drums. And it's really flying off the ground too. Fucking unbelievable. I've got a bet with Elliot that it'll be out before the end of September. After that we'll probably go out on a fall tour of 3,000 seaters. Me and Crazy Horse again. I couldn't be happier. That, combined with the bachelor life...I feel magnificent. Now is the first time I can remember coming out of a relationship, definitely not wanting to get into another one. I'm just not looking. I'm so happy with the space I'm in right now. It's like spring. [*laughs*] I'll sell you two bottles of it for $1.50.

STEPHEN STILLS GROWS UP

The trouble I got into
tryin' to live up to
what they said I lucked into
at twenty-five.

—"My Favorite Changes," Stephen Stills

BY LOWELL CAUFFIEL
Creem
November 1975

More than a year had passed since the CSNY tour of 1974 and it seemed no CSNY album was going to materialize any time soon. So Stills carried on with his own career. Journalist/novelist Lowell Cauffiel caught up with Stills when his solo tour hit Michigan, capturing the artist's creative energy and thought process at that time.

Stephen Stills. Photo: Roger Barone

Stephen Stills was dining/drinking with his band at a nightclub near Michigan's Pine Knob Music Theater, the first stop of a new tour with a new set of musicians and in the wake of a new album release with a new record company.

Those old cliches one might normally use in describing such events were absent: No hangers-on. No groupies, except for a few wide-eyed bar maids here and there. No limos, just Ford station wagons parked outside. And in the background, an MOR band brushed away innocuously under the laughter of Stills and the boys who were rehashing the ups and downs of their premiere gig.

Stephen was celebrating the opener by getting pleasantly lit on scotch. Glass in hand, he plopped down at a table where myself, another writer from a Cleveland tabloid and a publicist from Columbia Records were sitting. In the past, Stills had been tight in giving interviews. More were planned for this tour, however, because his "skin is thicker," as he would say later; or perhaps he just needed the ink.

155

"My way of dealing with things is different," Stills told the reporter from Cleveland. "It's called growing up. In my mind, I've gone through a pretty natural progression in life." A few quick thoughts came to mind: Stills was in his third year of marriage with French singer Veronique Sanson and had a 14-month, old son, Christopher Stephen. He had been overtly polite and friendly when he introduced himself to the table.

Now normally there wouldn't be any significance in the fact that a joking, polite family man had seated himself at our table. But with Stephen Stills in that role there was—at least in comparison with past reports where he'd been labeled "uncouth," "an arrogant superstar," and "an insecure egotist," along with tales of booze and drug revelry. Initially, then, I guessed all this would add up to a rock-rebel-goes-mellow story, but as the hours in Stephen's company began to tick by, it didn't.

Stills remains a turbulent character. "Out front, I've always been a pretty salty cat," he said. "I still am." His restlessness surfaces in a variety of ways—in his inability to sit in one position for more than a few moments, in his need to play ten different guitars during a show (and keep another sixty around the house) or in the fact he'll wear one T-shirt, two western shirts and five different football jerseys in the space of eight hours.

Stills likes to talk about his changes, but then again, going through a whole lot of them seems to be his most consistent quality.

The following day, Stills arrived at the Pine Knob stage several hours before his next show. Though the opener had been ragged, Stephen blamed it on the jitters and confidently told Michael John Bowen, his manager, he wouldn't be rehearsing with the band. We strolled into his intensely air-conditioned dressing room and Stills sprawled on a couch and placed his hands behind his head like a patient ready to unload to a shrink.

"I really don't deal with the star syndrome anymore," he said after the interview was well underway. "I used to. It was part of working it out. I used to get terribly paranoid about it...But I just realize it for the bullshit that it is but at the same time realize the phenomenon that makes it occur. I'm a star only because people think I am and if I'm not, I'm not.

"Jiveism," he added. "That's been the hardest thing to overcome. Partly on my own, partly by the British, partly by the press and the kind of trips people get into about music. It's just really jive. Jive is jive is jive. Trying to get your music past all that jiveness is the challenge."

In the past Stills has said he wanted deliverance from the "rock and roll circus." I asked him if he found it. He got up from the couch and leaned against the wall. "The circus I was talking about is the…hanger-on, the crowd that gravitates to the scene. I find it dull." The idea of making the gossip columns with Mick Jagger didn't thrill him, I ventured? "That's all glamour magazine stuff, part of the business. And I suppose I'll always remain a little bit of an enigma because of my distaste for it.

"I do enjoy, though, going out with Mick Jagger," he continued. "Because we always manage to find someplace and sit there quietly and get drunk and trade war stories. But I could never get into that Hollywood horseshit and who I was with. Jagger realizes it's a tool and uses it. That's probably one reason why he's infinitely more successful than I. But I don't begrudge him that."

As the sound of his band rehearsing rose in the background. Stills began to talk enthusiastically about his solo outing and the group he'd assembled. Bassman Chocolate George Perry and drummer Tubby Ziegler, former studio men, would be getting their first large audience exposure. Vocalists/guitarists Rick Roberts, an ex-Burrito Brother, and Donnie Dacus, once a sideman for Stills' wife, were themselves budding solo artists. Also in the group were organist Jerry Aiello and Joe Lala, percussionist and Manassas grad. Stills himself is playing surprisingly searing lead guitar these days, unleashing the power of two Marshall amps in many of the 24 songs in their three hour show. It brought the audience to its feet and in one of the two encores, the band even unveiled an all-electric "Suite: Judy Blues Eyes."

When he began talking about CSNY—"Merrill Lynch, Pierce, Fenner and Smith," he quipped—a tone of weariness crept into his voice. He said he "honestly" didn't know if the band would ever re-group. Stills claimed Atlantic Records hadn't backed his past solo efforts well, possibly, he said, as a ploy to pressure CSNY into making more albums. It was one of the reasons, Stills said, he signed with Columbia—"because they took me for me." "I've got a real problem," he would say later. "People seem to think it was one of the greatest fucking groups in the world."

"A lot of people seem to think CSNY should be in the studio, churning out the material," I said.

"Horseshit," Stills shot back quickly, punctuating it with a chuckle. "Neil and I could never do that. He knows it. I know it. And Neil and I are great friends. One of these days, though, and this is a direct quote from him: 'Stephen and I are going to make an album that will terrorize this industry,' which is absolutely true. We'll get around to it, when we find the right band we both can agree on. We'll just go in and make a monster."

There's another link with his past that Stills doesn't seem to be too happy about these days. As a patriarch of a drug culture that surfaced in the '60s, he said he feels partly "responsible" for the heavy drug abuse in subsequent years.

Stephen Stills and Neil Young at Roscoe Maples Pavilion, Stanford University, California. November 22, 1975. Photo: Dave Zimmer

"That's why I get incensed about people who keep writing about me being a big cokie," he said. "I mean drugs are…why fuck with people smoking flowers. So what if it makes them a little out of it. Or even blowing a little coke, it ain't gonna kill ya…I'm not going to be a hypocrite and defend anything but I feel partly responsible and it kind of makes me feel a little ashamed."

Stills walked over to a coat rack, grabbed it firmly and stared straight ahead. "On the one hand I see the danger of dope and on the other hand I'm part of the heathen defense league." He laughed, then continued seriously. "I don't want to pontificate about it one way or the other, except in the case of smack. Heroin incenses me. If we go into a whole thing, though, about cleaning up our act, then become like these puritanical figures that made us rebel and get into it…but a lot of kids are figuring out how out of it it is. I've buried a couple of good friends and had old friendships dissolve because of drugs. It's as real of a dilemma as power politics.

"There was always a reckless abandon to the way I did things," he said. "Consequently I spent hundreds of thousands of dollars learning how to make records and bullshitting around in the studio. Now I'm trying to apply some of the discipline I learned early in life, and just get it together to use the knowledge as quickly and as efficiently as possible."

158

With a personality as mercurial as Stills' had been known to be, I was interested in finding out what his fears were, what kept him up at nights?

"I have the standard fear of failure." he'd said. "I'd like to live long enough to do it all and I worry about being killed in a car crash, and all that stock stuff. What keeps me up at night is not any kind of fear, but I'll sit there and my mind will start churning for a song, a screenplay, for an arrangement or a certain business thing. And I'll just go fucking nuts trying to shut it off."

Rocky & Bullwinkle in Marin County

by Jaan Uhelszki
Creem
February 1976

This *Creem* article by Jaan Uhelszki portrayed Crosby and Nash enjoying a sweet spot. Secure with their success as a duo entity on stage and record, they acknowledged some frustration with CSNY's inability to complete an album following the '74 tour. But neither Crosby nor Nash seemed ready to close the door on possible future projects with Stills and Young.

David Crosby and Graham Nash at the Greek Theatre, Berkeley. September 13, 1975.
Photo: Dave Patrick

Ring! Brring! Ring!
"What d'ya want!" demands a rudely awakened voice on the other end of the wire. Taken a little off guard, the writer quickly explains her intentions: To consummate a prearranged 4:00 p.m. interview with Crosby and Nash, that reunited Rocky and Bullwinkle of rock.

"Absolutely not!" snorts the voice. "Graham has just gotten out of the hospital, and David is dead on his feet, and besides..."

"Listen, this appointment shouldn't be any surprise," I protest. My permapress had long before wilted due to a four hour car ride to a rural Michigan teaching college. "I'll be down in five minutes," I say.

"No way!" cautions the testy voice. "After the show or not at all."

A few angry phone calls and some record company politics later, I find myself hesitantly knocking on David Crosby's door, with the assurance, or should I say compromise, of a 20-minute "quickie" chat with half the duo. Crosby cracks open the door, looking none too pleased with the intrusion of me and my Sony. Trying to smooth the tense situation, I mumble something like..."poor baby."

"I am not a baby!" he retorts with the demeanor of a man who has been relentlessly accused of looking cute and cuddly—he's weary of being compared to a Teddy Bear. But nevertheless, David Crosby is cute in an engaging, Captain Kangaroo-ish kind of way.

Crosby's room is overbright, a spacious desolation, as only a Holiday Inn room can be. The only signs of habitation are dirty socks, carelessly opened suitcases, and unread skin mags scattered on the spotted shag floor. Mr. C. looks vaguely out of place in this pedestrian palace of Americana. After all, he did write "Eight Miles High," and was one quarter of one of rock's most popular groups. I mean, I'm sure the guy has probably bedded down in Conrad Hilton's finest. But here he is, scowling at me in a ratty red wool sweater, baggy brown levis, mismatched socks and a dirty pair of Topsiders. I am disarmed by the image. In fact my usual technique of studied but casual scrutiny had deteriorated into obvious gawking. Oddly he is more amused than irritated, and asked me, "What did you expect? I'm no superstar, and I've never been a fashion plate. See, I'm just the way I am, a little disheveled right now, maybe…I started out life as a chubby kid and things never got much better."

"Hey, come on!" I protest, a little embarrassed by his self-effacement. "You were the teen queens' heart throb with your bobbed hair back when you were in the Byrds. And I'd still give you a 6 and a half."

He screws his face up into a caricature of himself, and asks: "Do you get these headaches often?"

"What's the matter, can't you take compliments?"

He pauses thoughtfully, "No. After being with CSNY it was easy to let my ego get out of hand, buying my own bullshit. But now I have all the mistakes of ego behind me. I am definitely one of the funniest things I've ever seen. I can't even look in the mirror without getting hysterical. You see there's always this little guy standing there who looks like a pear with a brillo pad stuck on his head."

Back to the star sham: "Frankly, we're for real. Me and Nash aren't superstars or ubermen. It's a real straight trip. It's just us getting off on music, together. No mirrors, nets, or wires. Just a little kind of stumpy guy with funny hair and a good looking Englishman, and they've got these songs. Either you like them or you don't. It's right on the fucking line. The thing that I feel sorry for is that I see that kid Springsteen being flashpanned so hard that no way it's not going to damage him. They set a person up, aggrandize him beyond what he wants and way beyond reality. This cat is Jesus Christ, he's eleven feet tall, he's got chrome hair, he plays three guitars at once and he has wings. But he's just some regular guy people are building up so they have someone to tear down."

A knock on the door, and another voice booms simply, "Ten minutes!" "Oh I don't want to get to work yet," Crosby jokes. "Now, about that interview. After the show, okay? I'm sorry for all the misunderstanding, okay?"

Someone once said in a review of *Déjà Vu* that the principal weaknesses of CSNY were Crosby's singing and Nash's songwriting. But six years later, Crosby and Nash are growing gracefully older together. But that's not implying they're ready for the bone heap. Their enthusiasm and music is at full tilt. They've transcended the CSNY concept of vocal chords as the most viable instruments of rock, and have achieved something with their band that CSNY never even approached—music with teeth, metamorphosing into a more energetic, vigorous, and often funky mold. In this incarnation, you can justifiably say that Crosby and Nash are playing rock and roll.

Backstage, between sets, I spy Graham Nash, impeccably dressed and as perfect as a Ken doll. He is vaulting and ricocheting around the dressing room as if Slinkies are attached to the bottom of his Adidas, a remarkable feat considering that he had just been discharged from the hospital that day for— exhaustion. "I was so relieved that I didn't have pneumonia I celebrated by going out and eating a Big Mac," he quips and turns to go back on stage.

I move towards a folding chair. Before I reach it, David Crosby blocks my way, and somewhere between urging and insisting he says, "Don't miss this part, Jaan. You're really in for a treat. Go out there and see; no, go listen." What he is referring to is Nash's solo acoustic numbers. The crowd is suspended in enraptured animation. I too am impressed. But more, I am impressed with the mutual devotion of Crosby and Nash. They are each other's biggest fans.

David Crosby once said in an interview that Nash was "the most highly-evolved human being" he had ever met. When I ask for Nash's comments on this, he is a little embarrassed, fingering his collar. "I don't agree with him. Because of my shortcomings. He has a very high opinion of me, of that I have no doubt."

Crosby in the same interview had also proclaimed that if Nash were a chick he'd marry him, so I playfully interrogate Nash whether the two of them are lovers, and if that was the reason they made albums together. "Who? Me and Crosby? Go ask my old lady! Go talk to Nancy Brown! I'm staggered!" he answers in a flurry of denials. Then, silent for a moment, he asks me in a small voice, "People really don't think that do they?" Assuring him that his reputation is intact, I ask them what kept them together if it wasn't queer-baiting.

"Our differences. David is intense, fiery, bright red. I'm a little more mellow, a little more stable. It's not that he's unstable but he tends to have a short fuse. My character is a soothing one, so we balance each other out. It works on a musical and friendship level."

"But doesn't the friendship ever get in the way of the music?" I ask.

"My friendship only adds to the music that David and I make. I have nothing to hide from him; I know he's not going to stab me in the back so I don't waste my energy distrusting him. That frees my mind to explore just how far I can go with the man musically. I can definitely see a growth in David and I musically as well as friends."

Crosby: "Nash is the person I want to play with more than anybody else in the world. He knows that, man. He doesn't have to be territorial on me. I don't worry about him, he doesn't worry about me."

Well if nobody is worrying about anything, is everybody happy? Everybody except Atlantic Records, since *Wind on the Water* went gold—and it's on ABC. Crosby and Nash left Atlantic Records because they were sick of being the Ted and Alice of Crosby, Stills, Nash & Young. "When we were at Atlantic," fumes Crosby, "those chumps would say whenever we walked in 'Hey here's half of the biggest supergroup in America.' Big was the only thing that mattered, and we were only fragmentations to them…You wanna hear an ego trip? I think we're great. I think me and Nash are one of my favorite duets in history. I like us. I don't think we have to be the best. I don't think I'm the best singer-songwriter or guitarist in the world. But what I do with him is good music and I'm proud of it."

Logically my next question is about their "better half." I am curious as to how they would rate the other solo efforts that have come from the unit. "Any one of us is weaker than the four of us. But I really believe that the four of us, when we're really making magic—it's more explosive than any of our single efforts. Sure, I think *Tonight's the Night* is great. I thought Neil was incredibly brave to release it in its raw form. I'm also very pleased with our album, but David and I will both readily admit that there's magic the four of us can produce that we can't close our minds to," says Nash.

Me, I am more impressed with Crosby and Nash's current arrangement than with the celebrated quartet, so only half-jokingly I suggest to Nash, "Don't go back to the old band."

Looking me dead straight in the eye, Nash declares emphatically, "There is no old band, only the next one."

"So, there was never any rock 'n' roll divorce of the four of you?"

Nash looks somewhat aghast at the idea, but Crosby is the one that answers. "From the beginning we all agreed that CSNY wasn't a permanent entity. We'd regroup whenever we felt the inclination or need, and we'd save all the best material for the band. But there are times when it's good to do it, and there are times when it's not."

"So, the timing was off for that projected fourth CSNY album, *Human Highway*, that you planned after the tour?"

Crosby is candid about the project. "We had been at each other's faces for too long. I'm not Francis of Assisi. Graham is the *only* nice guy and if you put all of us together for very long we drain on each other quite a bit. Stills and me particularly are very cocky cats. We have different ways of dealing with it, but we are cocky. I'm feisty and not easy to get along with. At the end of that *long* tour, going into the studio was a hopeless cause. Stills was burnt out. I was burnt. Even Nash was less than his usual nice self. And Neil. Neil, Mr. Dependable. He came into the studio and said, 'Great, out of sight. I'll be back tomorrow night.' And never showed again. That kind of trip really doesn't encourage you to work. It wasn't anything more than the practicality that we couldn't get along with each other any more in the studio and we couldn't get into any of the tape."

CSNY were practically the steering committee of the Woodstock Nation and, as *NME* so aptly put it, they were the first post-Beatles band to be a major source of enlightenment and inspiration to the youth culture. They created some of the most topical music of the times, like: "Chicago," "Ohio," "Almost Cut My Hair," and "Teach Your Children." Midwest college students used to clutch CSNY albums to their bosoms along with copies of *The Greening of America*.

"People thought we were a political band. That's not what we thought. What we sang about were just isolated incidents that happened. Four people were lying dead at Kent State, and Kennedy actually did get assassinated. We commented on it," says Crosby. "Back in 1969 we thought that the change in value systems would sweep much further than it did. We thought our lifestyle would pervade the whole country. It has, but much slower than we anticipated. Certain values that had been heavily pervasive before were no longer valid. People were offered an alternative. We were only one of the art forms that expressed that. *Writers* were before us. But we're operating with an electronic mass medium and that ain't Gutenberg, baby. That's millions. At that level, we [CSNY] were the most visible, so people made us out to be priests. But in truth we were only reflecting the value systems. We didn't lead anything.

"If we were doing anything we were trying to build bridges between human beings. I don't think we were being political. I think we were being humanitarian. There's a lot of field worker in me. There's a lot of whale in me. What happened to the whales will eventually happen to humanity. You can't take away any part without affecting the whole. As the whale goes so goes man."

Since Crosby's view of the impending human condition is so dim, dare I ask about something as crucial as the future of music? I plunge: "Where do you think '70s music stands? In the hands of Roxy Music, Aerosmith, ZZ Top...?"

Crosby insists that he's insulted by any such suggestions.

"The heaviest people might be the same ones who were putting out the heaviest music at the end of the '60s. Dylan, Mitchell, Neil. Those people are putting out much more important music than the people you were talking about," he declares.

The way things are going, it looks like he just might be right.

For his sake...

QUICK END TO A LONG RUN

In which Neil Young and Stephen Stills
find that old magic and lose it all to a
sore throat.

BY CAMERON CROWE
Rolling Stone
September 9, 1976

A duo project by Stephen Stills and Neil Young in 1976 seemed like a "can't miss" affair. There had been some live teasers in 1975, when Young walked on at three Stills concerts in California, and as a New Year began, the two old friends saw it in together, acoustic guitars in hand, at a small bar in the Santa Cruz Mountains. But as Stills-Young recording sessions evolved into an attempt at another CSNY project, then morphed back into a Stills-Young album and was taken on the road, something was lost in the process. In this article, Cameron Crowe chronicled the promise of greatness, ultimate disappointment and the abrupt end of the short-lived Stills-Young Band.

Stephen Stills and Neil Young trail roadie Gerry Caskey backstage at the Spectrum, Philadelphia, before a Stills-Young Band concert. June 29, 1976. Photo: Roger Barone

Forget the balding pate and those wisps of gray. Stephen Stills and Neil Young, their hair cut summer-short, looked eerily like they did on the cover of *Buffalo Springfield Again*. But gone, at least temporarily, was the carefree abandon of those days. This was serious business.

The scheduled three-month-long Stills-Young Band tour had been rolling only two weeks, and while it came close to jelling in Boston just a few days before, the show still teetered on the edge of the magic that everyone knew they were capable of.

171

Even before they broke into their opener, "Love the One You're With," the sold-out crowd of 20,000 at the Capitol Center exploded at the sight of Stills and Young on the same stage again. In this, the summer of Aerosmith and ZZ Top, it was nothing short of astonishing to see the sustained drawing power of two artists who have not seen a solo hit single or gold album in years.

On paper, Stills and Young's set was a fan's dream. "Love the One You're With" was followed by a verse-trading rendition of "The Loner," then "Helpless," "For What It's Worth," the title track of their forthcoming album, *Long May You Run*, "Black Queen" and "Southern Man." After a ten-minute break, Young returned alone for "Sugar Mountain," "Old Man," a superb new song called "Stringman" and "After the Gold Rush." Stills performed his own solo set of "Helplessly Hoping," "49 Bye Byes," "Word Game" and "Four Days Gone." Together they did an acoustic "Ohio," then "Buyin' Time" with the band and another new song, "Evening Coconut," "Make Love to You," "Cowgirl in the Sand" and "Mr. Soul." The encore was an electric "Suite: Judy Blue Eyes."

Aside from the power of the songs themselves, though, it was another off performance. Stills had difficulty singing on mike and sometimes even remembering words. The harmonies sounded ragged. Young, in the process of keeping the vocals faithful, became too tense to cut loose on guitar himself. In typical style, Young did not hang around afterward. He went straight from the stage to the airport, where a Lear jet would take him to Miami for a day of remixing some vocals on *Long May You Run*. "If we both go," he told Stills, "neither of us will want to come back."

Stills spent the rest of the night in the Holiday Inn bar, nursing drinks and talking with fans. Somewhere in the early morning hours, he was even coaxed onstage for jams with the house band on "The Thrill Is Gone." Less than an hour after he finally headed upstairs to retire, the morning paper's review was out. The assessment was more bewildered than negative. Like most every other review thus far, it wondered why Young had ever taken on such a project.

Neil Young refused to be quoted in connection with the Stills-Young Band tour. He expressed a strong desire to just do the tour, bypass the hype and move on. He was fully aware of their ever-diverging paths, but he respects Stills as a musician…and worries about him. This tour, one sensed, was Young's way of helping Stills back on his creative feet. "It was," said one associate, "something Neil felt he had to do."

At thirty, Young has begun more than ever to realize his potential. Besides working on a screenplay, he writes several songs a day, has a few complete albums in the can and maintains an entirely separate career with Crazy Horse.

Stills, now thirty-one, knows full well that his solo work has lacked critical importance in recent years. "These last few years," he said, "I've been concentrating on my guitar work. I want to be considered one of the masters." As a result, the emphasis has gone off what was once Stills' strongest area—songwriting. When his last album, *Illegal Stills*, was ignored in most circles, including *Rolling Stone's* review section, he was very disappointed, but he said recently, "I'll tell you something. I'm gonna keep at this until I win back every last person.

"If I'm cruddy on my own, it doesn't bother me half as much as if I don't hold my own backing up Neil. The one thing that everyone has always assumed is that there's a fundamental competition between us. In fact, it's the difference between us that makes it work. When he comes up with those killer lines, I fall on the floor just like everybody else. And when I play something that blows his mind, he falls on the floor just like everybody else. It's the ultimate complementary relationship."

The changes that that relationship has undergone must strike Young as ironic at times. Stills was the one who brought him into the Buffalo Springfield and later Crosby, Stills & Nash. Young, at that point, was little more than a hired gun—another electric guitar to toughen up CSN's sweetness-and-harmony image. Young caught on quickly. Today it's that same hired gun whom everyone expects to call most of the shots. Whenever CSNY tries at another reformation, it is usually because Young has expressed the interest. But—and here's the snag—Neil Young is not a pressure performer. His constant frustration is that he must stand in a spotlight.

"I could have dug playing guitar with the Eagles," Young blurted late one night in the customized bus he designed himself. He jammed with the band three years ago at a San Luis Obispo benefit and never forgot how much fun he had. "I'd join any band I got off with. I'd love to play with the Rolling Stones…but they probably don't know my rock & roll side."

It's that same guitar player in him that brought Young back to Stills last summer. Young had just been released from the hospital after a throat operation when he dropped by a Stills concert at the Greek Theatre in Berkeley on July 25. He could not speak, much less sing. "It was truly great," Stills remembered. "He was passing us notes and playing up a storm. We both got off like motherfuckers."

Young did not forget. Four months later, he "just showed up" backstage at Stills' Stanford University appearance. Young watched the show and finally wandered out for the acoustic set. When he turned up the next afternoon in Los Angeles for Stills' concert at UCLA's Pauley Pavilion—again without warning—Young was equipped with his electric Les Paul. He and Stills dueled guitars far into the night, dazzling themselves and the audience to no end. "The spirit of the Springfield is back," Stills shouted in ecstasy. The commitment had been made.

The Stills-Young Band on stage at the Spectrum, Philadelphia. June 29, 1976. Photo: Roger Barone

Young went on to play a few Northern California bars, then visited Japan and Europe with Crazy Horse. The tour, by every account, soared beyond Young's highest hopes. "Every night was incredible," he recalled. "I really get free with Crazy Horse. They let me zoom off...and know me well enough to be right there when I get back. They're the American Rolling Stones, no doubt about it."

When it came to America, though, Young returned to Stills. The two flew to Miami and began work on an album. Midway into the sessions, Young had the impulse to turn it into a Crosby, Stills, Nash & Young project. Crosby and Nash agreed to give it a shot and flew down to Criteria Sound Studios to help out. For a few weeks it looked as if that third CSNY album would finally become a reality. Then, while Crosby and Nash took a break and returned to L.A. to meet the deadline for their own sessions on *Whistling Down the Wire*, Stills and Young continued working. They eventually decided to return to the original idea of a Stills-Young Band. Crosby and Nash's harmonies were replaced by Stills' band.

Said Nash of the near-CSNY reunion attempt: "We probably came closer this last time than we've ever come before. Stills was amazingly loose. Neil was great. I just have to say that I deeply resent David's and my vocals being wiped off the album. That hurts me. The four of us together have a special power...we make people happy with our music. The fact that we deprive people of that happiness by acting like children really bothers me sometimes. I don't care what anybody says, there's room for CSNY just like there's room for anything else we might want to do."

As for another go at CSNY, Nash admitted, "I'm not closed to the idea." Neither is Crosby. "Look," he said, "here's what it's like. If you were crawling through the desert and knew of a place where there once was a luscious fucking well...you'd go back to see if it was still there, wouldn't you?"

Stills, too, didn't close the door on some future reunion of the four: "The last thing I want is to have Graham Nash and David Crosby as enemies. But this Stills-Young album...I don't know, we just had to do it ourselves this time. No Richie Furays, no David and Grahams, no nobody between us."

After finishing everything but the final mixing of *Long May You Run*, Young and Stills took to the road together. Both canceled solo summer commitments. Although it was Stills' band (George "Chocolate" Perry on bass, Joe Lala on congas, Jerry Aiello on keyboards and Joe Vitale on drums), the tour was the same one originally intended for Young and Crazy Horse.

Following Washington, D.C., the next show, a muggy outdoor affair in Hartford, Connecticut, was unquestionably closer to the mark. The album now entirely finished, the band relaxed into a comfortable pace. The harmonies remained ragged but by the end of the set, Young and Stills' slashing guitar work was near-flawless. Stills, just after leaving the stage, gushed: "There's no place I'd rather be than right here, playing with *that* guy."

Young caught him in a bear hug, hopped in his bus and headed for Cleveland to beat the traffic.

On board his own bus—a more standard travel-only model he rents from Young—Stills spent the ride listening to *Long May You Run*. He was proud of the album, unabashedly claiming it to be his best work in years.

"There is one very special thing that Neil and I do for each other," he laughed. "Every time we play, I learn a little bit more about being real and he learns a little bit more about polish."

By the night of the Cleveland show, Stills was ready to kill. He ripped into "Love the One You're With" with an urgency that hadn't surfaced since he'd written it. Young responded with a blazing solo in "The Loner." Stills came back with a chilling delivery of "For What It's Worth"...and on it went. Suddenly, they were beyond the smiles and the backslapping. The Stills-Young Band bore down for a snarling night of what they'd all been waiting and hoping for. The magic.

Standing offstage during Young's solo act, Stills was enjoying the long overdue taste of victory. What happened? "Neil crawled all over me," Stills chirped. "He snapped me awake. I guess I was flaking it a little bit, so he jumped on my ass."

After the show, Young was similarly jubilant. Alive and animated, he told Stills not to consider the Cleveland show a peak. "Think of it," he coached, "as a new standard. Something you can't dip below."

Visiting the hotel bar before hitting the open road for Cincinnati, Young raised a toast. "Here's to the return of Stephen Stills."

The next night in Cincinnati, Young let Stills run with the ball. Stills delivered. The roughest part of the set for him—following Young's show-stopping "After the Gold Rush" with his own acoustic set—was a breeze. Stills sat down and began gently playing the chords to "Helplessly Hoping." When it came time for the vocal, gone was the whiskey wheeze of old. Singing slowly and into the microphone, Stills let the audience fill in the lilting harmonies themselves.

Young studied the sight, glowing like a proud father. "Now," he told the writer, "you have something to write about."

It seemed the proper place to bow out and do just that.

Three concerts later, it was over. Pittsburgh, Greensboro and Charlotte had been good shows—great by some accounts—and Young was reportedly pleased with each one. By Atlanta, though, a recurring throat illness had silenced him. Young flew home to California, was told to rest by his doctors, and went into seclusion at his northern California ranch. Rumors immediately pegged the tour's cancellation as intentional, and Young hasn't taken any phone calls or had any visitors.

Stills' reaction to the aborted tour: "I learned a lot and had a lot of good times. I don't think they're over, and I'm just not going to let this set me back."

In the meantime, both have canceled all appearances this summer. Young has a tentative ten-date tour with Crazy Horse scheduled for November, just about when he'll release his next album, planned as *Chrome Dreams*. Stills, recently sued for divorce by wife Veronique Sanson, is planning a fall tour with stalwart guitarist friends Chris Hillman and George Terry.

After that, Stills may well take a few years off to write a book and relax. "My hearing has gotten to be a terrible problem. If I keep playing and touring the way I have been," Stills shrugged, "I'll go deaf. I want to take care of myself and be around for a while...."

Whether Young has fulfilled or abandoned his drive to revive the affiliation with Stills is unknown. With *Long May You Run* just out, Stills is confident that he has not seen the last of Young.

THE ACTUAL, HONEST-TO-GOD REUNION OF CROSBY, STILLS & NASH

BY CAMERON CROWE
Rolling Stone
June 2, 1977

After the aborted Stills-Young Band tour, Stills was alone again, performing solo acoustic and with bass/drums backing during the remainder of 1976. Stills had also showed up unannounced at a Crosby-Nash concert at the Greek Theatre in Los Angeles in August. In this beautifully crafted article, Cameron Crowe recounted the road back to CSN and the making of the trio's 1977 album in Miami. Crowe had a great ability to let CSN's true natures and personalities shine through. He also deftly handled "the Y factor."

Crosby, Stills & Nash gather in the kitchen. Miami. March 1977. Photo: Joel Bernstein

T here are only two cars on Arthur Godfrey Road this early morning in Miami Beach. One, a Toyota, is full of punks looking for a party. They spot a rented Chevrolet carrying three men, older and looking rumpled in an eerie way. The Toyota pulls up alongside with a honk.

No reaction. Down roll the windows. It's five in the morning and an Aerosmith tape is blasting out of the Toyota. The guy behind the wheel leans out and yells: "Hey, let's go find some chicks!"

Then it registers. *What?* The driver nearly careens into a divider as he tries for a better look. It's...

The three men ignore him. The Chevy turns off on Pine Tree Drive and slowly pulls into the driveway of a miniature villa. Just as the driver is about to shut off the ignition, a familiar song—"Woodstock" by Crosby, Stills, Nash & Young—comes on the radio. The driver cranks it up, and all three begin to sing along.

"What a rush," whoops Graham Nash. He remembers his harmony line perfectly.

Stephen Stills is grinning broadly. His missing tooth is in full view.

179

David Crosby, the driver, stares straight ahead. "Yeah, we were definitely hot," he says, turning off the ignition at the song's end. "That love, peace and granola shit went over real big, didn't it?"

They laugh, grab their guitars out of the trunk and head inside. After five weeks of recording and living together in this spacious house, life has taken on a cuckoo-clockwork domesticity: up at 5 p.m., dinner at 6, Walter Cronkite at 6:30, recording studio at 8, then home for a sunrise breakfast.

"I'm just gonna put my guitar in my room," says Stills brightly. He bounds up the stairs. "Meet you guys in the kitchen for a nightcap. Save some Shredded Wheat for me...."

So Crosby, Stills & Nash—CSN—are back together. It's 1977, eight years since their first and only album became a rallying point for a budding Woodstock generation. But now, Richard Nixon is out of office, the war is over, marijuana is slowly being "decriminalized" and a Democrat is in the White House. Rock music is bigger business than ever, and artists like Peter Frampton and Fleetwood Mac easily outsell the entire CSN catalog (with or without Neil Young) with a single album.

And yet, Young is back with his band, Crazy Horse, and CSN are back in the studio. Another turn around the wheel....

There was a time in late 1970, with *Déjà Vu* at its peak, when CSNY were just about the American Beatles. The four of them had clear and separate, slightly adversary identities: Crosby, the former Byrd, the political voice, the California dreamer; Nash, the Briton, the former Hollie, the spiritually hungry searcher; Stills, the guitar hero from Buffalo Springfield; and Young, the brooding dark horse from Canada. They were, at once, steeped in mystique and still the guys next door.

"They always had that Judy Garland, tragic American hero aura about them," a former business associate remembers. "It's still going on. Were they strong enough to survive? Would they kill each other? Did they really like their audience? Were they leaders? Was it all for the bucks? Would they fall apart before reaching the top?"

In the end, they did fall apart. In 1970, after less than two years, CSNY shattered into four directions several months after recording the single "Ohio," backed, ironically, with "Find the Cost of Freedom." With the exception of a summer-long reunion for a tour in 1974, they never got together again. Apart and in partial combinations, their projects were mostly disappointing. But every year or so there was a tease. At least three times they announced attempts to record another CSNY studio album, but each one collapsed in bitterness. In their place, bands like the Eagles, whose members once idolized them, emerged.

And then, two months ago, I got a phone call and invitation from Crosby: "We're doin' it, man. It's CSN, just us this time, and it's coming out. C'mon down and have a listen." A plane flight later, I learned that he was right. For the first time since those nights in 1969, Crosby, Stills & Nash are in harmony. Only one question: does anybody out there still care?

Anything you want
to know
Just ask me
I'm the world's most
opinionated man*

—"Anything at All" by David Crosby

David Crosby is not quite ready for that one. He thinks about it for close to a minute, an uncommon silence for a man who calls himself "Ol' Motor-mouth." It is the next morning and Crosby is finishing off a snack of bacon and eggs. He dabs away the yolky residue caught in his waterfall moustache and smiles. "Sure, we may have blown it," he eventually admits. "But what constitutes blowing it? Not playing the game? I don't see any rules, anyway....Overall, I don't regret anything. I'm here and there's music...and it's being released. And I'm making it. Sure, the specific things I regret. Pieces of music that were never made or never came out...but I'm glad that we were smitten in the face with reality again and again. If we'd had to knock those corners off each other rather than just bounding down a couple of staircases of life, I think there might have been too much scar tissue between us."

It's hard to keep from gagging on Crosby's constant paeans to The Music, but he is sincere. Music, by choice, is his "entire being...with sex a very strong second." He lives his life from album to album and from tour to tour, rarely allowing himself any time home alone. At night he is often in the studios, either working on his own projects or cheering others on. And he spends his days ruminating over songs, letting petty business matters grow into problems.

Crosby, 35, has gained weight from lack of exercise, and he's sensitive about it. Propped up against the headboard of his bed, unshaven and wearing baggy cords and an oversized Pendleton shirt, he exudes a grand father-ly benevolence.

In Miami nine months earlier, the last attempt at a CSNY album had left a particularly foul taste in his mouth. Yet Crosby is back for more. "I look at it this way," he once said. "Suppose you're crawling through the desert, you haven't had a drink in days, you're parched, dehydrating. And then you remember where you once drank from this deep, crystal blue oasis. Would you go back there or what?"

Boats drift along the canal outside, and Crosby smiles wistfully at the view. He begins to stare. I wonder if he looks back at himself and sees naivete. "You always do," he says with a world-weary sigh. "My whole 'Wooden Ships,' wanting-to-sail-forever fantasy was bullshit. Where do you get off leaving the rest of humanity behind, even in your mind?...You live, you learn."

Crosby and Nash have remained close friends through the years. So all they needed to accomplish a CSN reunion was Stephen Stills. It is strange to hear Crosby answering for Stills' celebrated inconsistency. But he does so, and vigorously. "I'm not gonna hype him," he begins. "He's not a saint. He didn't suddenly change. The thing is...you don't get it for free. You can't ride on your fucking laurels, it doesn't work for long."

Crosby doesn't like to get into specifics about personality differences with Stills, and says only: "He and I used to go nose to nose about once every 15 minutes. And we haven't gone nose to nose *once*. Nothing. It's either amazing grace or great luck, but it's working...."

He leans forward and speaks in a stage whisper, overenunciating every word. "His chemistry is altered because he is not *drink*-ing....That cat, believe me, when he's heavy into the sauce, he doesn't have the chops, the attention span, the patience...he derails, he goes on trips...he can't make the music. But when he feels supported and when it's called up out of him, *bull-shit* on the people that think he can't do it. I'm proud to say that it happened to be us that could call it up out of him again. He says it, too."

They assume that Neil Young knows exactly what they're up to in Miami, using two months of studio time that Young himself wanted to book, But there has been no communication. He is spoken of in friendly but distant terms. Young views CSNY as an occasional marker in his own career, but CSNY comes first for the others, "I love singing with those guys," he said in 1975, "but CSNY tends to get too big. Too many people attach too much importance to them. I enjoy being able to visit, but I want to avoid people thinking, 'Oh, there's Neil Young from CSNY.'"

"At this point," Crosby says, "I don't know how to deal with my relationship to Neil at all. The last time the four of us were together, the psychic balance in the room, the level of trust, love or friendship was like"...Crosby whistles..."real strange."

That was last May, and the room was the very same Criteria Sound Studios. Recording sessions by the Stills-Young Band had reached an impasse. Young called Crosby to see about giving CSNY another shot. Crosby and Nash, close to finishing their own album, *Whistling Down the Wire*, in Los Angeles, flew to Miami Beach. It was a disastrous move. Besides a lack of material and some disagreement over the approach, there were rapidly approaching deadlines. A summer-long Stills-Young tour was scheduled to begin in June, and Crosby and Nash were already late delivering their own album. They finally had to rush back to L.A. to wrap it up, leaving Stills and Young to work on the CSNY album until they returned. Instead, the album reverted to a Stills-Young project. Crosby and Nash were not invited back to Florida, and their vocals were wiped off the tracks to make room for others.

Crosby was livid at the time. "I have nothing but contempt for those two," he said then. "I refuse to be on call for them any longer." Now, he can rationalize the incident: "Everything was wrong. I wish to fuck, man, that I had not felt so long an enmity for those cats over that."

In the end, the Stills-Young tour fell apart after a month. Crosby and Nash played throughout the summer, and the incredible irony occurred: the two harmony singers, the leftover pieces of the old group, outsold the Stills-Young album (*Long May You Run*).

The phone rings and Crosby snaps it up, as he usually does whenever a ringing telephone is within reach. It's John Hartmann, one of Crosby and Nash's managers. "Yeah?...I'm just shooting my mouth off....Well, how's things on that battlefront?...What did the Turk say?...Did you call the Russian? What did he say?...Well, play it for him. Our end is together...."

It is an easily breakable code since I know that CSN, still signed to Atlantic Records (where Ahmet Ertegun, "the Turk," is chairman), want to find out whether or not there might be another company that wants to buy them out, like, maybe, the only label that could afford them, CBS Records (whose president is Walter Yetnikov, "the Russian"). Crosby hangs up.

"We're having a huge business duke-out at the moment," he says, "which is what all that was about. You know, we're spread out all over the record business. At present we're on three different companies [Crosby and Nash are on ABC. Stills is with CBS as a solo artist]. It's weird that it should be fought over like 40 pieces of silver. But we know what it is in terms of its commercial worth. We know what happens when you make sounds as unusual and completely different from everything else as this does.

"If all somebody has to relate to, in terms of what's gonna come out of this, is *Whistling Down the Wire* and the Stills-Young Band, they're in for a monster surprise."

A striking blond woman, the cook and part owner of the agency that rented the house, pokes her head in the door and announces dinner. And so begins the prestudio ritual.

Downstairs, a spectacular spread is being attacked by Stills and Nash, by Joel Bernstein, their photographer of seven years, and by their young crew of three. Dinner is over in ten minutes; then they watch CBS news for their nightly crash course on the real world. CSN like Jimmy Carter. They had talked about announcing their reunion by singing "The Star Spangled

Banner" at his Inaugural Ball. Crosby, oddly enough, is the biggest fan of the president. The same man who had in the past proclaimed himself "ashamed to be an American" would gladly accept an invitation to the White House. "The Constitution is still strong enough to beat Richard Nixon," he says. "Bottom line, man: dude lost." As for Carter: "I feel that the guy is so intelligent that he knows how to be human and accessible and real. It's sheer genius...."

After Cronkite, they zip down to the studio. As he walks in, Crosby triumphantly claps his hands. "All right," he booms. "We're gonna finish the album tonight."

He has said the same thing every night at the same time for the last five weeks.

The album will be called simply *CSN*. Outside of keyboardist Craig Doerge, drummer Joe Vitale, bassist George "Chocolate" Perry and one track with drummer Russ Kunkel, the album is all their own work. It was coproduced by Ron and Howard Albert, the earnest young brothers who have had a hand in nearly everything that's come out of the Miami studios since Brook Benton's "Rainy Night in Georgia" in 1970, The Alberts are quick, thorough and determined to make a Seventies CSN album. They are succeeding.

Tonight, with the instrumental tracks finished, the moment of truth has arrived—after four days of rehearsal, it's time to record vocals. They've been singing all night, carefully bearing down to capture the harmonies.

Stephen Stills stands in the middle of the carrot-colored Studio B—the same gauche room where Eric Clapton recorded "Layla" and James Brown did "I Feel Good"—and madly smokes himself into a Marlboro cloud. He is on the crest of finishing a difficult, overdubbed vocal part on Crosby's "Anything at All." Graham Nash watches from Stills' left. Crosby is lying on the floor, staring at the ceiling and calling out suggestions, "Hey," he gripes, "I keep hearing the Average White Band gettin' down in the next room."

Stills ignores the gentle thumping and continues his last remaining line several times without much success. Ron Albert flicks down the intercom switch. "You're flat, Stephen."

"I've made a whole career out of singing flat," replies Stills. He returns to the line, tries more times, and then gets it perfect.

The Alberts, who've worked on most of Stills' solo projects, begin to talk between themselves. They don't know I'm sitting on a couch below their control board.

"Do you believe this?" asks Howard. "I don't believe this."

Ron chuckles. "Did you ever think we'd see the day when Stills worked this hard on a record? Is this for real?"

"He wasn't this on top of it for the first *Manassas*, even, was he? That was a great album…the last classic record he made.…"

Stills walks in and the musing immediately stops. He plops on a stool between the two brothers to hear his playback. "You know," Stills confesses out of the blue, "I've been getting away with murder. I think back on my solo albums, and there's some good stuff here and there…but it's mostly garbage, isn't it?"

I can see the Alberts' reflection in the studio window as they turn to each other. "Pretty much, Stephen," Ron says agreeably.

Stills begins to laugh heartily, something his friends say he's only recently capable of, until Crosby, still on his back in the next room, roars over the monitor: "All I wanna know is this—are we gonna have to give the AWB credit for percussion on this album?" Everyone cracks up.

They decide to knock off a bit and play me the 12 album tracks, chosen from a possible 17. All three stand and sing their unrecorded parts with the tape.

Here's the rundown: "Shadow Captain"—Craig Doerge wrote the music. Crosby the words…instantly recognizable, streamlined CSN, clear and strong. "See the Changes"—classic three-part harmonies huddled around an acoustic guitar; Stills wrote and sang lead. "Carried Away"—a beautifully stark Nash piano song with interwoven harmonies. "Fair Game"—Cubano Stills, well sung and brandishing a killer acoustic guitar solo. "Anything at All"—a deeply felt Crosby composition about a man who will answer any question. "Cathedral"—Nash started this song on his 33rd birthday after wandering into Winchester Cathedral on acid. Intense.

Side two: "Dark Star"—another great Stills song, overtly commercial and made for summer. "Just a Song Before I Go"—a breezy love song from Nash (whispered Crosby: "The girls are gonna fall in love with him all over again. I hate it."). "Run From Tears"—the best electric Stills in years, with chilling vocals and a fiercely real lyric about keeping his head above water. "Cold Rain"—written by Nash during the sessions after returning from his ailing mother's bedside in England. Gray and moody. "In My Dreams"— Crosby stretches out with a sinuous acoustic tune. "I Give You Give Blind"— more excellent electric Stills. A sophisticated, assertive closing note.

"I'm just hoping that it…just slays everybody. I really want it to so bad, you know. For me, it's kind of half out of responsibility to the kids and half 'I'll show 'em…thought we were washed up, didja?'"

Stephen Stills is a man with a reputation for being fucked up, coked out and/or fried to the gills. He concedes that he has done plenty to deserve that stigma, but, against incredible odds, he has survived. And his survival is one of the most important factors in the successful reunion of CSN.

To look at Stills today, at 32, you see a much different person than the gaunt, eager young man who confessed to the audience at Woodstock that he was "scared shitless." His face has spread out and hardened since then. He often wears glasses. He is smaller and huskier than you might expect.

"Right now, I'm a cripple," Stills says, taking a seat in the closet-sized mastering room at Criteria. "I've been sick through this whole thing. Then my back went…God knows what did that. It's probably all psychosomatic." He gets up to grab an ashtray and bangs his head on a tape machine. "Oh-ho. My body is rebelling. But…I've been working solid for six months. You know, the light is at the end of the tunnel.…I'm just hoping my poor body holds up long enough to get to it."

Stills is just now recovering from a particularly devastating stretch of his life that began with the release of *Long May You Run* last August. First Neil Young dropped off the summer tour of the Stills-Young Band after only a month, allegedly because of a sore throat. Others have suggested Young was bored. Says Stills: "All I know is that he turned left at Greensboro.…"

I remember calling Stills on the road in Atlanta, the next stop after Greensboro, for some backup questions on a piece I was writing. I didn't know the roof had just fallen in.

Stills, who was in a hotel bar, grunted something about wanting to be left alone and brusquely explained that Neil had disappeared and left him a goodbye telegram saying, "Funny how some things that start spontaneously, end spontaneously.…"

"I have no answers for you," Stills had said then. "I have no future." Chills. Two weeks later, still gamely making up on some canceled dates without Young, Stills' wife Veronique Sanson, a singer/songwriter, filed for divorce. Stills ordered everything packed and moved out of his home near Boulder, Colorado, where the marriage started. He now lives in L.A. and has not been back to Colorado since.

"Lenny Bruce was right," says Stills. "When you get divorced, the longer you've been married, the longer you throw up. I'm not over it yet.

"I went crazy for two weeks, you know, but I picked myself up off the ground and went to the studio. I guess there wasn't anyplace else to put my energy. It was like the coyote in the *Roadrunner* cartoons, just after he goes off the cliff…suspended in midair, scrambling to get back to the cliff."

Stephen Stills, David Crosby and Graham Nash at the Spectrum, Philadelphia. June 1977. Photo: Roger Barone

I am drowning
And I am fighting.
Something special
Is in me dying… **

—"Run From Tears" by Stephen Stills

Stills started writing his best songs in many years, all of them passionately autobiographical. He also started to think about his still bitter friends, Graham Nash and David Crosby. Stills humbly showed up backstage, uninvited, at a Crosby-Nash show at the Greek Theatre in L.A.

Nash: "I hugged him. And it amazed me. 'Cause I realized in the middle of the hug that the last time we'd met he'd wiped some very valuable work of David's and mine…but it didn't matter. We're all incredibly changeable people, God knows, and Stephen had come with his hat in his hand. So fuck it. I hugged him."

187

Crosby: "After that last debacle, I looked at Nash like he'd lost his total mind. I thought he was just out of his fucking tree. Completely. Then I hugged Stills too…the pencil-neck wimp."

Stills joined in for the last encore number, "Teach Your Children," and his bruised ego soaked up the tumultuous reception. Afterward Stills and Nash, long the weakest link in CSNY, went out and got drunk. "He was really the Stephen that I had always hoped I'd see back again. I piled him back into his room at 4 a.m." Crosby and Nash continued with a fall tour, as did Stephen with a series of solo acoustic concerts, but the reunion was already on their minds.

They met up in December, recorded some basics at the Record Plant in Los Angeles, then flew to Miami to finish the album. The key to the sudden harmony? "Everybody is a lot less sensitive," Stills replies. "We have a common, realized interest. We took a tremendous gamble the first time with Nash quitting the Hollies and everything….*Music From Big Pink* was out and all that…we really had to be good. And we were. We're up against the same thing now. We're taking a gamble with our reputations…the pressure's on."

I tell Stephen there are some who point to his lack of drinking as a major plus factor. He laughs tentatively. "I mean," he says, "I've always been a cheap drunk." He looks sheepish. "I've spent a lot of time drinking Scotch onstage and stuff…I just *quit*. It was seriously interfering with my ability to perform, to sing in tune. It made me braver, but I just wasn't pulling it off. I sat in with the Average White Band, man, the other night and I had three gulps of Scotch and I was just *blind*. Just…completely…on…the roof. I have definitely quit."

Directly after the CSN project, Stills will finish another solo album. He has asked Graham Nash to produce. After that, he says, he will concentrate on CSN indefinitely. He does not miss another guitarist, particularly Neil Young.

"The album we did was a nice avant-garde piece. I can see why it didn't do better. We were a little offhand about it. There were some special songs in there that we could have treated…a little more special.

"Neil is Neil and CSN is CSN. That has always been true. I think Neil does"…Stills sighs…"what the hell he wants, you know. And he puts as much energy into it as…he wants. That can be 100% or it can be 75%…and he really doesn't give a damn. My relationship with Neil is certainly not severed. I mean none of us are into closing doors."

There is always the specter of money looming over such reunions as this, just as it did when CSNY reformed in '74 for an album…and a summer tour. The album never happened…but the question begs to be asked: is it for the money?

"It isn't," Stills declares. He is, naturally, offended. "We're not broke. We've all got money coming in from other sources. But we're gonna make a lot of money, nice bucks. And we're also gonna deliver. We gotta…and we're gonna. And that supersedes the money and everything...I mean, there's not *one* disco track on the album. How could it be for the money?"

I thank Stills for his time and venture to tell him that there are people who will be very surprised by his strong showing on the *CSN* album.

"Hey, don't ever count this boy out," he advises. "Don't ever count me out."

Stills jumps to his feet for a dramatic exit on that line. And bumps his head on the tape machine again.

In the past few years Graham Nash has developed the public image of an exasperated Richard Benjamin struggling to reunite the Sunshine Boys. In the aftermath of the various breakups, it is he who has been left most dejected, wondering why everybody just can't act like *adults*. In the span of their history, Nash has never *initiated* any of their notorious blowouts.

Graham is the quintessential gentleman, able to make instant and lasting friends. A promo man he's just met can become "my friend Bill," a fan who wants to talk about "Lady of the Island" will not be ignored. He is good-humored, sensible, warm and open, yet very private.

This morning he sits on the expansive backyard lawn, next to the rushing canal, chipping away at an alabaster sculpture. From 20 yards away, I recognize it—an amazing bust of David Crosby—and ask why he would want to spend an excruciating amount of time sculpting the face of someone he has seen practically every day for the last eight years. Nash says he couldn't help it. The rock just *looked* like Crosby.

Nash is wearing tiny antique goggles. He throws his head back into the sunlight. "I feel fine," he says. "Some of the rushes I remember from that first album—when we hit a vocal chord or a vocal blend—I've had the same rushes here for the first time since. That's why I'm so peaceful about it all."

Last night, after first hearing the Eagles' "Hotel California," Nash had lifted a defiant middle finger to the line: "We haven't seen that spirit here/Since 1969."

Nash probably has the keenest sense of the group as something more than an old spirit. In recent years he's been responsible for compiling the *4 Way Street* and *So Far* albums, putting together set lists for their concerts and even sequencing the latest album. And he is a brilliant arranger and producer.

But he has loftier goals in life, you sense, than writing "Our House." "I tend to get a little into the importance of what I'm doing, because I'm so focused on it. I have to maintain the ability to be able to step outside and realize that all this doesn't mean shit to…that palm tree." He would rather see his friend and inspiration, Jacques Cousteau, on the cover of *Rolling Stone*.

Nash has gone through several complete life changes since growing up in Manchester, England. And he is certainly capable of several more. When he was 15, his father bought an antique camera from a friend. The camera turned out to be stolen and when the police came around, William Nash refused to divulge any information. He went to jail for a year and his only son, Graham, went to work to support his mother and two sisters. Graham took odd jobs in a wool factory, a brewery and a post office to keep the family afloat. He soon made enough money from singing and playing guitar with a buddy, Allan Clarke. Together they became the nucleus of the Hollies. Nash Sr. emerged from prison weak from pneumonia and broken in spirit. He died a year later while Graham was on tour in Sweden. Graham's chartered plane arrived a few hours too late. Missing a farewell to his father, he says, is his only regret in life.

The Hollies were a huge success. They developed a rigid, faultless formula that was something of a mixed blessing. By 1968 Nash had broken out of the mold and was writing "Lady of the Island," "Marrakesh Express" and "Right Between the Eyes," songs the other Hollies vetoed. When the group reached L.A. for a run at the Whisky A Go Go, Graham made friends with Cass Elliot, who brought him to Joni Mitchell's Laurel Canyon home. The rest has become well-drilled history. That night Nash met Crosby and Stills and sang with them. He promptly discarded a budding middle-class existence—the *O Lucky Man* syndrome as Crosby calls it with £100 in his pocket. His momentous departure from the Hollies is still remembered in England: "Every time I go back there," says Nash, "I still feel this strange edge.…"

I guess I'm taking a chance, moving out here to L.A., leaving my money in England and singing with David and Stephen. But it's what I want. At least it is for now.

—Graham Nash
Hit Parader, September 1969

We take a little break. Someone has brought wine and cheese and fruit and deli. Graham and Joni are getting silly together. Stephen is muttering about getting back to work. David is slumped on the couch, cuddling a bottle of wine. He closes his eyes and his mouth curls into a smile. "I've never had so much fun making an album in my entire life."

—*Hit Parader*, September 1969

By the time CSNY, Crosby, Stills & Nash—with Neil Young—reached the studio in 1970 for *Déjà Vu*, they were *the* American group. But the sunshine and light of the first album had dissipated. "When it's that enormous, all of the chemistry is heated up," says Crosby. "Everything takes place faster and bigger...your own emotions included. It went downhill as a relationship, and it's as equally divided a fault as I can think of...all four of us blew it. Everybody got paranoid about each other. We were all independent enough motherfuckers to go and do it on our own. We all thought we could."

There were personal difficulties as well. Nash and Joni Mitchell were about to break up, Stills and Judy Collins split, Neil and Susan Young were separating, and Crosby's "one true love," Christine Gail Hinton, had been killed in a car accident.

"It was an incredibly painful album," says Graham. "The first one, we were all madly in love. The second, we weren't even close." The sessions were moody, sullen marathons and the vibe even carried over to their subsequent tour. Stills was fired in Chicago, reinstated two days later, but when the tour ended, they scattered.

An attempt to reunite on record in '73 got as far as a finished package and title, *Human Highway*. They went to Hawaii to rehearse, came back and ran out of impetus. The cover photo, taken at sunset on their last day in the islands, tells it all—a clear portrait of four tanned men, all living in completely separate worlds. The print is now tacked up on Neil Young's bedroom wall at his ranch.

Another stab at CSNY happened in Sausalito after the summer '74 tour. It ended after several weeks, as a result of a momentous argument between Nash and Stills over a single harmony note. Neil Young left the studio and never returned. "It was an incredible thing to have happen," says Nash. "I didn't quite know how to deal with that for a long time. But it served its purpose by pushing David and me out onto the crossroads."

They were an obvious match, Crosby and Nash. They had already toured and made an album together, but this was a matter of an entire career. The turning point was an unexpected call from James Taylor, who wanted them to sing on his album *Gorilla*. They accepted (Nash: "We're music junkies, we'll sing for anybody") and in the course of one high, musical evening, recorded Taylor's "Mexico" and "Lighthouse." Graham and David, then living at the Chateau Marmont residential hotel, floated around L.A. in a haze for days, singing the chorus from "Mexico." They had proven to themselves that they were more than retread folkies.

Crosby and Nash—working without a manager at the time—rode the blast of confidence into a deal with ABC Records and an album, *Wind on the Water*, assisted by Carole King and Taylor. A successful tour was followed by another album, then the abortive trip to Miami Beach. And now this.

"Ah yes," Nash notes. "Here we are in the years, as they say." He chips away on his sculpture of Crosby. "Back on bended knees."

No, Nash decides, he would not take it all back. "It was so strange going back to Manchester this time," he says. "I still see the exact same faces and ruddy complexions and the people scurrying by...and they'll never change. But for a few good fortunes, I might still be there." He shudders. "No, I would not go back."

I mention the *Rolling Stone* interview in which John Lennon claimed he'd rather have been a fisherman in Surrey. A voice from behind responds: "Crap he would." It's Crosby, rubbing his eyes in the sunlight. "He just damn well wouldn't...he wouldn't have settled for it, because he's one of the ones that left home. Like us. There's always some of them that leave home....They're too dissatisfied or restless or horny or something. And we're the ones that left. You're one of 'em. He's one of 'em...or else he'd still be in the wool factory. I'm one of 'em...or else I'd be back in Santa Barbara now, working for Washburn Chevrolet."

"As far as I'm concerned," says Crosby, "the best thing for me to think about Neil Young is: *later*. Because if he showed up, right now, he'd just weird it out. He can't do the kind of painstaking work on vocals that we're doing right now. He doesn't believe in it. He can't even sit there while *you* do it. And he's proven that." Crosby chipmunk giggles. "He'd rather clunk around with that garbanzo band of his...."

> *Why do you ride that*
> *Crazy Horse*
> *Inquires the Shadow*
> *with little remorse...* ***

—From the song "The Old Homestead" by Neil Young

"I really wonder what he's gonna think when he hears this album," Crosby says. "I hope it makes him think. He's not doing justice to his records. And it's bullshit. I've done the same thing in another way, I'm sure, but I think that's really true. I hope he listens to this album and says, 'Oh shit, I shouldn't settle for less.' That would be great."

I remind Crosby that Young has gone on record as saying he made a commercial, technically perfect album in *Harvest* and "got it out of my system."

"That's just an excuse to not have to do it," Crosby retorts. "That's a shuck. He makes stuff, man, that if you listen to it the right way, it has moments of such startling art in it that you can be knocked out by it. But he could take his music much farther. He's also got this massive anti-God thing. He hates being so big and he tries to demystify himself by being funky. In music and in life. I've argued all these things with him, to his face. He laughs. He loves it. Bottom line? Neil's the most fascinating person I've ever met."

A laborious detailing of all the various unreleased CSNY tracks now sitting in the can follows, and Crosby begrudgingly admits each one's existence after much arguing. After several hours, we figure there is at least one great CSNY album among the tape archives of each member.

Nash, who has said little, interrupts as he senses yet another argument looming. "This is getting boring," he declares, and a few minutes later he grabs his sculpture and walks back inside. Not quite realizing the reason for Nash's departure, Crosby follows him. I follow Crosby. The conversation resumes in Nash's room.

"Please," Nash pleads, "don't drive me out of my room. I came in here to escape you all."

"Sorry," Crosby says, "it's *his* fault. He didn't ask me my favorite questions—what I have to say to the 15-year-old girls of America, what kind of weird sex trips I'm into, where I buy my clothes, *nothing*."

Nash remains serious. "None of the stuff we've talked about has been important…it's just part of a vast complex of much more important things. And we're a small part. Right now, cause we're all in this house, it's a large part of our lives, but if you take it from the point of view of the guy next door…he doesn't give a fuck, you know."

Back in my room, it's unnerving to think about this, staring at six hours of tape. Sure, it's historically valid to gather all the details, all the intricacies of each split, but…in the end, isn't the reality that CSNY are four guys who couldn't manage to sit down in one room long enough to make the very music they say they live for? In ten years, is that the irresponsible legacy they intend to leave?

I take that last question back to Nash's room. He and Crosby are engrossed in a Jacques Cousteau TV special. Crosby looks up, sees me and the tape recorder back again, and beckons. "What's your last big question of Doom and Destiny?"

It is a difficult question to phrase, and it comes out as: "Look at the fans who loved *Crosby, Stills & Nash* and *Déjà Vu* and thought they were some of the best LPs in their collections. They've followed you through all the breakups, the false alarms, the canceled tours and partial reunions, and there still hasn't been another album. Might they not be tired of it all? After all, there's the new Pink Floyd album...."

Silently, Crosby continues to watch television. "Look at the geese! Look at the geese!" he says. Another minute. "I don't know. It'll depend on how much music was the issue or the fantasy characters that the media tried to create. If it was the music that moved them, I'm sure that the on-again, off-again rest of it isn't that relevant.

"If, on the other hand, they were more concerned with the psychodrama of the group trips...and flashed by the bullshit star thing, then maybe they've moved on from that to something else, like gas stations and Parcheesi.

"Overall, you can't look at your life with regret...and do *shit*. So no, I don't regret. I...I look for my car keys and go to the studio." Crosby laughs and dangles the car keys from his finger.

Nash is troubled by the lack of sensitivity in his answer. "I agree, David," he says. "I totally concur. I was just thinking about the crux of the question, which was—do we think we were silly. In a certain way I think we were very silly...in not growing up quite so *fast*."

Joel Bernstein, their photographer and guitar-tuner of seven years, is also in the room and adds: "This all must seem so childish to someone on the outside."

"Fuck 'em," says Crosby, "I can't live my life for them. I'm telling you what the truth is."

"It's just," Bernstein resumes, "if you put yourself in the fans' place, you can maybe see how their attitude toward you guys may have changed."

Nash: "It's possible."

Crosby: "Okay...that's *very* distant from me, okay, but I'll respond. It is fringe. The only real consideration that anybody ever had to think about was whether or not the music got to them. Anybody that's into it to the level of following it as a psychodrama is fringe to me."

Bernstein: "I'm not talking about those people. I'm talking about your fans...the people who buy your records."

Nash: "Well, we're taking care of things. We're doing this album...."

Crosby: "I'm talking about *all* the fans, then. Everybody. Merely being *conscious* of them and what they care about and how they feel about whether or not we should or should not be playing is counterproductive to making art. So fuck you, number one.

Bernstein: "That's contrary to your criticism of Neil and his craft."

Crosby: "I'm not talking about *how* you make the music. I'm talking *why*. I'm desperately concerned with communication. Just let me finish. What went down is that…we tried over and over again because we wanted to do the *music*. We didn't try because we felt a pressure or need to satisfy these other people's predilections for one thing or another—fuck them. They can't help me or hinder me from making that magical moment on tape. Only my own personal love or hatred or feeling for…[the blood rushes to Crosby's face and he begins to bellow]…*Neil, Stephen and Graham has anything to do with it. Only. Nothing else. So their whole entire consciousness—whether they liked it, didn't like it…thought it was cool, hip, chicken, fucked…nothing.* It's all totally extraneous to me."

Nash stops chipping on Crosby's bust and looks up curiously. *"And it's totally, totally intimidating of the one fucking chance you got to break through and make this happen. The consciousness of that bullshit, the history and psychodrama and what everybody else is thinking about it is exactly why the four of us walked into the room the last time and…blew it! Because we were dragging that baggage. Can you dig it? Fuck you, number two!"*

Crosby catches his breath. "That's why we keep looking at each other, the three of us, and saying, 'No history—next subject.' That's not a joke. *That's trying to keep from drowning.* Excuse me for getting a little intense. But it's *our* music…that's why we make it for ourselves.

"People are gonna listen to this, I know, and wonder how 'right on' it will be. Well, CSNY and CSN was a rallying point because it was just a shared experience. Like *Easy Rider* was. Not because of anything we planned…we're not leaders. There isn't a leader in us. But if I started to think about all those people out there and what's gonna satisfy each and every one of them, how far am I gonna get?"

Nash: "He understands that. You explained to him about cheese. He thinks he tried to ask you about bacon."

"No," Crosby states flatly. "Suck cheese, English." For a moment, he sounds and looks like Larry Mundello, the easily bruised neighborhood kid from the old *Leave It to Beaver* TV show. "No, I nailed it."

Howard Albert had stumbled across someone pissing in the bushes outside as he walked into the studio that night. A few minutes later Albert had found out who he was when a wiry, bearded man in Levi's and checked shirt wandered in the front door.

"Was that you out there?" Albert asked.

"Sure, man," he said with a crooked smirk. "Jus' out there takin' a leak on a warm evening."

Neil Young had come to see Crosby, Stills & Nash. He walked into the control room unannounced and four men lunged to hug one another. "Big problem with CSNY," Young cracked. "Too much hugging." To see them all together in one dimly lit room was an incredible sight—like watching four big old gray timber wolves circling.

A tape of *CSN*—now completed and needing only final mixing—was slipped on and, with the opening notes of "Shadow Captain" booming over the speakers, Neil stared down in bemused fascination. When the first three-part vocals filled in, he looked up and smiled broadly. "It's nice to hear that," he said. "Real good to hear it again." Young listened on with warm enthusiasm. After the last track on side one, while the second was being hurriedly readied, he insisted on a break.

"Hey guys, c'mon," said Young. "You spend eight years making your second album and you want to get it over with in 45 minutes…

"Sheesh."

*By David Crosby, 1977 Staysail Music
**By Stephen Stills, 1977 Gold Hill Music, Inc.
***By Neil Young, 1974 Silver Fiddle

DARK STAR: WORKING THE VAMPIRE SHIFT WITH STEPHEN STILLS

BY PETER KNOBLER
Crawdaddy
December 1977

This late 1977 feature by former *Crawdaddy* editor Peter Knobler is an absorbing portrait of Stephen Stills. Knobler pealed back some layers surrounding Stills' muse and his tortured soul. An author, journalist and songwriter, Knobler obviously has a deep understanding of Stills—portraying him as a driven musician, a creative artist and a very sensitive man with strong convictions. When this interview was conducted, Stills was in the midst of recording some songs that would ultimately be part of his 1978 solo album, *Thoroughfare Gap*. Stills put CSN in perspective and provided answers to many interesting questions, such as "What are the qualities of a friend of Stephen Stills?"

Stephen Stills. Photo: Henry Diltz

They were lying in wait for David Crosby. The body of the consummate harmonizer—not a svelte figure to begin with—was out of harmony with nature and the guys felt that David was getting a little, uh…excessively round. When they caught him in the kitchen with his hand in the chocolate chip cookies they got on his ass real good.

So maybe it was embarrassment, maybe it was pique when, more abuse being a little much to take at five a.m. after a hard night's recording on the

Crosby, Stills & Nash comeback album, Crosby turned to Stephen Stills—himself hardly Mr. Physical Fitness—and said, "You couldn't run a mile if your life depended on it. I'll bet you a thousand dollars you can't." Graham Nash just laughed, knowing a race was on, maybe wondering who would sing bottom after they hung Stills upside down.

"You're on!" grinned Stephen.

By the time Stills hit the street—T-shirt and sneakers and jogging in place—it was six a.m. Crosby was asleep. The sun and Miami were just beginning their morning intimacies but Stills had on his hustler's glow; he'd gotten up at five that afternoon and this was simply an early evening jaunt for the Kid, a lock. The pace car—he would run till the speedometer turned a mile—sidled alongside him. "Okay, let's do it."

Down two blocks, then back two, then down, back—he did it, easy. And with witnesses! Upstairs, David rolled over. It's a thousand bucks Stills will never see; Crosby stiffed him. But it was worth it.

Standing in the studio, headphones and tortoise shell aviator glasses giving him a fighter pilot flip-down effect, Stephen Stills seems every bit the impenetrable pop star. His arms are folded tightly and he moves from foot to foot, head down in concentration, as he listens to a playback.

The song is a shuffle, and he is having trouble with it. You can hear where the horns will go—make it ten black guys slinging cornets in soul choreography—and the organ sounds like a vamp out of a steamy club, but Stills hasn't yet gotten on top of the vocal. He had opened with a nice dispassionate groove and developed a soul show composure, which was great—the surprise of a Stills understatement against such a hot track—but then he couldn't resist a strut. Now he is flatting all over the place, that patented Stills growl that works so well live is just not translating onto tape. The Criteria Studios control room in Miami is clucking—obviously he'll have to do that part over.

"Uh, Stephen...." The talk-back rings hollow in the studio proper. "The feeling in here is that the first part's real good but that tag at the end could be much better." Howard Albert, co-producer (with his brother Ron and with Stills himself) of the Stephen Stills solo album on which they're working, leans back in his swivel chair.

"Really?" Stills says. His voice is distant, surprisingly childlike at this hour of the morning. As if wondering whether he could have a hall pass. "I thought it was pretty good."

"The opening I think we can keep," says Ron Albert. "But that tag I don't know."

Stills manager and confidant Michael John Bowen tries another tack. "Wanna listen to it again?"

"No, man, I *like* it that way. That's what I was trying to *do*," Stills says. He is biting off his words now, all of a sudden not a pupil. He strides into the control room and plants himself behind the board.

Now, keep in mind that the tag is an outrage. There's no way it would get anywhere near a Crosby, Stills & Nash album. But this is Stills solo work, and he is adamant.

There is no quick reply. Howard looks at Ron, Ron looks at Michael John. In a room built to absorb sound, the silence is palpable.

"Well, I don't know. The take was good until the tag. We can use it until there, definitely," Howard says.

Another silence.

"It's real good up until after that chorus," Michael John offers. "Play that part again." They rewind and play the tape. Again the errors are obvious.

"Well, whaddaya say?" says Ron.

Stills rises wordlessly from his chair, pushes past the console and yanks open the door. When it has closed he stands, muscles tense, chin rigid against his chest. You can almost see him shake. He slams his fist into the wall.

It takes him two hours to get back to serious work. And the tag doesn't get done.

Stephen Stills is fair game. Everybody's got some drunk and disorderly Stephen Stills story, and there is the sense that he is touched by them all, that he listens acutely. One too many thank you's on-stage; damaged autobiographies on record. He's got Principles, and he has made what may be the mistake of displaying them to his audience and then perhaps not always living up to them. After the phenomenal success of CSN/CSNY, his solo career has been a roller coaster of hits, failures and tall tales. Yet he is a figure not to be dismissed, an affectingly human performer with a personality which comes through in place of image.

Crosby, Stills & Nash pioneered the public blending of voices and personalities, writing gloriously harmonized vignettes of each man's interconnecting passions; Crosby and Nash's mostly hopeful, Stills mostly not. When Neil Young signed on, the fragile brotherhood gained some rock 'n' roll punch but had a hard time absorbing the loner. They opened wide, then stepped aside.

But Crosby, Stills & Nash found it in themselves to reunite, and did it successfully after several failed attempts, and now Stills is back on top.

"We figured if it worked eight years ago, it should work now," he laughs. "I think what it boils down to, when you get to the bottom line, not to be vain, but we're really good."

It's this kind of accurate bravado which has gotten Stills in trouble many times before.

We are lounging in the Criteria office during a break. Stills has surprised me with his directness. I watch as he plays me four new tracks and then says without a pause, "Okay, I'm ready to talk."

Stills' sixth solo album is being created, due out in March. The next Crosby, Stills & Nash album is scheduled to begin recording in December, and Stills is feeling good. "Here's these three guys," he says, "35, 34 and 32. One of them's real fat, one of them's got a recessed tooth—we're not what you'd call John Davidson! But I understand them and they understand me better than anybody except my old lady, and Neil sometimes, too, when he decides to take off his cloak."

The CSN rebirth seems to have taken some of the edge off Stills, eased him a little.

"Well," he says, "I feel a lot more secure. I don't feel like I'm gonna be washed up at 38. I'm 32. A mere child! Give me one of those kids who jumps and leaps around and plays so fast. I'll stand over on the side of the stage and just burn his shirt off." He looks at me deadpan. "That's the Stills you want to hear from: vain, egotistical."

Has the CSN tour been a return to the rock 'n' roll crazies?

"No," he says, "very relaxed. I don't like all that crazy shit on the road. It's very easy to stay away from it; just have a few intelligent people to hang out with, and do something besides throw televisions out the window. My manager, Michael John, is a very intelligent man. And David and Graham too. And everybody on our crew are interesting people to talk to. They don't live, breathe and die rock 'n' roll; there's other things—talk about what you read in *Psychology Today* last week, theorize on all kinds of bullshit. Some of the conversations are asinine, some are groovy. It's a very atypical rock 'n' roll tour.

"I did my share of being crazy," he says. "I just don't like to party too much anymore. I don't drink hard booze, except for cognac. Booze is nice but I don't like to get falling-down, knee-walking drunk anymore. I used to hit the stage in that condition...." he looks at me again, "...and pull it off, but God knows how. I'm getting away from red meat, and gradually I'm getting away from sugar. Sugar is poison, and I've been through enough poisons.

"I've done a lot of self-analysis. At some point in one's life one must examine oneself for motives, clarity of thinking, existence, realization of limitations. You've got to look into the real mirror and look for the shadows, and try to drive away the ghosts."

"People want answers, not questions. The kids aren't going to plunk down $6.98 for questions!"

Michael John Bowen is holding forth in the Criteria hallway. A hard-talking, persuasive man with the manner of an off-duty State Trooper, Bowen takes care of Stills' business, and his own. He seems genuinely concerned for his charge, always keeps an eye out, as if in the middle of any conversation he may be needed and will respond. He looks you in the eye when he talks to you, chin to chin, a rock 'n' roll Leo Durocher.

"Look at the Beatles," he says quickly. "'I Want to Hold Your Hand,' 'All You Need Is Love'—*answers*! Look at Crosby, Stills & Nash—'I'll light the fire'—*answers*!"

It's Bowen who took Stills aside when the session was bogging down and started joking with him. "Four o'clock," said Howard Albert. "Must be time for the Jimmy Reed imitation." And it worked.

"Stephen needs a little distance from the song," Bowen says in the hall. "Got to step back from it, let the story tell itself. Gotta be *coool*. Boz Scaggs, man, the band starts playing and then he *glides* in—" Bowen takes three Scaggs steps.

"Gotta be on top of the song. Stephen's too *inside* it. Gotta step back. He'll get it, don't worry. Sometimes he hears things that nobody else hears and when you go back and listen, there it is, he heard it and you didn't. The man's got it all. Are you kidding? He plays guitar, sings, writes songs, paints, sculpts; we're writing a screenplay—Stephen hasn't got time to put two hands on his ass!"

It's mid-afternoon after locking up the studio at 5:30 in the morning, and Stills is just beginning to get it together. ("It's a little early for celebration," Michael John says knowingly.) Breakfast is served and cleared at the nine-bedroom, Spanish-style home he has rented rather than be cooped up in a hotel. (Stills and his entire crew are living at this bayside villa together, as the CSN family had done last winter and spring while recording.) The vibes, as they say, are definitely mellow.

The day is overcast and the Miami skyline across the water is taking it lying down. The sky is two-toned and turning; even the birds have tucked themselves under eaves expecting a shower. Not much is moving when we begin to talk. He seems prepared to be pensive.

"At what point did you start thinking about yourself?" I start.

"Well, I don't know." He is nestled comfortably into the corner of a couch, one leg tucked under him, arms resting on the cushions at right angles. "I was going so fast the first 30 years of my life that I kind of went, 'Hey, hold on a minute!'"

"Was there a specific moment that made you do that?"

He sits up a little straighter. "Yeah," he says. "I did a show in New York at Carnegie Hall and it was right at the beginning of my solo acoustic tour [Autumn, 1976] and I was just a little too drunk to do the crowd justice. And I really got furious with myself and so I quit drinking onstage. I mean, three scotches isn't too bad, spread over two hours," he begins to cover himself, then laughs, "but I was fairly well lit by the end of the show!" Stills' laugh is remarkably winning, a truck-stop wheeze of the reformed but unrepentant. "I'd been a little nervous about Carnegie Hall and I kind of overdid it. The basic element there being fear."

"Have you always been that nervous about performing?"

He looks to his lap for just an instant. Speaks slowly. "Let's just say I need a lot of encouragement. Not encouragement like stroking, but…I'm not that confident." He looks straight at me again, at once making an admission and beating a retreat behind the backstage star stare. Apparently, people don't ordinarily try to follow him there.

"Where do you figure that comes from?" I ask quietly.

His words are clipped, his chin raised perhaps a fraction. "I don't know. Probably something happened when I was a kid." There is an awkward silence. "Sometimes you've just got to close your eyes and charge," he says finally. "One of the things I like about the stage is it's such an immediate art form. When you're on, you're on and that's it."

"Are Crosby and Nash supportive?" I wonder.

"They let me psych myself up however I want to psych myself up. But they're very supportive," he says, "Graham's really supportive…." Stills pauses. "And I'm supportive of them," he adds. "Crosby's even worse than I am. Crosby's terrible!" he laughs amiably. "He moans and groans, says, 'Oh, man….'" Stills does a good Crosby.

"What are you afraid of? What could possibly happen?"

"I don't know," Stills says. "I have no idea what the show will be like, so it's fear of the unknown."

"But you've done the show so many times…."

"Yeah, I know," he says sheepishly. "It's really neurotic, obviously. But every time I walk on the stage to play in front of people, I get real professional real quick. But also exploratory with my guitar. I never play the same solos. We always skate real close to the edge. I put one foot over," he laughs, "and ski on the inside ski." He laughs again, then chuckles, then coughs. We look outside for a moment.

What is this fear?

"I can't really answer that," he says. "That's what I talk to my *doctah* about." He leans on the word like a New Yorker and lets out again with that brotherly belly laugh, then checks for response. "I have a great guy who lives in Santa Barbara and we see each other about once a month. I just started this last year. I mean, you know, I think it's something everybody needs. I used to scoff at it when I was in New York, all these people in analysis and everything. And then I went, 'Welll, hold on,' you know. There's a certain amount of neurosis that goes with going out there and doing a psychological striptease in front of 10,000 people, and you've got to learn how to deal with it."

"When did you start with the doctor?"

"Oh," he says, "I started when my marriage fell apart. [Stills is married to French singer Veronique Sanson; they have one son, Christopher.] 'Cause I was definitely on the roof. That was last year. I've since put it back together. I mean, it was incredible. August of '76 will go down in the history of my life as being the worst. I hope I've seen the worst!" he laughs. "The Neil Young tour fell apart and I went home and my old lady had left me. So that can make you stop and look—maybe these people are trying to tell me something."

"What did you figure they were trying to tell you?"

"I don't think Neil was trying to tell me anything. As far as my wife goes, there's just a year of building up things and she finally took off....She's a very volatile French lady."

There is another pause and I just have to ask.

"Why have you been so crazy so often?"

Stills answers evenly. "Self-destructive." He looks down. "I don't know. That's one of the things....I guess maybe I don't like myself."

But he has friends, has written some classic songs, plays excellent guitar. Strangers love him.

"Strangers love me," he agrees. "And I have some very devoted friends and it's totally ridiculous. But some old bugaboo down there, some old bugaboo inside myself doesn't like me for some reason. I mean...it's...It gets hard to verbalize. It's what I see my doctah for," he laughs, "to ferret this little guy out, whatever he is. Isn't it funny to be a writer and try to verbalize some kind of...."

"That's what writing is about," I offer.

"I put it in my songs," he says.

Sometimes it has appeared to me that, in his songs, Stills pulls back from good lines, as if afraid to say them for fear they will go unappreciated. He disagrees, about his songwriting: "I'm a little more committed than that.

But I did it with women—not wanting to hang out my emotional laundry so that just one person could rip it all down and stomp on it in the dirt. It's a rather interesting little picture of what I mean, but it pretty much says it. I bleed." He laughs. "I'm brave, but I'm a coward too. I'll face down exterior forces, but my interior forces scare me to death,"

"There's something of a bravado in facing down exterior forces," I add.

"Yeah," he says, "until the first punch. Then you've got to swing back—'*Alright, motherfucker*!' And then it's to chairs, two-by-fours, television sets. The few fights that I've had in my life I've won, just because I won't quit. I just keep going and going and going and going until someone picks me up and throws me across the room.

"I was once in Alaska and this great big Alaskan guy, something about all the chicks were going to the rock 'n' roll show and he was pissed off. And I said," he breaks into a barroom slur, "'Well listen, motherfucker'—I was just pissed to the gills!—'Listen, motherfucker, *I'm* the rock 'n roll show!' He said, 'Oh yeah?' And *Kaboom*!" Stills sprawls back in his seat. "So I just picked up a bar stool and...." he has it pantomimed by the legs and smashes it with two hands over the guy's back. He's laughing. I'm laughing. You can almost see the splinters and sawdust fly. "Oh, it was a classic. I finally got him and the bartender says, 'You better get out of here. That guy's gonna wake up and pound your ass.'"

Spirit moving at a dreadful pace
Slowing dying, I can see it in my face
Sadness and anger, all that keeps me going
Tired of nothing but my outside showing.

　And I'm lowdown
　Get me out of this place
　I'm lowdown
　Like a hole in space. *

—"Lowdown," Stephen Stills

It was five in the afternoon at the Caribou Ranch in Nederland, Colorado, when Stephen Stills arrived for the session. The dead of winter, 1975—Souther, Hillman and Furay were a band for the time being and Stills had been invited down to add a few hot licks to their second (and what was to be final) LP. But he peaked too soon; recording didn't begin until nine and by that time Stephen was loaded. He tried to put on a few lines but nothing was doing; his fingers stuck and the music wasn't there. He blamed the guitar, the new strings, the setup. As if in restitution he tried to teach the drummer a new beat that would liven up the take. Sitting behind the drum set at four in the morning, all flopsweat and hard talk, Stills was a sorry sight. When he left at nine there were no intoxicants of any kind on the ranch. He had made a raid and downed them all. Nobody seemed surprised.

Orchestral tune-up cacophony and violists' smalltalk fills Criteria Studio B. Twenty-six string players and a French horn have been gathered for an evening of recording with Stephen Stills. Mr. Stills intends to sing and play acoustic guitar against the background of live accompaniment; errors will not be tolerated.

Ron Albert has broken out the double-breasted black velvet blazer for the occasion. Stills is wearing his tortoise shell glasses and a neat sports jacket. He is clearly nervous as preparations are finalized, pacing with arms folded as the moment arrives. Among other spectators, his wife is watching in the control room. All is ready; the studio quiets. Conductor/arranger Mike Lewis intones: "Ladies and gentlemen, allow me to present to you Stephen Stills." The room is filled with the staccato timbre of bows tapping music stands, a string section's ovation. Stills nods a respectful bow back and walks quickly to his place. Surrounded by wires and microphones, he seems fairly frozen with self-control. Lewis raises his baton and they begin.

The music is lush, almost every note in place, and it is Stills who must play to capacity in order to complete the evening. He does, the rich tones of his heirloom D'Angelico guitar blending significantly with the wealth of strings. Stills' voice complements the full sound by rounding its own rough edges and flowing almost milky throughout the song. The ballad suits its setting:

There is really no describing
How I love you, 'tisn't fair
Deep and rich and trusting
Building on the things we share

I am with you, girl
From your eyes I take a curl
Dream on peacefully, girl
Sleep deep and sound
I will be around
*I am with you, girl.***

It doesn't take long. Stills is obviously prepared; the sound is right, there is little to do but go for the fine tuning. The song is finished to everyone's satisfaction rather quickly.

The next number, "Beaucoup Yumbo," starts out in similar fashion. An acoustic, gut-bucket blues with strings for counter-balance and horns for the hell of it, the tune is burning until it hits the bridge. Stop. Something is not right.

Stills is not satisfied with the playback. He hears something, knows it's there—now if he can only find it. Ah. The string charts must be rewritten, on the spot. ("String players?" says Michael John out of earshot. "After midnight these people get paid by the note!") Stills and Mike Lewis huddle by the podium and scan the song. What's to be done?

It's getting late. Some violists are grumbling; they're not used to this rock 'n' roll disregard for daytime, but they are trying to understand. Finally, Stills and Lewis reassemble the multitude. They've come up with the evening's saving "head chart"—a seat-of-the-pants orchestration meets the Top Ten.

Damned if it doesn't sound real good. The orchestra responds, the new chart is just right, and when the session ends, at 2:30 a.m., Stills is feeling fine.

Veronique ("Vero") Stills arrived in Miami only today. An attractive woman, she watched intently as Stephen worked and now talks animatedly with her husband in the studio. They kiss with the distraction of lovers in public and embrace as they part for the night.

"I'll be home soon," Stills tells her.

"I hope so. For your sake," she says. "You must take care of yourself."

"I will. *Je t'aime.*"

"*Je t'aime beaucoup.*"

Stills watches her leave, then lifts his head to a mike and shouts to the control room, "Let's do some vocals." Dead on their feet after a hard session, not fully prepared for Stills' enthusiasm, the Alberts gamely oblige. There are perhaps eight unfinished songs to be sung and they slap on the first one.

Stills is active behind the mike. Shifting from one foot to another, a familiar motion by now, he begins the song and something happens. Where first takes are normally warm-ups, used simply to accustom the singer to the song, Stills is getting it right. Half-paid attention is replaced by sharp focus. Eyes turn, ears perk. Even Stephen has not expected this. Halfway through the vocal the pleasure/tension grows, as if we are ballpark boys and Stills is going for a no-hitter. At the next-to-last verse, he peeks ahead and stumbles over a word, then glides home safely. He lets the track fade over his silence to an end.

"Amazing." The talk-back clicks the voice out to him. "All you've got to do is that one line over and I think we've got it," says Ron Albert. Stills redoes the line, then sings the song all the way through again. His voice is supple this evening, not strained. He is singing under his arrangements instead of crying over them. He moves on to the next.

Again, the first take is usable, the second is better, the third is there. He is running through his repertoire. He could sing the whole album tonight! Do it once on tape and it's forever.

He tries another vocal on "Beaucoup Yumbo" and it shines. He finishes up the disputed tag in one take, knocks off a ballad and finally unleashes his Stephen Stills wail on an ace version of "Midnight Rider." At seven in the morning as the pipes are beginning to tighten, and leaving very little undone, he calls it quits.

Cocky and calm, wanting to crow and not wanting to blow it, Stephen is ready to talk. "How're you gonna fit that into a psychological analysis of Stephen Stills?" he laughs. "That's what I mean about time and chops and being able to cut it. Old reservoirs."

We take a couple of folding chairs and sit in the studio. The carpeted floors and thick walls absorb all sound except our words. It is a silence one rarely hears.

"The union Vibe Guy was here tonight," Stills says. "And pulling off that head chart...the confidence factor was built up by that. I'm sensible enough to recognize when I get hot."

And sensible enough to have given himself a lot of thought. "What," I wonder, "is the most telling song you've written about yourself?"

"Oh boy," he says, "I really can't answer that. 'My Favorite Changes'...I know there are better ones. 'The Myth of Sisyphus' is a bust on myself. But I can't really put my finger on any songs that really pin me down. I'm much too elusive for that." He sits more comfortably in his chair.

"Before I played music I was into a gig that demanded I be able to be anonymous. I was really into just being invisible. So there's that quality about me that still remains. No matter how big a star they make me, I can become totally innocuous and invisible."

"Do you want to be?"

"Yes."

"Why?'

"It's where I can observe." The hour is taking its toll. Words come more slowly, pauses are longer. "My antennas are out all the time."

"But you very rarely act as an anonymous person."

"Not when I'm working, certainly," Stills says. "When I'm working it's, 'The boss is here, let's go.' When I'm not working I can go to a party full of a bunch of well-known people and let them kind of 'Hey, howareya, blah blah blah,' and then I'll gradually fade into a corner and watch the movie."

"But only surrounded by celebrities," I suggest.

"Not so," he objects. "Sometimes on the road I'll run into a bunch of kids that kind of interest me and I'll take off and go to their joint and we'll play for a while and I'll let that barrier slowly drop and just fade a little bit. Just keep wandering around the house until everybody's kind of doing their own thing, and they talk about me for a while and then they start getting real. Thereby I become invisible. And then I can observe."

There is a pause. "You've said that something inside doesn't like you. What kind of person would you rather be?"

He lounges in his chair even lower. "I don't know. I'm not going to delude myself into thinking I can be something that I'm not. I already tried that and it didn't work. It was transparent."

"What role was that?"

"Several different ones. Just trying to be what I thought would fit...." he waits, "...with the people around me. As to the specifics of it, I can't recall or don't really care to."

"You said you were afraid of something," I say slowly. "What of?"

"I don't know," he says. It seems a reflex response.

"You've been giving it some thought."

Stills definitely understands. Perhaps he is considering whether to answer at all. "I guess I'm afraid of that guy inside me that I don't like," he says quickly. "I detest embarrassment, and I'm afraid that guy might pop up and embarrass me. I'm actually *afraid* of embarrassment, but yet make a fool of myself time and time again. But yet, making a fool of oneself is not that...it doesn't mean that much to me, but...I mean, that's not the end-all and be-all, it's just..." he searches for another word but can only find, "...embarrassing."

"But you hate it."

"Absolutely. Down to my toes. Can't face it. Can't take it at all."

"But you seemed at one point to be embarrassing yourself regularly. Why did you do it?"

"Hey," his voice shows some anger, "read a few books. Self-destruction is a very common ailment."

I am a bit shaken. "I always figured you had a lot of strength...."

"The strength to destroy myself," he breaks in.

"But you haven't done it," I say. "Other people have gone out and done themselves in."

"There's a difference between drinking yourself to death and eating your gun," he explains. "There's a difference between being a fool when you're not, and just being a fool."

"There are forces at work...."

"Self-destructive, almost masochistic forces."

"Brought on by something."

"Maybe...maybe..." Stills is searching his psychic pockets for loose change. "Maybe I feel I'm not doing my best. 'Cause I've felt for a long time that there's more to me than this....I'm gonna write a book. I'm writing a movie. When I do write, I write well. I paint, sculpt. I'm catching up on things I missed in high school and college. I'm catching up on physics and I want to grapple chemistry next. I hope you don't regard it as egotism or vanity, but I feel like there is more to me than just music, no matter how gifted I am or am not. I make records. I do it well. Some of them are good; some of them are mediocre, blah, blah, blah....

"I want to go back to school and become a doctor. I could teach music. It's just a question of how long is this going to hang me up as much as it does, which it does."

"The career?"

"No, the music. The career is a secondary element. Going for it—every few nights in front of twenty some odd thousand people—that's where I like to live. Performing to 26 string players, and singing to the violist and watching her just melt and forget her part is one thing. But reaching back to the last row of Madison Square Garden, that's then again a different story. Now, I think I'm good at it."

"Tell me more about Crosby, Stills & Nash," I ask after a pause.

"We make up for each other's inadequacies," Stills says with some resignation. "We help each other through each other's stupidities. And I play guitar and I try to help them get the best out of their songs and their music, and they try to help me....Without taking over," he adds. " 'Cause sometimes I'll get a flash on one of David's songs and know exactly how it should be done, and I can be totally wrong. Then I'll get hung up and cut him a mind-blowing track. Or he'll say, 'No, man, that's not what I want to do, man.' It's a *gestalt* mentality. Very interdependent—and we finally admitted that it is.

"Graham's the only one with the patience to go in there and take four or five partial vocals and make one good vocal out of all of them. David can put together really neat harmonies that sometimes are incredible and sometimes are not incredible. I set the feel. I get the band together. I make everybody play like there's no tomorrow. And I make double goddamn sure that David is satisfied with the performance of his song, and Graham is satisfied with the performance of his song...even if I lay out."

"So, are they friends, brothers, acquaintances...?"

"You can't get away from your brothers." Stills tries on his soul voice. "I didn't have no brothers, so I adopted some. Ain't a whole lot of jive goes down on my stage...or Graham Nash's," he adds, "or David Crosby's. When we're singing out of tune, *we*'re Out of Tune. When we hit something spot on, then it's 'Aaay, awright!' I mean, we all lead different lives, but nobody can understand what I'm after when I hit the stage as well as David and Graham.

"We get downright cold pro, and it's great. Just like I did tonight. I had to stand up in front of 26 violinists and move them to where they started playing with me. Same thing is true of 26,000 or 90,000 or 122,000."

"Isn't it hard to keep individuals in mind when you're playing in football stadiums?" I ask.

"No," he says firmly. "You take the mass as an individual."

But Stephen Stills rarely sees the individuals in that mass; they simply don't get past backstage security or into the crowd he runs with. The people out there are almost entirely a concept for him.

"Do you," I wonder aloud, "make friends easily?"

"Not particularly," he says. "Because of my vulnerability."

And what are the qualities of a friend of Stephen Stills?

"I don't know," he says. "To be my friend? Gotta be loyal. Gotta be absolutely trustworthy. I mean, don't be blowing my cool, 'cause I won't be blowing your cool. And don't cross me, 'cause I'm a real hard-ass in a lot of ways. And just operate on a level of respect and trust. Keep your mouth shut—Don't put *my* bid'ness in the street and I won't put *your* bid'ness in the street. I do a bad enough job blowing my own cool.

"But I don't think anyone'll see me blow it that bad anymore."

Like smashing studio walls?

Stills runs back the scene in his mind. "I was getting totally negative vibes from everybody, no positive feedback."

"But if they really thought the tag had to be redone, what would you have expected them to do?"

"I don't want to be bullshitted," he says, "but at the same time I only need to be told once." Again, the schoolboy voice. "I'm not deaf. And I came back in thoroughly in mind to fix that tag. And I don't need 15 people telling me the same goddamn thing over and over. *I heard it*, for chrissake. Shut up, gimme a break! I mean, nobody knows what the hell I'm gonna do next anyway....And I wouldn't have it any other way." He slaps off the tape recorder. "I like that, that's a good way to end."

Stephen Stills would like you to care what he does next. It's a natural desire. (As he says, "Neurosis is rampant in our land. What am I copping to?") His best work—Buffalo Springfield, CSN/CSNY, Manassas—has come when he's been surrounded by a family of one kind or another. He needs that reinforcement; he hasn't, to date, given it to himself. Sometimes he promises more than he can deliver—med school? backstage *Psychology Today* seminars? the straight and narrow?—but his earnestness, his desire, is his most appealing characteristic. He could be a consummate liar, and I could be being had, but there does seem a sense to him of the kid in summer camp who is always one award away from security. He seems, happily for the time being, to have found his families. Yet he is the man who wrote:

It gets harder as you get older
*And farther away as you get closer.**

One hopes he's closing in on it.

*©1977 Gold Hill Music, Inc.
**"I'm With You, Girl" by Stephen Stills ©1977 Gold Hill Music, Inc.

GRAHAM NASH:
THE WINDS OF CHANGE

BY DAVE ZIMMER
BAM: *The California
Music Magazine*
February 1980

I'm fully aware that it may be bad form for an editor to include his own work in a book such as this one, but I just couldn't leave this interview out. Graham Nash and I "locked in" to the point where when our sessions ended, we both physically shook ourselves back to present consciousness—as if we had slipped into a kind of time tunnel. Neither CSN nor CSNY were happening, so Nash was deep into his latest solo project; but, as you will read, the man is a master storyteller with an historian's eye for detail, focusing in on a number of turning points in his musical life.

Graham Nash at the Pantages Theatre. March 1980. Hollywood, California. Photo: Henry Diltz

Integrity, more than any other word, seems to define what Graham Nash is all about. Whether as a member of the Hollies, a part of various CSNY groupings or on his own, Graham's integrity, his ability to remain true to himself and his musical art form, has resulted in a consistent flow of creative compositions and performances that not only honestly reflect a myriad of sensitive emotional feelings, but often create a vivid awareness for what he views as social and environmental atrocities.

During the past year, much of Nash's musical energy has been merging with efforts to combat the growth of nuclear power, something he has been concerned about since the late '50s. Multiple benefit concerts (he had only three paying gigs in 1979) to support the anti-nuke cause, several of them with Jackson Browne, coincided with his work as a Board Member of the MUSE (Musicians United for Safe Energy) organization and climaxed with his participation in the five-night MUSE concerts project in New York last September. Then, Graham's tireless production work, along with Jackson Browne and several others, throughout an unprecedented "marathon session," made possible the release of *No Nukes* (a three-record set of music from the September shows) by Christmas. It's amazing that amidst all of this activity, Nash also managed to recently complete his third solo album, *Earth and Sky*. This new record exhibits startling musical dynamism, in terms of instrumental fire, pointed lyrics and vocal strength, by this vital recording artist who turns 38 February 2nd.

• • •

The following interview was conducted in the warm, leather and wood-filled Hartmann and Goodman offices at the Crossroads of the World in Hollywood. I met with Graham there on two different occasions—first, in mid-October, for a two hour conversation; and again, for another hour, right before Christmas. Throughout our talks, Graham was open, friendly and showed an incredible memory for detail. When recalling a particularly vivid experience, the cadence of his rich English accent would quicken, his eyes would sparkle and it seemed as if he were reliving the moment right before me. Never once did he seem to just churn out a stock answer; rather, Graham would expand into remarkable elaborations that were startling in depth and insight. During these three hours of conversation, Graham Nash definitely spoke from his heart.

Why a solo venture now?
The thing that I go through that results in a solo album is an interesting process of collecting songs that can't be done, for whatever reason, by a lot of people—specifically, CSN and C&N. And so when I get a wealth of songs and no vehicle for them, I put them out myself.

I like making music with other people better than making music by myself, but this album is exciting to me. Something very special is going on and I feel very confident that I'm not wasting people's time.

What were the specific stages that led up to *Earth and Sky*?

Crosby, Stills & Nash at Survival Sunday, Hollywood Bowl. May 25, 1980. Photo: Henry Diltz

It started out as a CSN album, way back about a year and a half, almost two years ago. And that project crumbled because of lack of material, lack of energy, lack of respect, whatever. So, I proceeded to the next course, which was a Crosby and Nash album and, lo and behold, that crumbled *too*, leaving me alone with all this stuff and nothing to do.

So I decided to just keep on going. I took one of the tracks I'd recorded with CSN and a couple that David and I had recorded, and used those three songs as the basis for starting my own album.

How would you compare *Earth and Sky* to a CSN project?

It surprised me, this album, I must confess. I can hear one man's music there, although the music was made with a lot of really fine musicians. Nobody makes a solo album totally on their own, but I got off on *Earth and Sky*, because I had nobody to answer to except myself. Normally, I never have anyway; but when you're making an album with David and Stephen, one is answerable to the collective cause. So it's very interesting to have total control over what I do. Alone there's no one looking....

That was what was so thrilling about the Universal Amphitheatre gigs [August, 1979]—selling out three nights with no partners and no record. It was an amazing feat; I was rather pleased about the whole thing. And John and Harlan [Hartmann and Goodman, Graham's managers] really set me

straight on opening night. They said, "I only saw *your* name up on the mar-
quee. I didn't see Stephen's or David's or Neil's, and look at 'em pouring in
and filling this place. I guess they're just coming to see you, aren't they? So
you better dig it." And that was a really interesting perspective. I was totally
shocked. Then I walked into the parking lot and heard this woman shouting, "Get your Graham Nash T-shirts." And it stopped me cold, because it
was so odd to hear one's name, out there alone, with T-shirt sales. "Get your
Graham Nash T-shirts." [Laughs]

**What are your feelings towards *Earth and Sky*, in comparison with
your two previous solo albums?**

I've been equally thrilled with each of my solo albums. I think they
have shown a side of me, an angle of me that was relevant right then. My
songs are just my reaction to my environment: if I fall in love, if I go blind,
if I lose someone dear to me, if I get angry, if I'm elated. They're all just bits
and pieces of my life. And each of my albums is that way.

This new album reflects exactly how I feel right now. It's up, it's direct,
it's easy to listen to. I'm not interested in complex music that leaves people
behind. I like to talk to people. And I feel there is a directness with this
album, so that once you start listening to it, it's hard not to continue.

Will this album change your "musical image?"

Hopefully so. This is not the same old Graham Nash. Hopefully every
day I'm not the same old Graham Nash. Because I hate conformity and I hate
staying in the same place. I like to get out there on the edge. And that's what
I do with a lot of these songs and a lot of the musicians I have on these songs.
Instead of saying, "Okay, you play this and you play that," I said, "Here's the
song, how do you want to play it." Between six or seven people, it all works
out very well. Like I said, nobody makes solo albums alone.

**How do you react when journalists put labels on your music, try to box
you into an image?**

I've always just made my music and hoped that it represented a
growth and a movement forward, and that people would like it. I've never
thought, "Boy, I'm just an old folky and I'm trapped in my image." I just
make my music.

But I do think this album is very different, musically, from any album
I've done before. [Long pause] I'm definitely going for the throat.

The album cover for *Earth and Sky*...

[Goes and gets the cover and spreads it out on a table in front of us.]
When I saw this picture that Joel [Bernstein] had taken of me, I decided that
it was good enough to put an album between. Here I am, standing on the
edge of this canyon. It's a 2,000 foot drop there, and I was standing there for
about 15 minutes. You can tell from the pant legs that there was an awful
lot of wind there. That is exactly how I feel. The music that goes inside is
what this album cover shows. It's light, it's airy, it's a little ominous in the

darker areas. There's hope in it. There are rainbows, good feelings...being blown around.

On the inside is *this* picture [a black and white close-up of Graham], which also reflects a certain amount of the music, too. It's much more direct, a starker image.

I maintain that an album is a totality. I don't separate the music from the cover. They have to marry, they have to match, they have to bounce off one another.

That's why I had so much trouble with Columbia. Because they thought I was just fooling around when I didn't want a computer scan out bar code on the cover. I said, "Listen, let me send you the cover photograph, then you'll understand why I don't want a bar code on there." Now, I understand the need for inventory methods that will eventually be able to pinpoint each album, but only two percent of the stores can currently deal with it anyway.

But with Capitol, here it is, and there's no bar code. So it couldn't have been that important. But to Columbia it was important enough for them to want to ram their corporate policy down my throat and say, "We say that's where it goes, so that's where it goes." They said that to the worst man they could say that to on the planet.

I have a photography collection that is priceless to me, some of the greatest images that have ever been seen from 1845 to 1979. I know what I'm talking about. If I didn't want a bar code there, for whatever reason—if I didn't like the color of black and white stripes going by—CBS should have understood and at least thought about it artistically, and given me an unbiased, balanced point of view, as to why it should go on. If they had done that, I could have been convinced...maybe. But for them to say, "CBS says it goes there, that's it," that's total bullshit. You can't say that to me. So I gave them back their $700,000 and told them to stick it up their ass, and went to a company that would give me total artistic freedom.

Every Capitol record has a logo on it. They even moved that for me. They were sweethearts to me. When they saw this picture, they said, "Of course you can't have a bar code there." A lot of people at Capitol said, "Are you telling me that Columbia lost a several million dollar deal in signing Crosby and Nash because of a goddamned bar code?" It amazes them that Columbia's corporate policy could be so stupid.

Back to your songwriting, what percentage of your songs would you say are autobiographical, about real situations?

Every one of them. I stopped manufacturing songs when I left the Hollies. That was the cause of a lot of my musical mistrust and unhappiness with them. Because we could really invent a pop song...from nothing. We could really do it well. We had great success manufacturing songs that weren't based in reality. But since I came here in '68, actually before that, in '66–'67, I started to get more introspective, more personal and more real.

221

Can you think of any songs you have shelved because they were too dark, where there was no hope?

Oh sure. I have lots of them. I think every artist does. Specifically, I started to write a set of changes about a man called Abu Daud, who was the man theoretically responsible for killing the 11 Olympic team members at Munich. The reason I got into that was because I was in England at the time, seeing my family, and I saw the French let this man go, for no reason. Then I saw the president of France go, the very next week, to Saudi Arabia and clinch a deal for 200 Mirage jets that the French were selling to the Arabs. It doesn't take a genius to work out what's going on there. That's filthy.

So this song was called "Mirage," and started out, "Blood is thicker than water, but it looks like oil is thicker than blood." It's dark, and sometimes I don't feel like laying bummers on everybody.

And is it sometimes also because you don't want to be too preachy?

Yes, I never try and preach. I've never enjoyed being preached at and I don't try and do it to other people. I try and allow them to look at me going through my changes and make up their own minds.

Some of the changes portrayed in your songs seem rather painful. Doesn't performing them again and again bring back that pain?

Sure, every time you perform a song, you have to think about what it is you're doing. But, however I deal with it is what the show is. That's it. There are no stacked heels, no glitter, no glamour. It's just me and my guitar up there.

How do you feel about performing your older material, the hits. Do you feel an obligation?

I'm not sure obligation is the right word, but I definitely know that an awful lot of people love certain songs, and who am I to deny them some of those songs? I have played "Our House" *thousands* of times. I got bored with "Our House" the day after I recorded it. But there's no way that occasionally I won't sing that song, because it does mean so much to so many people.

So I try and balance a show 50–50. I figure that's an equal balance. I don't want to bombard an audience with 15 new songs. I like to entertain, not that I can't entertain with new songs. But, I recognize the value of good memories, fond, warm memories, and I will always sing what we are referring to as "old songs."

Are you put out by people wanting to talk to you in public when they recognize who you are?

No, I'm thrilled. Because, back in 1960 I saw the Everly Brothers live in Manchester. I was a teenager, and me and my friend Allan Clarke were there. We hadn't formed the Hollies yet and were singing a lot of Everly Brothers material, into their two part harmonies. So we waited till four in the morning for them to come out of this night club. And at four in the morning, in the pouring rain, they took the time to sign autographs and just talk to us. And that impressed me greatly. They didn't have to do that. They could have gone straight to their hotel rooms.

Consequently, I've had a policy ever since of never refusing an autograph and never refusing to talk to someone who wants to just say a couple of words. What the Everly Brothers did to me, I hope I can do to other people. They inspired me. They were gentle, not off-putting, weren't drunk out of their minds. They inspired me to get more into music.

Can you recall any other specific incidents or experiences that drew you to music initially?

There were several of them. But one made the most impact on me: When I was growing up as a teenager, the local dances were all important. That was the way you met ladies, learned how to dance and hear new music. And I remember specifically going down to this dance hall with my friend, Allan Clarke, and getting half way across the floor, when somebody put on "Bye, Bye Love" by the Everly Brothers, with that acoustic guitar opening. I'll never forget the feeling that sound had on me. It stopped me dead in my tracks, I wanted a part of it, I wanted to know how to do that, wanted to know what it was about that musical passage that made me feel that way.

And I've been trying to do that my whole life, to make music interesting enough to stop people and make them think a little more.

When did you start writing original songs?

'57–'58. We'd been singing skiffle songs, and some Big Bill Broonzy, Lonnie Donnigan, great songs. Then me and Allan got a band together, I started writing some then, and then we formed the Hollies in '63, put these songs on the B-sides of singles. The B-side of the first record was called "The Whole World Over," a totally naive little pop song. That's what we were writing.

Around the time of the Hollies' fifth album, I started to write songs that were influenced by my life, more introspective, rather than manufacturing pop songs like "Carrie-Anne." I began to not make them up, began to draw on my personal life for their source.

What was the Liverpool scene like in the early '60s?

Very exciting, very funky, very raw, very earthy, very human. We used to play lunch time sessions at The Cavern. It was mystifying. It was magic.

Did you have any personal contact with the Beatles?

Yes I did. We were playing the same circuit a lot and I got to know them a little personally. But they were very protected by a filtering system between the four of them. They were always together, even if there was a room full of people and they were all separated.

It was a very interesting perspective on musical history for me, being there at the elbow of it all, watching it all go down. I've always felt very lucky that not only was I involved in some sort of musical history, in terms of the growth of rock and roll and pop music, but I got to see it all unfolding before my eyes and I was *aware* that it was historical. When you saw the Beatles and saw the effect they had on people, you *knew* something was happening, especially during the early years, around '63.

In 1967, didn't the Hollies back the Everly Brothers on a record of theirs?

Yeah, we did. They made a record called *Two Yanks in England* and I think they did six or seven of our songs. We helped them out in the studio, played and sang on various tracks. It was just a total thrill...to go from 1960, waiting in the pouring rain for the Everly Brothers, to '67 and being in the studio and singing on the same mike with Phil Everly was a mind-blower for me...*mind* blowing! One of the real high points of my life.

What initially started to draw you away from the Hollies?

Basically, I was the only one that smoked dope in the band, and although it may seem like a silly answer, it was deeply obvious that there was a giant rift developing between us. Once you start becoming more self-aware, more deeply aware of surroundings and feelings, and heightening all your experience levels, which marijuana did for me then—and LSD, to a certain extent—you also become more open, more perceptive and are more eager to experiment. The other guys were not into smoking; they were still the "five pints every night lads," and would end up scrapping, a little drunk. So, the more dope I smoked, and the more beer they drank, the deeper the rift between us became.

When did you seriously consider leaving the group?

Early '68. I'd decided that I'd had it, that I was being stifled. You see, I'd written what I thought were some interesting songs at that time— "Marrakesh Express," "Right Between the Eyes," "Lady of the Island"—and the Hollies weren't interested in them. And when I said in the first "Sleep Song," for instance, "I'll take off my clothes and I'll lay by your side," they said, "Hey, you can't bloody sing that. We're not going to sing that *filthy* stuff." Saying those things to a stoned musician is ridiculous. So I began to realize there was no way that I could exist with these people. They were still my friends and I loved them dearly, but there was no way I could continue to make music with them.

This happened at the same time they wanted to make an album with Dylan tunes. I thought even that was sacrilege, because we were doing them like [Graham starts singing "Blowin' in the Wind" in swing fashion, snapping his fingers] "How many roads, yeah, would a..." a Las Vegas type thing and it was driving me nuts. I couldn't handle it. At the same time, when I sang with David and Stephen, I saw and experienced what musical delight that was. So all these things happened at the same time, in early '68.

- **So you left the Hollies.**

February 14, 1968, and I can tell you specifically why I remember that night.

The Hollies were in Los Angeles at the time. We had a free day, and we figured no one knows who the hell we are on the West Coast, so why don't we do a free gig. We called Elmer Bernstein at the Whisky A Go Go and asked him if we could use the hall, throw a free gig. It was Valentine's Day; that's the reason I remember. It was a really fine concert, one of those shows I was telling you about, when we were experimenting with tapes. We blew a lot of people's minds. Buffalo Springfield, the Byrds, the Mamas and the Papas were there. But after the show, once again the band wanted to go drinking and I wanted to go hang out with David and Stephen and get wasted. [Laughs]

So I was in Stephen's Bentley and sittin' in the back with Crosby, and Stephen looked over and says, "Well, which one of us is gonna steal him?" And we started talking about the inevitability of singing together, and that was the night I made up my mind to move to America and move musically and get on with someting else.

People said, "You're crazy, to leave all that wealth and fame and notoriety." But I wanted to explore new music. I wanted to do something different. So, the change was easy. It was just something I had to do.

How did you meet Joni Mitchell?

[Very long pause]

I was just reliving the moment as you asked me the question. I know exactly how I'm going to tell you.

The Hollies did a gig in either Toronto or Ottawa, I think it was Toronto. And the radio station that was promoting the concert threw a party in the Holiday Inn afterwards. I remember going in and getting changed and showered and coming down to the party. I walked into this room, got myself a Coca Cola and I see this woman sitting in the corner. She's got long blond hair and bangs, is wearing a necklace and a sort of a blue-grey silk dress, and she has a large Bible on her knee. And the manager for the Hollies, Robert Britton, whispers in my ear, "I want to introduce you to this person," and I said, "Please don't bother me now, I'm checking out this lady. I'm really interested in who the 'ell is sittin' in the corner." He said, "Well, if you'd just shut up for a second, that's who I'm talking about, too. This lady's name is Joni Mitchell. She's a friend of David Crosby's and she wants to talk to you." So I walk over and say, "So *you're* Joni Mitchell," because David had played me some of her material and you don't have to be a fuckin' genius to realize she's one of the greatest talents on the planet. [Laughs]

So I struck up a relationship with Joni and she took me back to her hotel and sang me some songs. We just had an incredible, insane, beautiful time. And it developed into a great, deep love that continues to this day.

How do you think your relationship affected your respective creative developments?

I'm sure it affected them a lot. The time that Joni and I were living together was really interesting, because I had left my band successfully, I had left my country successfully, I had been accepted successfully here, and I was feeling great. And Joni was feeling great, too; she started to realize who she was and the fantastic work she was doing. She was painting and designing her second album cover, doing that self-portrait. And I remember being totally in awe of her. She'd go and make some supper and come down and we'd be eating, then she'd all of a sudden space out, go to the piano and write this insane shit…just insane shit. To see her sit down and write "Rainy Night House" and all those other things was just mind blowing. My music meant nothing compared to how I felt about her music.

How did you react to "Willy" [a variant of Graham's middle name, William, which serves as a nickname] on *Ladies of the Canyon*?

Just to know that by my presence and by my actions I can provoke a song such as "Willy" thrills me and makes me a little uncomfortable, because she's laying it out there. And I can remember the specifics…I remember looking out the window at the moon, and I remember talking about hearing wedding bells too soon. I remember all those incidents that came together to form that song. So, it's pretty scary.

But just to have been a part of that woman's life thrills me beyond belief. We have and have had a deep, deep relationship. She is an incredibly special woman. I have incredible respect for her.

What was the Laurel Canyon scene like, circa 1968?

Very young, very fresh, very energetic, very loving. At that time, all of us musicians had been kept from the board for so long; from [slaps his hand] "Hey, don't touch that knob, that's a union gig." We had gone from that sort of reaction in the studio to being able to call up and say, "Hey, Wally, I need three weeks." "Okay, I'll see you tomorrow." You'd go down, run your own session. They actually let us hippies do it. I mean, look at that place [points out the window to his home studio, Rudy Records]. That's my place there. Fifteen, twenty years ago, you couldn't get involved with that The point I'm trying to make is, during '68 and '69, musicians were coming into their own. They were able to make their music however they wanted to do it. They didn't have to, as on the first Byrds album, use session musicians at the request of the record company, because the company didn't think McGuinn, Crosby or Hillman could play worth a shit. Then, in the late '60s, musicians became totally in control of their own musical destiny, and Laurel Canyon was a place for the meeting of musical minds, which made for an atmosphere that was very Bohemian and very enjoyable to me.

What attracted you to Crosby and Stills?

I'm a people-watcher. I really love to watch people. And Crosby fascinated me. I'd never met anybody like him. He was a total punk, a total asshole, totally delightful, totally funny, totally brilliant, a totally *musical* man. And I enjoyed his company. He introduced me to Stills, and the rest is history.

Do any Crosby, Stills & Nash "living room" sessions in Laurel Canyon stand out in your mind?

I remember me, David and Stephen rehearsing our entire first album and being able to play it on two acoustic guitars. We would sit people down and say, "Listen." And then we would sit down and play "Suite: Judy Blue Eyes" right in front of them, great. And we would follow it with "Helplessly Hoping," "You Don't Have to Cry," "Marrakesh Express," "Right Between the Eyes," "Guinnevere," "Long Time Gone." By the time they'd sat down and listened to this hour of music, they were *on the floor!* We used to play deliberately to blow people away.

We would go down to Elektra-Asylum, where Paul Rothchild was recording John Sebastian, and they'd say, "Oh no, here are those three lads again!" [Laughs] We'd totally bring the session to a halt, because we'd learned a new piece of music that was so exciting that we had to play it for Sebastian. It was great, a very enjoyable time.

And we *knew*. We weren't fools. We'd all made a lot music in the previous ten years and we knew that the certain chemistry that happened when I sang with David and Stephen was not the same as when David sang with Stephen alone, or I sang with David alone, or I sang with Stephen alone. There was something that happened when the *three* of us put our voices together that was magic, and we knew it.

On the morning that we left the studio with the two-track of *Crosby, Stills & Nash* under our arms, about to send it off to New York to the great pressing plant in the sky, we knew we had something going. We knew we had a #1 record. Maybe that was youthful naivete; but we *knew* and it went to #1 and it went *fast*. Because everyone was doing heavy metal, Jimi Hendrix, stacks of Marshalls, King Dick kind of music, and here were these three guys with an acoustic album that just created an entire scene. We knew that it was exciting and we knew that it was different, and wanted to let people know about it. So, we would just go and wander in places and just sing. Sounds corny, but it's true.

How would you compare how the first CSN album sounded to the living room performances?

It was very close. The effect that we had when we put on a tape of "Suite: Judy Blue Eyes" and the effect that we would get when we sang it live was very close. I thought we really nailed that album. But obviously, a piece of plastic with music coming off of it can't *compare*, in a certain way, to a live performance of me, David and Stephen sitting down in front of you and singing a song. But we definitely got *more* of what we were doing on tape with that first album than we did subsequently.

How did you react to Stephen's multitracking, instrumental prowess?

227

I was fascinated, because I've always been involved with the physics of making records, and I saw this maniac create tracks *overnight!*

We tried to do "Long Time Gone." We had a demo of the song that David and Stephen had done earlier…slowed down a little, dragged out a little; we tried to do it in the studio and it wasn't happening. So, we left Stephen and Dallas Taylor in the studio one night. The very next day, when we come in, Stephen says, "Well, listen to what we've got to sing on top of," and he played us the track that he and Dallas had constructed on "Long Time Gone" and blew me and David away. We sang on it and that was the track.

So, he was great. When Stephen's on it and he's clear, there's nobody better.

Is it true that "Blackbird" was being considered for inclusion on the first CSN album?

Yeah, sure was. As a matter of fact, I wrote "Blackbird" down on a piece of paper yesterday and put it to my mind that we should record it. And we have recorded it millions of times before and played it in live performances, but never just *hit* it. What we do to "Blackbird" is very special, I think.

How did you feel about Neil Young joining the group?

I felt threatened at first. But my initial feelings had nothing to do with my musical opinion of Neil, which is very high. My favorite song of his at the time was "Expecting to Fly," and I played it and played it and played it. But I felt a little threatened, because the three of us had made this *thing.* The thing of CSN, this album, this image, this *sound* and I felt afraid that it was going to change. But, as normal, when faced with change, I took a deep breath and dove in. And, subsequently Neil and I have become great friends.

What was Neil like back then?

Neil was protective of his space, protective of himself, friendly, funny, hard working and…totally unexplainable.

Can you remember the first CSNY concert?

The first CSNY gig was at the Chicago Auditorium, a beautiful little theater opened up by Isadora Duncan in 1890. That was the first time CSNY played live in front of anybody, it was the first time CSN did. There were no CSN concerts back then. When we went on the road it was CSNY. And the very next concert was…Woodstock.

What are your clearest recollections of Woodstock?

Almost gettin' killed in a helicopter flying over the crowd and physically having to walk on in front of all those people and *sing* with one acoustic guitar. We were nervous; it was okay; we did all right.

I also think that Woodstock was the first time that the youth of this country came together *en masse* and realized they could have a good time for three days without grown-ups looking over their necks or the police force bumming them out. They could just have a good time and it was great.

In the initial CSNY grouping, were there certain roles that you found yourselves filling?

It was forever balancing itself, like a little gyroscope. When one of us was weak, the other was strong; if somebody was a little out of it, somebody would be more stable. It was an ever constantly moving thing that pivoted on the music, and when we could pivot and focus on the music, we did make some good stuff.

You have to understand that there's something that happens when the *four* of us get together, which is totally different from when the *three* of us get together. I don't know why and I never question it. I am just thankful that we've managed to make any music whatsoever, and I'm a little disappointed that we haven't made more.

Can you understand why all of your personalities became such news?

When a record changes music to the extent that the first CSN album did; and I really believe it changed the way people approached making records and approached singing. When that happens, and the record goes Number One, and Woodstock happens right after that, with a half a million people—all of a sudden the media want to know who the hell is making this music. And, they tend to focus on personalities, because that's the stuff that fills *People* magazine. They want to know who we've slept with, what color our socks are, do we like bologna, all these things.

And there also seemed to be dress imitations at concerts, people looking like Neil.

I saw more people mimicking Crosby than anybody. He had this decidedly *hippie* image, with his long hair and moustache and fringe jacket and colored socks.

I believe we definitely got treated to the "hero syndrome" by a lot of people. Not that that's bad and not that it's good; it just happened.

Do you think the *Déjà Vu* album captured CSNY?

That was a difficult time for everybody. It was very uncomfortable for everybody. You must realize that during the CSN album, we were all in love. We all had ongoing relationships. During the *Déjà Vu* album, David's old lady had just been killed, my relationship with Joni had fallen apart, Stephen's relationship with Judy Collins had fallen apart, and Neil was having trouble in his personal life. It was not the greatest of times. The feeling of the music reflects that, I think.

How would you describe the climate in the studio?

It ran from total elation to...I ended up crying one night, as a matter of fact, during those *Déjà Vu* sessions, out of total frustration. We had so much to give, and because there was so much bullshit in the way, we were truly in danger of seeing it all just turn to a piece of shit. So, I remember just crying, *losing* it, out of frustration. So I'm amazed that the *Déjà Vu* album was as good as it was, frankly. Because we were all at each other's throats.

There were many late night sessions. When we'd finish at 3:00 in the morning, Stephen had developed a habit of continuing until 8:00, which made the crews late and made *him* late, which made the session start late the next day; and it went later and later....

We were all staying in this goddamned Caravan Lodge Motel, up in San Francisco. And Neil had these two bush babies in his room—Harriet and Speedy. They were jumping around, the bath tub was overflowing, it was *nuts*. I swear, I thought I was on acid, thought I was in a *Fellini* movie....You ever notice how much Neil looks like a bush baby? [Laughs]

What made you decide to record Joni Mitchell's "Woodstock?"

When CSNY did Woodstock, Joni wasn't scheduled to play, but she wanted to go and be a part of it. Only, the very next day, after Woodstock, she was supposed to do the *Dick Cavett Show;* and that was a pretty heavy show at that time. So, it was decided between her and her management, that if she went to Woodstock and couldn't get out, she'd blow the TV show the next day. So she stayed in New York. She was totally upset about that, because she wanted to hang out with lads and rock and roll.

When we came back to the city, we were enthused tremendously about what had just gone down. And she, in talking to the four of us, got such a depth of feeling for it, she was able to write a song about Woodstock and she wasn't even there. And as soon as I saw her writing it, I said, "Oh, God, what's this?" [Laughs] And it was such a great song, the whole *feeling* of the song...It pinned exactly what had happened, in terms of being a wheel in something turning. As soon as the four of us heard it, we wanted to do that record so bad. And we did.

At the CSNY live shows, there seemed to be magic happening between the four of you that was definitely transmitted to the audience.

The music was great. We were four mysterious individuals, we all looked totally different. We were like little folk heroes, in a way. We were doing it for everybody out there, for every musician that felt the way we did. When they saw as up there, they saw *themselves*. It was a very interesting thing that happened between the artist and the audience, a very close, symbiotic relationship.

Did *4 Way Street* capture this feeling?

Yeah, but we made a judgment that, in retrospect, I agree with totally, and yet I feel uncomfortable with. We let a lot of wrong notes get by in our quest for it to be real. But we've made records every which way; we've made totally perfect, in-tune records, and we could do that forever. But several of the tracks on *4 Way Street* leave a lot to be desired in terms of in-tune singing, and we decided as a policy, to let it go—if that's what it was then, fine, that's what it was. I thought there were some very high musical moments. I didn't think, personally, that it should have been a double album. I was not crazy about the graphics and…yeah, I thought it was a little indulgent to do two records of that music.

How blown out of proportion was the CSNY "ego clash" issue?

A lot, I mean, *musically*, it makes no fucking difference what any of us think about anything. They're all just individual thoughts that are musically manifested. But at times I thought people were more interested in who hated who most, than in the music. We got *bombarded* with it; it was very hard. So we stopped doing interviews all together for a while, which made 'em just make it all up anyway.

How did this kind of press affect the group?

I think it had a negative effect on, specifically, Stephen and me. Giant rifts opened up between us because of stuff that was said and stuff that wasn't said, and stuff that was done and wasn't done. It was *everybody's* business, when it was really nobody's business but ours. Stephen and I weren't talking for a while. But it's all so foolishly childish, thinking about it now in reflection.

This may be delving into that personal area you just spoke of, but, just to set the record straight, a popular rumor at the time was that the first CSNY split was because of a conflict you and Stills had over a mutual girlfriend.

The relationship between Stephen and me and Rita Coolidge was the straw that broke the camel's back. Let's just leave it at that. There was something going on between Stephen and me that was manifested and brought to a head because of that specific incident. It was just a question of two guys falling in love with the same woman. It's no big deal.

So after the first CSNY break-up, you and Crosby went on a sailing cruise.

…which had an effect on my *life…totally*. I'd never really been on my own and decided that I just needed to just go and be alone for a while. I know that's hard to do with four other people on a 60-foot boat, but as far as not dealing with other areas in my life, I was relatively alone. And I saw some *incredible* things, just great stuff. The most mind blowing thing was seeing an 80- to 90-foot blue whale come within 50 feet of us; it had a blow hole about six feet across. And to feel a monster like that, with a couple of dozen dolphins swimming around it…that's basically where "Wind on the Water" came from.

Even though *Songs for Beginners* was your first solo album, the title seems inappropriate, given so many really engaging pieces of music.

Carole King said the same thing to me, going into the Roxy one night. She just looked at me—and I didn't know her at the time—and said, "Songs for beginners, eh?"

It was a beginning, my first solo album. But also, *beginning* means songs for people who *act,* begin things. Because people think a lot, but then don't act on their thoughts.

Was Crosby and Nash a natural union?

Yeah, absolutely. I've always been drawn to David's musical insanity. And we went on this acoustic tour, had a great time. David and I were really close then. We were happy to be getting away with what we were—some funny times on stage and some great music. God save us from a *real* job. [Laughs]

There's a song on the first Crosby and Nash album, "Black Notes." What's the story behind that song?

David and I were doing an acoustic show at Carnegie Hall. Then, just before we were about to go on, Stephen shows up with his guitar. So, we hurriedly decided that after a certain song, David would leave the stage, go get Stephen and bring him on. In the meantime, I would talk to the audience and introduce the next song. So during the concert, we did this song, and David left and I started talking, and David's still not back, so I talk a little more....Crosby's *still* nowhere in sight. So, I'm beginning to feel a little uneasy now, here I am alone in Carnegie Hall. So I look, and when I still don't see Crosby, I go and sit down at the piano, and get an idea for this song: about when I started to learn how to play the piano, and how it was so awesome, unapproachable.

With this song, I tried to deal with overcoming the difficulty of approaching and starting *anything*, especially piano playing. I started to just bash anywhere on the black notes, not using any white notes, and wrote this little song, right on the spot. And if anybody could see me, on stage at Carnegie Hall, just thumping with my arms and my elbows on the black notes and making up a song, they should have realized that they could play and they could write songs, because I'd just done it. I'm very fond of "Black Notes."

How did the single "War Song," recorded with Neil Young, come about?

Neil called me up one day from his place just south of San Francisco and said he'd written this song that he wanted to cut *today*, as Neil always does. He wants to cut it now, at the instant it's created. It's a feeling I agree with.

So I went down there to his ranch, and Kenny Buttrey [drums] was there, and Tim [Drummond, bass], [Jack] Nitzsche [piano], Ben Keith [steel guitar], Neil and me. So we cut it and sang it live. It was kind of an anti-war, anti-George Wallace politics song.

What circumstances led to the CSNY reunion try in Hawaii, the summer of '73?

We were all sort of on vacation and there was great music to be made. We had these great songs, like Neil's "Human Highway" and "Maui Mama," and we were rehearsing them on David's boat, and it was sounding great. We tried to put an album together—and it would have been a *great* album.

Then Neil went back and it all turned to shit. That spaced us out for a while. Because it's hard—you get so high with the prospect of doing a great album, that the temptation to just put up with other people's bullshit is great. But this just turned to shit.

So *Wild Tales*, your second solo album, came out in its wake. Can you understand why that record wasn't more successful?

A combination of a pretty stark looking album cover and a pretty stark record company that didn't get into selling it. It was squashed at a very early stage by the record company, a fact that I've been pissed about for years. Because I'd spent three years thinking that it was my basic failing, and to find out later that there was an actual move afoot to quell the record, to not even put any energy into servicing it, was an astounding fact to find out.

When CSNY re-grouped in '74, how did you feel about playing baseball stadiums?

I loved it and I hated it at the same time. It was amazing to play and sing and overcome the situations; it was amazing to try and play acoustic guitars in front of 80,000 people. It was amazing to think that probably most of the audience saw you as no bigger than a postage stamp. And it was amazing to see that much money made and that much money disappear.

How do you react when people bring up the possibility of money being a motivation behind the CSNY reunions?

I honestly don't believe that money has been a motivation. I know that it's possible to think that, but I believe it is basically just an attempt, on our part, to get together and make more music and more albums.

When CSNY came together, we realized we couldn't do a folk club tour. We'd have to tour for 50 straight weeks before we'd be able to have the amount of people hear us and see us that want to. There are certain physics involved with a band of that size. So, in '74, we made a decision to go into stadiums. We had subtle pressure from management and promoters, and we went for it and lost it, frankly. We didn't make that much great music, we did have some great times and we did keep a lot of people really high with our music, I think. Artistically, it was dissatisfying to most of us.

Now, again to confirm or refute a rumor, is it true that the sessions to record a '74 CSNY reunion album came to a halt because of a disagreement between you and Stills over a single harmony note?

Yes, that, specifically, is what happened. That just shows you how three people, four people can get. The thing was, *musically* to fit a major progression through a minor chord is…it's impossible. Everything in my musical soul rejected it. Even to this day, I feel what Stephen was asking me to do would not work. And, back then, that was the final straw, because I felt like I was being manipulated and that my opinion wasn't being listened to. David's opinion was the same as mine, as it happened, not that it was important. So that broke it, that one specific minor note on this real jazzy thing of Stephen's...[after pause he remembers the title] "Guardian Angel."

So after this session...

I decided I'd had enough of this bullshit and that David and I were just going to concentrate on David and me. We made a couple of really fine albums, *Wind on the Water* and *Whistling Down the Wire*. And, with the help of our manager friends, we managed to get some lucrative contracts.

How did Carole King enter the picture during this period?

I'd met Carole when she shouted "*Songs for Beginners*" at me at the Roxy. And when we were in the middle of recording *Wind on the Water,* we got a call from her. She had written a couple of tunes and asked if David and I would be interested in helping her sing them.

So we went over to Carole's house and met her beautiful 14-year-old daughter, who is now her 19-year-old daughter and all the more beautiful. Then David and I sat next to Carole at the piano and sang three-part harmony and gave Carole King the famous Crosby-Nash "ear fuck," which consists of one of us on either side of each ear, singing directly into the ear. [Laughs]

She did good on our albums, we had fun doing several things of hers. It was a really nice feeling. She's a fine artist and really loved by a lot of people, too.

When you were recording *Whistling Down the Wire*, why did you decide to give CSNY another try?

Once again, it was done as it was normally done. Neil came to my house in San Francisco and played me and David a cassette of a couple of things he'd written and a couple of Stephen's, and we had some new songs in excess of what we were using for *Whistling Down the Wire* album. Basically, the music intrigued us, so we left for Florida two days later. We did some really fine work down there, sang really well. I have a tape of the five things we did and they're really special.

But the vocals you and David added were eventually erased, right?

How do you know all this shit? [Laughs]

That's what happened, but here's why, basically. What we wanted to do was work on this CSNY album, take a break and finish me and David's *Whistling Down the Wire* album, which was about 90 percent done, and then go back with some more songs. But the timing wasn't right, they [Stills and Young] had booked a tour, wanted to get the album out as soon as possible and realized they couldn't wait for me and David; so it reverted back to a Neil and Stephen album [*Long May You Run*, 1976]. But they needed the tracks, and David and I were really pissed at the time, thought it was a rotten trick. I couldn't care less now, but it hurt a lot at that point. We insisted they couldn't use our voices, so they took 'em off and re-did the tracks. It's that simple.

234

What was your reaction when Stephen showed up at the Greek Theatre in L.A. at a Crosby-Nash show, after all this had occurred?

Lots of heart thumping and dry mouths, but it was okay. It was good to see him. And that night, Stephen and I went back to my house here in Los Angeles, got drunk and decided that we would try *one more time* to get this ship asail. [Laughs] And that resulted, ultimately, in the second CSN album, done in Miami.

How did you feel about that record, compared to the first one?

It was different, but it was exciting. I was very proud of that album. I thought there was some fine singing and some fine songs on that album.

As for "Cathedral," I know that you wrote the song about your experience on acid in Winchester Cathedral, but what was involved in the songwriting process?

It was the longest one for me. It took about four years. After the experience, I began to write a piece of music with no lyrics and that was the *feeling* of what it was I wanted to say. But trying to hone down the overwhelming series of feelings I had into some cohesive form, understandable to other people, was a long process. I really had to work at it. "Teach Your Children" came in an hour. I'm not trying to equate the two songs, but sometimes it happens very fast and sometimes it happens very slow. "Cathedral" happened to take a while. "Wind on the Water" took a couple of years. Obviously I don't work on a song continuously, but I don't force my songs. There's a certain point where I can take them, then I have to wait for the rest of the information. I was proud of myself for waiting for "Cathedral." I think it was worth waiting for.

Do you ever suffer from writer's block?

I don't believe in writer's block. I believe that everything comes when it's supposed to and it just takes patience, sometimes, to wait for it. I never stop writing; because, for me, writing is experiencing and I never stop experiencing.

I go through periods when I don't physically sit down and put things on paper; but I'm thinking, I'm a writer, I can't stop thinking about it.

Now, the '78 CSN session in Florida...

...was again just bad timing. We started to work on it, it didn't happen, so we all went our merry ways again. David and I started to pick up the threads, and that didn't happen either.

I read in another interview that you and David were supposedly "musically opposed."

We were musically opposed and socially opposed. There are certain areas of his life I don't agree with and I just have to express my opinion and stand aside. But musically, I didn't feel David was working hard enough, but far be it for me to say, but I don't think he was putting enough attention to his music. I thought he was fucking off, so I told him that. You see, he's capable of being a brilliant, brilliant artist, and it saddens me, when I see him not realizing his full potential…as a person and as an artist. But I love him dearly and it's hard for me to be objective about it.

So how did the CSN MUSE reunion come about?

Before we ever got to Madison Square Garden, the MUSE people had asked me to get CSN together and I totally refused. Because I didn't feel we had anything to contribute. Our music depends on our personal feelings and love towards one another and when it's not there, we can't perform. It's that simple.

So I rejected it on various personal grounds, and I wanted to make my own stand; I was doing my own album. I was tired of this shit. I wasn't up for it.

The day I got to New York, I went to see Jackson [Browne] in his hotel room. And Jackson said, "Hey, we're going to have to cancel the fifth night." I said, "What do you mean?" "We don't have a headline act," he said.

I've done a lot of shows in my life, so I know that the first three nights cover expenses, and it's the fourth and fifth nights that are the gravy, the profit. So, I was determined not to cancel that fifth night.

Jackson looked at me and said, "I know how you feel about it, but I'm going to ask you one more time, can you get David and Stephen, would you want to do that?"

I thought about it for about seven seconds. And I went through all the changes by the micro-second. I went through *everything*, and I figured this cause was greater, more important, than whatever personal differences might exist between us. So I called them up. They were more than delighted to hear from me. And they were on the next plane…literally.

We had a couple of hasty rehearsals of a couple hours each; we were a little disappointed that we hadn't worked up any new songs; we hadn't been together long enough to. But we made a very spirited attempt and our hearts were in it. They came to the rally. So, I'm thrilled that we did get together. I've since strengthened my relationship with Stephen. We're singing better. And I'm just glad to have included them in what I consider to be an historical social event.

So the CSN cycle continues.

I crave that music. It's great when it's good and it's painful when it's not. But I'll take a little pain for greatness. So, I never discount them.

How did you react when, during the last decade, groups like America and the early Eagles were in so many ways jumping off from the groundwork CSN had laid?

I didn't react at all. It was complimentary and flattering, and it was obvious that part of the musical change that we helped give music at that time was being manifested in groups like the ones you mentioned—not by imitating our sound, but being affected by it enough to want to do it their way.

Dewey [Bunnell, of America] specifically told me at one point that they wanted to make an album like the first CSN album; not that they wanted to copy it, but they wanted to make a thing that was as powerful as that. And that's a great thing to instill in people, to inspire them to do things like that.

How do you view what's going to happen musically in the '80s?

I think it will be the same process of building it up and tearing it down, rebuilding it and tearing it down. It's just what the punks are doing, new wave bands. They're kickin' ass and I love it. It's really great to see it. They're keeping us old fuckers on our toes. It's great. They still have a lot to learn, but that's where I was. When I was their age, I was exactly where they are.

I intend to plow right through the '80s and into the '90s. I feel I've got a lot more to offer and I'll be doing it until they pull the plug.

Do you view your current solo status as a fairly permanent thing?

It's always been a permanent thing, with diversions into other areas. But I feel stronger now than I ever have before on my own.

How do you view your current audience?

I view them as forceful, changing people. I personally have been thrilled with what I've come to understand as my audience, right now. I'm treated very respectfully. I'm never rough-handled. I'm only smiled at. I feel really loved.

So what are the personal rewards you now get from your music? What aspect satisfies you the most?

I still like to write a song and get somebody off with it, that's basically my joy, right there: to sing a song, where you can smile or just shake your head. That's still the main joy for me…writing and sharing.

Any regrets at this point?

I have two main regrets in my life. I would have loved to have been present when my father died and I wasn't. And I was sorry to get somebody out of prison who later murdered a close friend of mine. I would never have done that. Those are basically the only regrets in my life.

What dreams have you been able to fulfill?

All of them. My life is a dream. I mean, this is a totally ridiculous place to be in this society.

What goals lie ahead?

I would like to bring a little more sanity into the world, a little more balance, a little more careful thought. I'd like to continue to make music, to create, to have children. And I would like to help stop the nuclear power policy of the globe.

CROSBY, STILLS & NASH BURY THE HATCHET AGAIN

BY DENNIS HUNT
Los Angeles Times
November 27, 1982

Graham Nash delved into some of the factors behind the conflicts and complicated relationships within CSN and CSNY in this November 1982 *Los Angeles Times* article by Dennis Hunt, which ran in a Thanksgiving weekend edition when CSN played live at the Universal Amphitheatre. Taped for broadcast on cable television, this concert footage was later released as a home video/laser disc. Crosby was in visibly shaky shape on stage, but few in the audience knew the true depths of the man's problems.

Crosby, Stills & Nash at Zoetrope Studios, Hollywood. July 1982. Photo: Henry Diltz

Only three times during their illustrious but battle-scarred history have David Crosby, Stephen Stills and Graham Nash been able to stomach one another long enough to record an album together. During these truces, the singers/songwriters have at times worked with a fourth combatant: Neil Young.

During a recent lunch, Nash probed the nature of their conflicts. Philosophical and musical differences? Nothing that sophisticated.

"It's always stupid stuff," Nash explained. "We've been guilty of the most infantile behavior. For instance, arguing over somebody playing the wrong chord. 'You deliberately played that chord, what the hell's wrong with you!' Then we wouldn't speak to each other for months.

"Once, years ago, we argued over a girl and never spoke to each other for 2 ½ years. That girl was Rita Coolidge. We were really young and stupid then. I shudder when I think of the dumb things that have kept us apart and all the time we've wasted. When you get to be around 40, like we are, you're too old to be acting like kids."

This love-hate relationship is unique in pop music. Usually when musicians discover that collaboration leads to conflict, they avoid one another. They figure that making music and making money isn't worth it if it means making war.

But it seems that no conflict is fierce enough to keep Crosby, Stills & Nash apart forever. It's not that these guys are gluttons for punishment. They're simply gluttons for Crosby, Stills & Nash music.

"It's very special music and well worth fighting for," Nash insisted. "The best thing we do is make CSN music. The harmonies turn us on, the songs turn us on."

Crosby, Stills & Nash music—basically romantic, melodious, soft pop-rock—also turns on many fans. Their first Atlantic Records album in five years, *Daylight Again*, has been a huge fall hit and their tour, including a weekend Universal Amphitheatre engagement ending Sunday night, also has been a success.

Fans of Crosby, Stills & Nash music savor each new album because they fear it may be the last. In recent years it did seem like *CSN* (1977) was the group's grand finale. *Daylight Again* was a surprise to everyone, including the group.

The album began as an oddity: a Stills-Nash collaboration. Outside CSN, Stills basically is a solo performer and Nash usually works alone or with Crosby. But Nash had asked Stills to sing with him in a benefit concert in Hawaii, Nash's home. The duet was so successful that they decided to record an album together. A harmonious Stills-Nash relationship certainly was unexpected.

"Stephen was the one I was always arguing with," Nash pointed out. "Sometimes he thinks I'm really stupid and sometimes I think he's really stupid. Or if I said, 'Stephen, that's dumb,' he'd want to hit me. But this time we were getting along OK. The problem was that when we put all the songs together we realized that a lot of them were CSN songs in disguise.

"We needed Crosby's voice. So we had a decision to make. We could force the album through as a Stills-Nash album and forever hear in our heads what those songs should really sound like, or we could get Crosby."

The quest for artistic excellence wasn't the only factor in the decision to contact Crosby. "There was pressure from the label (Atlantic Records) to do a CSN album," Nash admitted. "They would pay for that but they didn't want to pay for a Stills-Nash album. Stephen and I paid for it. By the time we had spent $400,000 of our own money, we said maybe we had better get Crosby. I knew Stephen would never have called him so I finally called him."

Once again, Nash, the charming, gentlemanly Englishman, was the mediator. Of course, he can be temperamental, too, as temperamental as those renowned rowdies, Stills and Crosby. But Nash also has the ability to put his personal feelings aside and organize truces.

"Sometimes I think I'm the only sane one in the band," he said. "I think Stephen and David are mad. But I've got to be as crazy as they are in my own way. Still, I've been the one to calm things down when we all hate each other. This current tour and album wouldn't have happened if I hadn't worked

Graham Nash and Stephen Stills at a CSN concert, Universal Amphitheatre. Los Angeles. November 1982. Photo: Henry Diltz

extra hard to keep things together. The music is the important thing. Sometimes we have to overcome our own pettiness for the good of the music. We're all relatively screwed up but somehow we make good music together. That always amazes me."

Why didn't *Daylight Again* include Neil Young, who worked with Crosby, Stills & Nash on *Déjà Vu* (1970), the live album *4 Way Street* (1971) and on tour? It certainly wasn't because they didn't want him. Basically, they were afraid to ask him. To Crosby, Stills & Nash, he is this mysterious, revered, almost unapproachable figure who is more of an idol than a colleague.

"It's hard to approach him," Nash admitted. "We're so afraid of rejection. We're scared of him. I swear we are. Can you believe that? We've had so much heartbreak with him. Who wants to be rejected by a mad musician? It's grief I don't need.

"But I still consider him a friend. I last talked to him four months ago, but if he called tomorrow and said, 'I've got these three tunes and I can hear you guys singing on them,' we'd be ready to work with him right away. Every day I expect Neil to call. It's my fantasy."

Crosby, Stills & Nash on *Daylight Again* Tour. 1982. Photo: Henry Diltz

Even if they did start an album with Young, there's no guarantee it would ever be finished. "We've started three albums that have fallen apart," Nash said. "It would be hard for us to start another one and have it fall apart. Working with Neil, that's very likely. We could be in the middle of an album and Neil would say, 'Well it's 6 o'clock, I'll see you tomorrow.' And we wouldn't see him again for years. That's the way Neil is. He only does what he wants to do when he wants to do it."

One of those aborted albums still is a painful memory for Nash. Crosby, Stills, Nash & Young recorded an album in 1976 in Miami that wound up as a Stills-Young album. "Stephen and Neil wiped David and me off those tracks," Nash recalled, cringing.

"David and I wanted to do the album but we didn't want to tour. But Neil and Stephen wanted to tour, so they figured the album should be just them. But they didn't consult us. They just wiped our voices off the tapes. It was so depressing, so crushing. All that great work down the drain. I was mad at Neil for years after that.

"Then Stephen got a taste of what Neil is like. They were touring as a duo and Neil suddenly left in the middle of the tour. Stephen found out about it because Neil sent him a telegram the day he left. The rest of the dates had to be canceled. But that's what you expect from Neil."

Despite Young's eccentricities, Nash still wants him to work with Crosby, Stills & Nash again. Nash, however, did express one fear: "Maybe

244

Neil doesn't think CSN music is very good. I don't know how he feels. I haven't asked him."

Nash has been a fanatic about Crosby, Stills & Nash music ever since he, Stills and Crosby first got together in 1968. "When I first sang with David and Stephen in Joni's [Joni Mitchell] living room, I flipped," Nash exclaimed. "I left my country [England], my wife, my family, my group [the Hollies], everything I had to sing with them."

At that time, pop music was in the grips of acid rock and heavy-metal music. Because it was so different, Crosby, Stills & Nash's soft, folky, acoustic sound stood out and received lots of attention. It also got lots of attention because CSN, with Nash from the Hollies, Crosby from the Byrds and Stills from Buffalo Springfield, was considered a supergroup.

Though he's busy with Crosby, Stills & Nash and all his anti-nuke activities, Nash still found time to record a Hollies reunion album that will be out next year.

"The Hollies are unfinished business to me," Nash said. "It's the same guys I worked with in the '60s. It's a chance to go back to my roots. I like Hollies music. It's pleasant, pop music, but, you know, it's not like CSN music. CSN music means more to me. CSN music is like a god, a sinister god. It haunts me. No matter what I do, I have to go back to it."

A Long Time Gone

He's been called rock's favorite threat to society.
But David Crosby is a bigger threat to himself.

BY Mark Christensen
Rolling Stone
November 11, 1985

Two long articles came out within a short time of each other in the Fall of 1985. *Spin* published "The Death of David Crosby" and *Rolling Stone* ran this one. Both pieces painted a pretty doomish portrait of Crosby, with little hope that he could pull out of his drug-fueled descent. I chose to go with the *Rolling Stone* article by writer Mark Christensen for this book because it was less sensationalistic and dealt more fully with the impact Crosby's drug use had on his musical career. It's a sobering tale.

David Crosby and three empty chairs. Photo: Henry Diltz

He hates being an addict. He fights it as much as he can, and I know that he knows he's losing. He has a self-hatred deeper than any man I've ever known. He looks in the mirror and sees a guy who is fat, ugly and forty-five. He only sees the self he chooses to see. This is not anything he's enjoying. This is not a joke. He's sick.

—Graham Nash

Freebasing is the worst addiction.... It's not too late for him to come back from a bad problem, to be very strong and show young people how you can beat drugs. Either that's going to happen or he's going to die.

—Neil Young

Autumn 1985. Dusk at David Crosby's. His brown clapboard house is perched high on a hill above Mill Valley, near San Francisco, at the end of a mouse's maze of skinny avenues and asphalt switchbacks. As the sibilant squawk of an alto sax floats from the thick tangle of woods below the house, Jan Dance, Crosby's girlfriend, comes down to the pool. She is very thin, and her skin is nearly translucent. Several of her teeth are missing, and a long, red comma of ruptured skin curls down her cheek. She serves Cokes in paper cups, then slips back inside the house.

Twenty minutes later, David Crosby comes out the back door, acoustic guitar in hand. Big and bearlike, a ski hat pulled low over his eyes, he sits down beside the pool and plays a new song. It's lovely, complicated.

"I gotta come up with a lot more like this," he says when he finishes the song. "Capitol rejected my last album. Said it wasn't enough like Devo or Elvis Costello or something. Stupid jerks. I spent damn near every last cent I had just buying back my contract. I gotta make a statement. I can't hack this. I'm such an easy target. I've obviously had terrible problems with drugs. But I'm not a vegetable or some vacant-eyed lump of flesh in a corner, with disarrayed clothes covered in blood and spit. I'm a human being with a mind, a spirit, a soul and a heart. It's when…"

Suddenly, the startling sound of a woman wailing comes from the house. Crosby gets up, strides around the pool.

"It's Jan," he says. "She's just real upset now all the time." Crosby takes the steps to his back door three at a time. "Things have been real bad for us lately, man."

Back in the summer, as Crosby, Stills & Nash prepared for a tour, the stories were terrible: that Atlantic Records had dropped CSN; that their voices were so far gone that ghost vocalists had to be employed backstage to counterfeit their famous harmonies; that David Crosby was freebasing $600,000 of cocaine a year and that the Hell's Angels had assumed ownership of his Marin County house to cover his drug debts; and finally that Crosby would be arrested and jailed by the Texas police the minute he set foot in the state on the nationwide tour—this in the wake of his cocaine and illegal-weapons conviction in the summer of 1983.

Crosby, Stills & Nash seemed to be in trouble. Crosby, especially. During the last several years, he had been tracked by police and press and plagued by coke busts, an assault-and-battery suit, arrests for possession of illegal guns and knives, you name it. Said to be living like a wino and dubbed "rock's favorite threat to society," Crosby was portrayed as a fanatically unhappy man, too zonked to engineer a successful overdose, his life a Möbius strip of trials and tribulations substantial enough to earn him a place in the Bible.

What had happened? This was the man who was a founding member of the Byrds, whose spacey sixties folk-rock is still emulated in the Eighties. This was the man who formed Crosby, Stills & Nash, the last and longest lived of the sixties supergroups—and the most successful. (With Neil Young sometimes joining them, they sold more than 20 million records within sixteen years.) This was the man who wrote classics like "Guinnevere" and "Long Time Gone" and helped voice the concerns of the sixties peace-and-love movement. "Wooden Ships." "Triad." You remember.

"I have literally gone home and cried over that poor guy," says one Crosby associate. "*He is going to die*. He *has* to have those drugs. He can't deal with people without them. When he's high, he's fine. He's normal. It's when he's straight that he has problems."

"But isn't that the way it is with all addicts," says Graham Nash, at Rudy Records, his studio in uptown Los Angeles. "They are fine so long as their drugs are fine. This has been a very sad episode. I've tried everything—extreme anger, extreme compassion. I've gotten twenty of his best friends in the same room with him. I've tried going one-on-one. I've tried hanging out with him. I've tried *not* hanging out with him."

Nash is trim and nimble and looks less like a rocker than a rugby player slightly long in the tooth. Off the road, he spends most of his time with his wife and kids in Hawaii and tools around L.A. in a fifteen-year-old Volkswagen. For almost two decades, he has served as friend, banker and one-man family to Crosby, whom Nash credits with "saving my life." It was Crosby who brought Nash into what was to become CSN after members of Nash's previous group, the Hollies, decided Nash's songs, like "Marrakesh Express" were "not right" for the band. It is a debt Nash remembers. Lately, though, he has become fed up with being, as one associate puts it, "the forty-three-year-old father to his forty-four-year-old son."

"David has pushed his karma so far to the wall," says Nash. "I'm a great believer in cause and effect. But he's made me question my belief. Maybe you *can* go trash yourself over and over and over and destiny finally doesn't go, 'Naughty boy. *Zap!*'"

The next CSN album is scheduled for release after New Year's, and Nash is working on a solo record. He has written thirteen songs, three of which he will contribute to CSN. Will he let the band have the pick of the litter? "I must confess that in the past I've done so," he says. "But I'll also confess that I see CSN on a downward slide. Not musically. Not energetically. But I'm worried about David, about his ability to contribute. CSN is equal energy. Equal thought. And that's not happening now."

A situation that also became apparent to Atlantic Records. "We had an [eight-album] deal for $1 million per album and have only completed four,"

Nash explains. "They look at David and don't know if he's going to be alive next week. So we agreed to take less per album, with a chance to win big if an album really takes off. And it can! Music is David's most motivating force, aside from his drug habit. I don't think he has the stamina he once had, or the voice, or the patience. But he still has the fire."

Stephen Stills is seated on concrete steps outside soundstage 3/8 at the former Zoetrope Studios. As he waits for David Crosby to arrive for a CSN rehearsal, he explains his inspiration for his composition "For What It's Worth," the Buffalo Springfield classic that many people consider to be the best song about paranoia ever written.

"This was, what, 1965? And it turned out to be kind of indicative of what was about to happen. But it didn't have anything to do with Berkeley Free Speech or Mario Savio or any of those guys. I mean, I thought he was a bore…not to mention a fucking communist! Heh, heh, heh! I mean, I'm just a musician."

In the triumvirate of Crosby, Stills & Nash, Stills was the one who wrote the most forceful songs, the tunes with the harder, rawer edges. He also cultivated an image—what with his horses and cowboy boots—as a sort of Marlboro man of rock & roll. Tonight, however, outfitted in wire-rimmed glasses, a navy flight jacket and a sailing shirt emblazoned Tex, he looks less like a cowpoke than, say, a renegade orthodontist.

To Stills, the relevant questions about the band today are simple: "Are we awake? Are we alive? Do we still sound real good? Are we still a valid entity in showbiz?" And he doesn't care much for all the attention Crosby has been receiving of late. "Dave'll be fine," he declares. "Pity the man who says another word about him. I'm sick of this Perils of Pauline attitude in the press. It really makes me ill. It's not like this is some rare disorder or something. You got ballplayers with the same problem."

Stills is beckoned back inside the soundstage, a structure big enough to house a 747. He finds Graham Nash waiting, a tad impatient.

"Stephen, have you talked to David?"

"How come?" Stills asks.

"He's late."

"He'll show."

"That's not the point. The point is, I asked him to be here on time. It's important that we start maintaining a reasonable schedule for this, or we're in trouble."

Nash talks softly and carries no stick, but it only takes thirty seconds of watching his dealings with the band to figure out who is at the helm. While Stills' music may be more thrustful and vertebrate, and Crosby's the most beautifully melodious, it was Nash who delivered the most CSN hits— "Teach Your Children," "Our House" and "Military Madness" among them. And it has been Nash, especially of late, who has found a finger for every hole in the dike.

Moments later Crosby strides into the room accompanied by a bearded man seven feet tall. Big John Bloom, star of *The Incredible Two-Headed Transplant* and bad guy in many television shows, has been hired to "watch over" Crosby. Built along the lines of Santa Claus but wearing his usual attire, a work shirt and jeans, Crosby looks more like Ben Franklin gone to seed. He is greeted enthusiastically by the band.

CSN assembles onstage, and rehearsal commences. By the time they are into "Long Time Gone," David Crosby is singing like a bird.

David Crosby's parents were blue bloods from New York, denizens of the Social Register, who moved to California before David was born so David's father could pursue a career as a cinematographer. Floyd Crosby would go on to win Academy Awards for his work on both *High Noon* and *Tabu*.

David's childhood seems to have been as tempestuous as his later years. "His older brother, Chip, was tall, thin, handsome," says Nash. And the obvious comparisons were made. "David comes home from school one day and there's a note from his mom: 'Chip, your dinner is in the fridge. David, stay out of here, fatty.'"

Crosby was not an early achiever, either. "Without exception," he would later recall, "I was thrown out of every school I ever attended." Deciding to call academia a wash, he quit college to get a head start in life. He began burglarizing houses, an activity that ended when he got caught and was confronted by one of his victims. "I'd stolen the last remaining picture of this woman's old man…and lost it.…I thought I was gonna die."

In the early sixties, he found a job singing at the Unicorn, in Los Angeles, where he met folk singer Travis Edmundson. "Travis was also the first person ever to give me a joint," he told CSN biographer Dave Zimmer, "which was really a wonderful thing for him to do. I've got to thank him a million times for it. I took a toke and just went to heaven. I thought, 'This is for me!'"

After Crosby abandoned his pregnant girlfriend, he bounced all over the country, sleeping by roadsides, introducing himself to Bob Dylan in New

York and eventually to LSD in California. He showed up on the album *Jack Linkletter Presents a Folk Festival*. And while playing solo at the Troubadour, he was approached by Jim, soon to be Roger, McGuinn and Gene Clark. Did he want to be in a band? Sure.

The band was the Byrds, and Crosby was to become a prince in the blooming L.A. rock aristocracy. It was 1964. Local clubs like Pandora's Box, the Whisky A Go Go and the Troubadour were becoming legend-making venues, and the Byrds were there at the beginning. Bob Dylan would stop by to watch them play at Ciro's, on Sunset Boulevard. Crosby, for one, felt the Byrds had become a better interpreter of Dylan songs than Dylan himself. The title track of the band's first album, *Mr. Tambourine Man*, was a Dylan cover, and it was an almost immediate success.

"We were all cruising down Sunset Boulevard in a black '56 Ford we'd bought from Odetta," Crosby remembers. "All of a sudden, we hear '*Dum-de-da-dud-dle-de-dum-de-da-dum-dum*—Hey, Mr. Tambourine Man.' They play it once, then they play it *again!*"

During the Byrds' trip to London in 1965, they were feted by various Beatles and Rolling Stones, and when they returned to America, they released their classic album *Turn! Turn! Turn!* They were certified stars. "David handled success better than any of us," says Byrds leader Roger McGuinn. "He was very idealistic, looking for love and recognition—but smart. He didn't go out and blow all his money on cars like Gene Clark and I did."

"I remember back when Roger McGuinn was still singing Beatle songs by himself at the Troubadour," says Henry Diltz, folk singer turned photographer, "and David was just, like, hanging out. I was in the Modern Folk Quartet, and David came up one night completely impassioned and said: 'I envy you so much. I want so badly to be in a group and be able to sing and just *have* something.' The next year the Byrds exploded, and he did. He was so *pleased*. He'd walk around in his Borsalino hat, with a little smile on his face. He would give away the greatest things. And he had unbelievable women! One on either arm. And they loved him! He also had the best dope in the world. Two tokes and you were boxed. He was a leader of that whole 'Get high and there'll be no more hate or war.'"

Success with the Byrds brought Crosby validation as a musician, as well. "He became one of the best rhythm guitarists in the business," says music publisher Kenny Weiss. Even more impressive was the power of his voice. According to former Byrds bassist Chris Hillman, "He had an astonishingly innovative sense of harmony. Not church or barbershop but jazz. Something that Brian Wilson picked up on, too. Unfortunately, David always loved being the bad boy. And when he'd get scared, he'd lash out. We were booked on *The Ed Sullivan Show*. It was going to be live, and David got scared. So he started in on Sullivan's producer, who also happened to be Ed's son-in-law, telling him, 'You fucking asshole, you don't know *da-da-da...*'

254

and the guy just looked at him and said, 'You may be right, but you and your friends will never appear on this show again as long as you live.'"

Crosby was eventually fired by the Byrds, but he left, essentially, a happy young man. He bought the sailboat he still owns, the Mayan, with his settlement and left for Florida. There he "discovered" Joni Mitchell playing in a club in Coconut Grove; he would go on to produce her first album. "That was the best time in his life," Mitchell recalls. "He was clean as a whistle, his eyes were like star sapphires. He was a great appreciator. When he liked something, you could almost hear him purr. He'd left the world to go sailing. He was so good at it. Those were very magical times. You could make a whole evening out of just going down to the docks and listening to the masts clink. The calm before the storm."

Meanwhile, Stills had found his way to Los Angeles. He had auditioned for the Monkees before forming the legendary Buffalo Springfield with Neil Young and Richie Furay. While playing at the Whisky, the group caught Crosby's eye and soon found themselves opening for the Byrds. Shortly thereafter, Cass Elliot of the Mamas and the Papas introduced Crosby to Graham Nash, an established phenom with the Hollies. Both Nash and Stills were having problems with their respective bands. What would they think, Crosby asked, about forming a trio?

Less grubby than the Grateful Dead, less fun than the Beach Boys but lots more fun than the Doors, CSN provided a soundtrack for a generation at war with authority. But between the time Steve Stills confessed to 400,000 at Woodstock that "We're scared shitless" and Richard Nixon bombed Cambodia, CSN began their long history of family feuding. Crosby and Nash were angered by what they felt were Stills' attempts to dominate the band. Stills, in turn, felt Crosby and Nash were not sufficiently committed. "If a voice of reason could have cleared that fog," Stills once remarked, "we would have realized our full potential and CSNY would be mentioned in the same breath with the Beatles and the Rolling Stones....So we all lost, right there, to indulgence. We lost it all."

Crosby was feeling the pull of other gravities. He had found the love of his life, Christine Hinton, a beautiful blonde who would inspire his ballad "Guinnevere." But, in 1969, she died in an automobile accident. "It was the worst thing in my whole life," he says. "I was on top of the world. She goes to take the cat to the vet and never comes home. I wanted to die. Nash stayed with me the whole time. He practically wouldn't let me go to the bathroom by myself. He was afraid I'd kill myself."

Although Crosby, Stills, Nash & Young went on to record the highly successful *Déjà Vu*, the bloom was off the rose for Crosby. More and more, he relied on pharmaceutical diversions. "For a while," recalls a friend, "the drugs were there to make the music better. Finally, though, the music was there to make the drugs better."

"I'm not ashamed," he once said, "of being stoned....Everybody's been on my case so long, saying I'm so smashed, so stoned, strung out. But I was stoned for every bit of music I've ever played. Every record, every performance....If they can match the music, let them criticize it. Anybody who can't ain't got no fuckin' right to tell me nothin' about gettin' high....I *want* to get high."

"I should have seen it all coming," says Nash. "David was always the world's ultimate consumer. He always had to have the best. The best wines, the best pot, the best women, the best guitars. He just could never get enough out of life. I mean, after Christine Hinton died, the two of us literally went around the world smashed."

But the extent of Crosby's problems didn't strike Nash until the late Seventies. "We were jamming with some guys, really getting into it, when David knocked his freebase pipe over. It shattered, and he stopped the whole session to pick it up. That's when it hit me that this whole thing was out of hand."

Nash, along with Jackson Browne, concert promoter Bill Graham and the Jefferson Starship's Paul Kantner and Grace Slick, got together and confronted Crosby. "We did it AA style and got him into a rehab center," says Kantner. "It was nothing but a turnstile. He went in, then walked back out." More and more, the music community perceived Crosby as a wastrel, a relic, a prophet for a future that never happened.

Crosby's legal difficulties over drugs began in 1971 when he was arrested for allegedly jettisoning pot from the bilge pumps during a police visit to his yacht in Newport Beach. But things didn't start to snowball until a decade later, when he plowed his car into a freeway divider on his way to sing at an antinuke rally in March 1982. The police extracted Crosby, cocaine residue and a .45 automatic from the vehicle. His explanation for the gun: "John Lennon."

Three weeks later Crosby was surprised by Texas police in his dressing room at Cardi's nightclub in Dallas, where he was performing. Their booty? Another .45 and more cocaine residue. Then he was picked up in September of the same year on an outstanding warrant for an assault-and-battery suit brought by two women in Culver City, California. The following summer he appeared in Dallas for the Cardi's nightclub charge, and according to an account in the *Dallas Times Herald*, "Several times he fell asleep and snored loudly, his head tilted back and his mouth open. When the snoring became too loud, one of his attorneys leaned over and shook him awake."

Judge Pat McDowell hit Crosby with five years in the Texas state penitentiary. Crosby told reporters from *People* magazine, "I'm being treated like a murderer. They put manacles on my hands and put me in solitary. And I didn't do anything to anybody. I didn't....This is *now*: This is happening to *me*....They got me for a quarter of a gram of pipe residue. For that I'm going to spend five years in the state penitentiary?...Please just say this isn't fair, okay?" He began to cry. "If I ever made you happy with my music, if I made anybody happy out there...help me. If there's anybody out there who loves me, please, try and do something."

"We got money and Bibles for six months after that," recalls Crosby's press agent, Wayne Rosso.

While out on appeal, David was arrested in Marin County on a motorcycle, carrying a dagger and a pharmaceutical buffet consisting of heroin, cocaine, pot and codeine. Then, good news. In December 1984, Judge McDowell agreed to allow Crosby to enter a drug-rehabilitation program in lieu of serving time in jail. Next, his charges were reversed on the grounds of illegal search and seizure, though McDowell ordered Crosby into detox anyway, pending the state's appeal.

Right after Christmas last year, he entered a drug-treatment program at Fair Oaks Hospital in Summit, New Jersey. But within seven weeks, Crosby had "eloped," in McDowell's words, from Fair Oaks. He simply jumped into a waiting car and split. He was arrested the following evening at a friend's New York City apartment.

Though Crosby immediately volunteered to go back to the hospital, McDowell said nothing doing. Crosby waived extradition and returned to Dallas. He went to jail March 7th and was released in late spring. His conviction was reinstated. He is now out on an appeal bond, on the brink of spending his emeritus years eating fish sticks and mashed potatoes at a Texas penitentiary—a first-class candidate for hard time.

"Ho-ly Shit!" Steve Stills grips the bars that separate him from the gathering crowd at the Pacific Amphitheatre in Costa Mesa, California. It's one of the largest arenas in the country, and it's full to the gunwales.

"I don't believe it," says Stills, grinning. "We're gonna kill 'em. This is fan-tas-tic." He wrings his hands conspiratorially. "Wait'll you hear this," he says to no one in particular. "My mediocre is better than your best. Heh! Heh! Heh!"

So far the 1985 tour is going well. On their first two nights out, CSN broke the house attendance record at the Concord Pavilion—and tickets for the rest of the two-month tour are selling quickly.

From song one, it's an enthusiastic house. High on the lawns this early evening, people engage in—get this!—tribal dancing. Hippies. Yes, hippies. *New* ones. Young boys with hair down their backs, girls in granny dresses. They undulate like seaweed in a changing tide as CSN whirls through "Wind on the Water" and a slew of other chestnuts.

Nash performs with a passionate calm, setting the pace of the show. Stills vamps like a bandit on "Suite: Judy Blue Eyes." Crosby remains impassive, playing almost as if he were underwater. Suddenly, though, during "Long Time Gone," he comes to life. In seconds, he looks ten years younger, beaming like a jack-o'-lantern as the crowd goes crazy. A group of stoned fans has made a long banner that reads, *David, we love you.*

"You have to consider the Bad Dave factor here," says Crosby's agent, Jay Jacobs. "A lot of these people figure this is the last time they'll see him alive."

After the show, Stills sits in his dressing room, a drink in hand. "Crosby's problem with his drug treatment was he got this too-cool-for-school mentality," he says. "I asked him, 'Why would you walk out of Fair Oaks after you had everything beat?' And he says, 'Because I realized that others were controlling my life.'" Stills leans forward on his chair. *"Welcome to the human race, man."*

"I'm like a guy who does everything right nine days in a row, then stumbles on the tenth day. That's all anybody ever wants to talk about, the tenth day. It's not fair, it's just not fair."

It is night in Las Vegas. David Crosby sits in the Lab, as the band calls his bus. The Lab's décor can be best described as Attempted Holiday Inn. Formica. Dim fabrics. His entourage includes the bus driver and…that's about it. No family. Few friends. While Nash remains the genial tour director and host, and Stills banters with anyone who will listen about everything from Shakespeare to his tax problems, Crosby keeps to himself. In the Lab. Alone.

Crosby, who had rallied his energy again and again during tonight's concert, is subdued. Staph infection has raised hell with his skin, and in this light he looks like an eighteenth-century pirate sorely in need of vitamin C.

"Look, man, I've never hurt anybody in my life," he says. "I don't do bad stuff to people. But I've had my name dragged through the dirt.

"Those two girls that brought that assault-and-battery charge?" he continues. "I'm a gentleman. I've never hit a girl in my life. Not once. They filed a civil suit to make money. They saw their chance to make big bucks."

Crosby swallows. "I'm not violent or dangerous. All I ever wanted was to make people happy." As for his fracas in Texas, he says, "Apparently the whole thing was bought and paid for in advance, 'cause the guy just walked into my dressing room and said, 'You're under arrest.' A dozen cops were there instantly." He sighs hoarsely. "Right now I'm on appeal bond. If we lose, I'll probably have to do three years in the Texas Detention Center—40,000 guys.

"I've been a good boy, man," he goes on. "I went through such a long period of time in jail kicking, getting clean.…It's an immense psychochemical readjustment, okay? I've been getting high for *twenty years. Constantly.* And I stopped. The readjustment was turbulent. Like being in the center of a cyclone. I was very crazy.

"The other thing was, they were so hard-nosed. Wouldn't let me have a tape recorder or a Walkman or the synthesizer Nash sent me. I asked to form a band, 'cause there was a drummer, bass player, lead guitar. They said no. I said, 'Look, you don't understand. I have to play music. Music is the best thing in my life, the strongest faith I have, the most positive force. It gets me much higher than drugs ever will. It's my salvation, man.'" Crosby's voice starts to crack. "'Why won't you let me play music?'"

He takes a breath. "They said, 'We think it'll get in the way of therapy, and besides, it's against the rules.' So I vented my anger and frustration by leaving. It was a mistake. I was getting better every day. But I was frustrated and feeling crazy."

So, goodbye New Jersey, hello the Dallas County Jail. "Jail is hell on wheels, man. Guys made it hard on me. Imagined I was rich. Imagined I was a star. They think a star is real. They don't know that it's nothing. It was really bad. I cried myself to sleep every night, man."

Which apparently has led him to change his tune about freebasing. "Don't do it," he admonishes. "It's a blind alley, a definite dead end. I think reefer is the only thing that doesn't fuck you up. I can't recommend hard drugs to anybody. I've been through 'em. I've seen too much pain, too much suffering, too much death. Just look at all the friends I've lost. Cass, Jimi, Janis. I'm decent. I don't want anybody to think I'm just some outlaw rebel giving America the finger." Minutes later Crosby begins to weep.

"Freebase is the most addictive substance we know about," says Dr. Mark Gold, director of research at Fair Oaks Hospital, where Crosby spent seven weeks last spring. "It's the ultimate euphoric. Far worse than heroin. Lab animals will freebase till they die."

Nash wants Crosby to get back into a drug-treatment program. Crosby's claim that he has cleaned himself up cuts little ice with Nash. "David's father, Floyd, is dying," he says. "As a parent myself, I think I'd find it terribly sad at eighty-four, when you're knocking on heaven's door, to know that what you've created has turned into a total piece of shit."

Henry Diltz is more optimistic. "The frog has taken over the prince, but the prince is still fighting to get out," he says.

Other friends and associates aren't so sure.

Paul Kantner: I used to get whole songs just from David's *tunings*. But the freebase has made him a total horror show. Robbed him of himself. Success has destroyed him. That drug would be too expensive otherwise— unless you're somebody out every other day sticking up banks.

Kenny Weiss: Musicians want to sustain the high they achieve onstage. Some start chasing that euphoria. But David's been overwhelmed. He's lost control. The evil is winning. If he goes, people will say, "His friends should have tried harder." Wrong. His friends have tried everything. Seriously self-destructive people will seek out the thing that will do them in. David has found his.

Chris Hillman: David was seduced and ruined by the myth he helped to create, that getting high would make a better world. It was the biggest fraud of all time. Want to know how to cut drug problems by half in this country? Have David go to the schools and just *display* himself.

Bill Graham: To the media and a lot of his fans, David Crosby is just a product. They eat him when they are hungry. But to the people who love him, he's a man worth doing most anything to save.

"Hi, Texas! I came back! I came back for you!" Crosby shouts into the microphone from the stage at the Southern Star Amphitheatre in Houston.

Crosby, Stills & Nash are still soaring from their appearance at the Live Aid Concert in Philadelphia the night before. They had played five songs altogether—three by themselves and two with Neil Young.

Crosby was jetted into Texas by charter. The plan was cautious and simple: get him in, get him out. But even Judge McDowell, the man who sentenced Crosby, now seems conciliatory. Shortly before Crosby's arrival, he had said, "He has a very realistic chance of beating this charge. He was

David Crosby. Mill Valley, Calfifornia. Photo: Henry Diltz

arrested because of a provision of the Texas Alcohol Beverage Code which pretty much allows the police to search a club anytime they want. If he gets this overturned on grounds that the code violates a citizen's reasonable expectation of privacy, well, that'll be it. You can't have rabbit stew without the rabbit."

Outside the arena after the show, Crosby is deposited in a limo aimed for the airport. Asked about the rumor that the Hell's Angels have taken owner-ship of his house, he begins to laugh. And laugh. *"You have to be kidding!* I swear to you on my mother's grave, the Hell's Angels do not own my house."

The chauffeur slides into the driver's seat. "Goodbye, Texas," Crosby says. "I'm about to leave a great smoking hole in the sky."

With pancake makeup smeared across his face, Crosby sits in his drive-way on his Harley-Davidson, pumping the throttle. He has returned from placating Jan, who remains inside the house. Friend and photographer Henry Diltz is choreographing Crosby for some pictures.

"People say I've let all my cars go to hell. I don't own one of these things," he says, pointing to a beat-up Audi and Peugeot and a Mercedes with the entire front end missing. "None of 'em." As he speaks, color comes to his face. Anger almost makes Crosby look healthy.

"Want to know the latest wrinkle?" he continues. "That I'm already dead. Not a dope addict anymore, not even a zombie or a vegetable, but already dead. Man, that hurts. Reading that shit. You know people who take a lot of drugs get paranoid. Start thinking people are out to get them, start seeing people at their windows, bugs on their arms—*millions* of bugs. I try to avoid that. It's hard, though. I've been living my whole life in the public square. People think you're a star, you're fair game. Guys came sneaking up here one night, screaming, '*Crosby! We're gonna kill you!*' Scary. I feel like a bug on a wall. You hear about the time I shot the place up? Guy at my bedroom window, wearing a ski mask. His gun lines up on me, right? Got a bead. But he's got to bang the glass out. Numskull. I pull my piece. A .45. Ka-pow! *Ka-pow! Ka-pow! Ka-pow!* I stitch the whole clip frame to frame. That son of a bitch fled the entire area."

The CSN tour is almost over, forty-six shows down, a handful to go. There have been only a few glitches. In Virginia, for example, Crosby walked off-stage in the middle of a show. "Daddy was *pissed*," recalls one of the CSN entourage, referring to Nash. "The Croz just cruised into the band's hospitality room and lay down on a couch and said he was too sick to play. Stills ran off-stage and dumped a bucket of water on his head. Then Graham came in and nearly killed him." Nash says it was less dramatic than that: "David caught the stomach flu. It's tough to sing, vomit and shit all at the same time."

Now Crosby is feeling and looking a whole lot better. "I love this motorcycle," he says. "Rice rockets—Jap bikes. God, they're fast. *Incredible!* But Harley's are the best. Why is riding a Japanese bike like fucking a homosexual man? 'Cause it feels great until somebody sees you." Crosby parks his Harley, says, "Back in a sec," and goes inside the house. He is gone twenty minutes.

When Crosby reappears, it is night, and he's up for some dinner. He decides to drive into town in a big, new Lincoln Continental he's rented and invites Diltz along. On the way, Crosby checks his mail.

"'Dear David,'" he says, mocking a recent missive. "'Jesus told me to write you....' Myself," he continues, "I talk to God. I call God Ernie. Less pretentious. 'Ernie,' I says, 'Why?'"

Crosby speeds through the narrow, twisting roads into Mill Valley, pulls into a parking lot, spots a diagonal slot marked *compacts only* and whips the Lincoln right in, front tires bumping up over the curb. Its snout sticks three feet across the sidewalk. "Just another Pinto, officer," he says, getting out.

Crosby leads the way into D'Angelo's. "This is a fantastic place," he says, stepping into the large, airy restaurant. Waiters constellate around his table. He orders a steak, a salad and several kinds of pasta. Then he pulls a walkie-talkie from his herringbone jacket and calls Jan. "Hi, listen, we're at D'Angelo's," he says. "You want me to bring back something? Veal Parmesan? Antipasto?...Anybody call?...Linda from Sausalito? Never heard of her. Love you. Bye."

Then Crosby says: "The other day I read that Graham tells this guy I'm going to die. How could he have said that? He's my best friend. He said I was just going to *die*." Crosby's voice wobbles. "How could he have said that? So cold. I would never have said something like that about Graham in a million years, man. It was so crude, so out of hand.

"What does Graham think, that I'm so stupid he's gonna shock me into some perception I haven't already attained? You think I haven't thought about this every minute of every day? There's not a damn thing he's gonna teach me about this that I don't already know! I know more about freebase than anybody! You think you plan to become an addict? It sneaks up on you. Oh, I'll just get a little high. I've kicked cigarettes, heroin, booze, everything. But this is the most horrible drug in the universe. It stays with you. I was in jail four months. Want to know how long I stayed clean when I got out? Two days. It never lets you alone. All I want to do is be clean, man. But I'm scared I'm gonna crave it *forever*."

Crosby sits there, breathing noisily in and out, as if exhausted. Then, an epiphany, of sorts; "Hey, John Coltrane was a junkie. And who could ever make better music than him? I'm gonna beat it. Really I am."

The food arrives, and Crosby passes the plates around. "I love fish," he says. "Last time I sailed to Hawaii, we had hand lines trailing out. Three days out of the islands we caught three mahi-mahi."

A waiter appears. "Cheese for the pasta, David?"

"Just for the fettucine. Whack it on there. Lots." He knifes his steak in half. "This is not quite medium. Just a couple minutes more, please....What a trip. Bearing the windwards—motoring the windwards lots of times— Mexico to Hawaii, 3,000 miles in the trades."

Crosby plans to return to the South Seas next year, a trip to Australia for the America's Cup. "Tahiti. One of the few things on earth as good as you thought it was going to be. Their music is crazy. Sexy. Wonderful people. All they want to do is get smashed and fuck. That's their whole program. *Ooooooh, let's get drunk! Make schooner, baby!* Fuck the white boys, get the bloodlines mixed up. Paradise. *Crosby, Stills and who? Whaaat ess you name? You are one auf Bing's boys?* Trade winds at ten knots. Baby's breath, man. No circular storms. No typhoons. So rich with life. You'd have to be blind, deaf, dumb, ignorant and have a lot of enemies to starve there. Ocean's not fished out. Air so clean and sparkly..."

Crosby picks up his walkie-talkie and calls Jan again. "I love you," he says. "I love your skinny little ass. I wanna grab ya! Sounds like a good idea, huh? Well, I'm gonna come home and stuff ya. All right, sweetie."

His steak returns. "Money is fun, but it'll trash you out," he says. "I've got guys who've invested in me, yeah. Saved me from the IRS. I give 'em what I can. That's it. Sometimes things get hard. Jan was crying last night. Called it eyelash soup. But there are good things, too…"

Crosby falls asleep. Instantly. His eyes are closed. They look as if they're about to slide off the side of his head. He begins to snore.

"Gimme something hard and heavy," Crosby says to the clerk at the Mill Valley 7-Eleven. The clerk hands him a hammer.

Crosby has just bought forty dollars' worth of cat food, soda pop and ice cream and discovered he's locked his keys inside the Lincoln. Diltz's flight is the last one for the night and only an hour away.

"Maybe we should call somebody," says Diltz.

"At this hour?" says Crosby.

"But…"

"You don't want to miss your flight, do you?" Crosby raises the hammer, his arm comes down in an arc. *Wham!* The Lincoln's window is history. Little diamonds of smashed glass everywhere. Then Crosby carefully cleans out the car and sweeps the parking lot.

"Don't worry," he says, "I'll pay for it. It'll just get stuck on my bill with everything else."

THE CONFESSIONS OF
A COKE ADDICT

BY DAVID CROSBY
WITH TODD GOLD
People Magazine
April 27, 1987

On the other side of prison and drug-free, David Crosby, speaking to *People's* Todd Gold, offered up to-the-bone details about his years as a drug addict, its affect on his music, his incarceration and how he remarkably lived through it all.

David Crosby. Photo: Henry Diltz

*L*ots *of rock stars succumb to drugs, but few have nose-dived as publicly as David Crosby. The prototypical '60s folk-rocker began using marijuana and hallucinogens during his heyday with the Byrds and Crosby, Stills & Nash. When his girlfriend, Christine Hinton, died in a car wreck in 1969, he says, he began turning to harder drugs. A decade later he was headed toward the abyss. In 1982 he wrecked his car, and police found a .45 pistol and a freebase pipe containing cocaine residue in the vehicle. Three weeks later Dallas police found him with another .45, another pipe and more residue. Convicted on drug and weapons charges, he was caught with heroin and cocaine while out on appeal. Sent to a drug treatment center in 1985, he ran away. He grew fat and splotchy, and even his best friend, CSN co-founder Graham Nash, despaired of helping him. "I've tried everything—extreme anger, extreme compassion," Nash told* Rolling Stone *in 1985. "I've gotten 20 of his best friends in the same room with him. I've tried hanging out with him. I've tried not hanging out with him." Said longtime friend Neil Young, "Freebasing is the worst addiction. It's not too late for him to come back. Either that's going to happen or he's going to die."*

Crosby spent 11 months in Texas jails and was paroled last August. He says he's been straight now for 16 months, and even Nash believes the change is fundamental and genuine. "I always prayed that David would come back from the land of the dead," says Nash. "Now he's 100 percent with us—none of this going away

267

for 10 or 15 minutes. It was insanely difficult to be his friend, but I feel as if I've been paid off in spades."

Crosby himself has the zeal of the born-again. He's living in a rented two-bedroom house in Los Angeles, writing music for the first time in years, and on May 16 he'll tie the knot with his steady of eight years, Jan Dance, 35, who is also a recovering drug user. He's now delighted that Donovan, 12, his daughter from an earlier relationship, is finally getting to see him in his right mind when she visits.

Crosby, 45, talked to reporter Todd Gold about his addiction and recovery.

Most people who go as far as I did with drugs are dead. Hard drugs will hook anyone. I don't care who you are. It's not a matter of personality. Do them and it's a matter of time before you are addicted. You can give me any rationalization you want, I know better. I have a PhD in drugs. Fool with them and you'll get strung out. Then there are about four ways it can go: You can go crazy; you can go to prison; you can die; or you can kick. That's it. Anything else anybody says is bull.

I kicked a huge freebase and heroin habit, but it didn't start out that way. You don't sit down and say, "Gee, I think I'll become a junkie." When I started out doing drugs, it was marijuana and psychedelics, and it was fun. It was the '60s, and we thought we were expanding our consciousness. There was no harm in it. It wasn't interfering with anything.

But after my old lady, Christine, was killed, I was unable to handle it and the drugs became more for blurring pain. I was very much in love with her, and she just never came back from the store. That incident was just one contributing factor to my problems, but that was when I got more into hard drugs. I'd been doing coke for a while, but after Christine died, I started doing heroin too. You don't realize you're getting as strung out as you are. It sneaks up on you. And I had the money to get more and more addicted.

The biggest alarm, I think, was that the drugs made it harder and harder to make music. I worried about that. I was still able to play and sing, but not as well, and it became more and more difficult for me to work with the other guys. It slowed my writing down too. Anyone who tells you that hard drugs increase your creativity is full of s——. I noticed I wasn't writing music, believe me. It's my life's work, man, but when you are severely addicted, you don't really have control.

I got busted a couple times, and there were a couple of car wrecks. The most serious was in 1982 on the way to a show in Southern California. I wrecked my car and had a gun with me. For a long time I used to carry a gun. I like guns. I don't have any now, but as a kid, I was a member of the

National Rifle Association. When John Lennon was shot, I said, "See. We draw nut cases like flies, and when it gets so crazy that a guy will shoot somebody as harmless as John, you have to think about protecting yourself." Twelve years ago two guys in ski masks with guns showed up at my house in Mill Valley [Calif.] to rob me. I shot first and they left. But for a long time after that, I couldn't go to sleep until it got light. It was very frightening.

So I had a gun on me that night the car crashed. I don't think I had any drugs. I think all they got was some residue in a pipe. But that counts the same. I was busted, taken to jail, then released in a couple of hours. Later they dropped the charges. But these things weren't registering much. When you're in that state of mind, man, you don't really accept the data. People whom I love would say to me, "David, this is really bad," and I'd say, "Hey, I don't tell you how to live your life." That was total bull——. Their lives weren't screwed up and mine was.

A short time later I was busted again. I was playing Cardi's, a small club in Dallas. They busted in and caught me red-handed, pipe, gun, all of it. The cops knew. By that time my habit was a matter of national knowledge. I went to jail, was out in a few hours and then went through a long legal process. The judge gave me five years. I thought I was being made an example of. Now I think the judge was very fair to me. He let me appeal the sentence and gave me a chance to straighten myself out in a hospital. But I blew the appeal when I was busted for drugs after I ran away from the hospital. Finally the judge said, "That's enough. You're going to jail." I spent four months in jails in New York and Texas. I came out and went straight back on drugs. When you're as strung out as I was, your life is primarily just trying to find drugs, figure out a way to get the money to get drugs and hustle and beg drugs.

I got busted again a few months later in Marin County, and was sent back to prison. And frankly, although I hated prison, I don't regret it. Before then my life was horrible. On tour I functioned badly. There was constant paranoia. I knew I was doing the wrong thing. I lived with a great deal of guilt and loneliness because I'd isolated myself from everybody. My daughter wanted very much for me to get off drugs. She'd come to visit and I'd spend most of the time in the bathroom.

At the peak of my consumption I was doing anywhere from an eighth of an ounce to a quarter of an ounce of cocaine [$500] a day and at least a half gram of heroin [$200] a day. When you're as well known a junkie as I was, it's easy to get the drugs. Dealers come right over. They're faster than a pizza delivery. Over the years I spent millions of dollars, although I never reached the point that I was broke.

I was constantly feeling the weight of disapproval of all my friends. Some of them just finally backed off. They couldn't stand to watch me go down the tubes. One time Jackson Browne, Paul Kantner, Nash and a bunch

269

of my other friends did what's called an "intervention." They all confronted me and got me into a hospital. What happens is that you have short periods of lucidness, when you know you are doing the wrong thing, and you say to yourself, "I'm going to beat this somehow." But I left the hospital the next day. I did this six times.

The prospect of going to prison was devastating. I was so afraid. But I was more afraid of having to kick the drugs. I thought I would die if I didn't have them. Rather than go to jail, I became a fugitive. Jan and I fled to Florida. There was a warrant out for my arrest and we were going to get on my boat and leave the country. Jan also had a drug habit, and we were going to sail away and try to kick on the boat. We knew we had to beat it, but we couldn't face doing it and we couldn't face going to prison and we couldn't face being split up. But the plan was totally ridiculous.

When we got down there I realized, "I can't be this guy." Music was my life. I couldn't run away and not do any more Crosby, Stills & Nash. I couldn't not see my daughter again. I had one of those lucky moments. From somewhere I finally had the courage to do something. I called up the FBI in Florida and said, "You have a warrant out for my arrest. Don't anyone freak out. I'm coming in and surrendering."

They took me to Texas, and I spent the next four months in solitary in Dallas County Jail. My cell was about 6 by 13. They fed me through a little hole in the door. There were two big fluorescent lights above that never went off. I slept very poorly. I was kicking coke and heroin under the worst possible circumstances. They wouldn't give me an aspirin. I did it as cold turkey as you can do it, and it was hell.

After four months the judge gave me the choice of staying in County Jail or going to the Texas Department of Correction. I chose TDC. I couldn't stand being alone anymore. Also I knew that if I went to prison, I could play in a prison band.

It turned out not to be as bad as I thought. I'm not saying the Texas prisons are nice. There was a great deal of violence and cruelty of every sort. There are a lot of guys walking around like loaded bombs, so you have to be very careful. People related to me in every way, from, "Wow, are you really...?" to "That sonbitch, Dave Crosby. He's got more money than I ever seen. Kill that sonbitch." But I never got beat up. I had to get up at 5:30 every morning and make mattresses for the next six hours, measuring and cutting material. Man, that's not fun, but there's lots of talk and it kept me from being bored.

Ironically, the main thing about prison for me was that I had more freedom. I got to be out and move around. And my friends could send me books. My cell turned into a library. I could also play guitar, and I got into a rock 'n' roll band. We did shows for the inmates and had a good time with it. Jan and I would write each other constantly. She went through detox in a hospital, then recovery in a rehabilitation place for a long time. We used to keep each other alive with letters.

It took me about six months to wake up. I hadn't written any music for nearly three years. When the words started to come I knew I was on the way back. I started to be able to think again, to be able not to have dreams about drugs all the time. It felt the way I imagine it would feel if you took a sparrow, tied a five-pound weight to its feet for about 10 years and then untied it.

I got out of prison last August 8th and spent some time in a halfway house in Houston. Graham came right down and did a gig there so we could play together and I could have the feeling of going back onstage. He's that kind of friend. My real friends, like Neil, Stephen Stills, Jackson, they stuck by me. A lot of people had written me off. The general feeling was, "We lost him. He's going to die or stay in prison." Wrong. I'm writing like a fool now. A couple of the songs are about my experience with drugs. In the last four or five months I've turned out a couple songs that Nash says are among the best things I've ever done. Nash loves me, but he won't give me a quarter inch unless I earn it.

Crosby, Stills & Nash are going on a tour this summer, and we're getting back with Neil to make a record. We seem to be bigger than ever. Stills, Nash and I recently did an acoustic tour in the East and found half our audience was between 15 and 20 years old. I'm not complaining but I don't understand it. Who told them?

Sure I regret the missed years and the music that didn't get made, but I don't beat myself over the head about it. I'm ashamed of some things. But you have to learn from the mistakes. I had time to think, believe me. In a prison cell, you have a lot of time to think.

When I got out of prison I was in very bad shape. My health was trashed. Since then I've lost 30 pounds and I'm losing more all the time. I work out and I'm on a diet. It's getting better all the time. I'm a growing person. I grew into drugs, I grew through drugs, I grew out of drugs. I'm now growing into being a parent, being the best writer and performer I can be. Also, Jan and I are getting married on May 16. Through all the hardship, we never came unglued.

I learned a great deal from all this. I learned that instead of instant gratification, I needed to learn patience and humility. I learned that music, love and friends are more important than getting high. But the biggest surprise was that I could quit drugs, that I had a choice. I thought I was going to die on drugs. When you've been as severely addicted as I was, you're real surprised to be alive.

NEIL YOUNG ON CSNY

Excerpt from
"Blue Notes from a Restless Loner"

BY DAVE ZIMMER
BAM: *The California
Music Magazine*
April 22, 1988

As David Crosby began to piece his life back together, Neil Young made good on a promise to get "the Mothership" afloat again. When this interview took place in March of 1988, Young was in the middle of recording a new CSNY album at this Northern California ranch studio and preparing for more road work with a solo group dubbed the Bluenotes. Sitting face-to-face with Young in the front seat of one of his vintage Cadillacs in the gravel parking lot of a restaurant not far from his ranch, I was prepared with a binder full of questions about the Bluenotes, other aspects of his career and CSNY. Demonstrating relaxed enthusiasm, periodic humor and focused care, Young patiently answered every question—including several about CSNY, which are excerpted from that interview here. His warm affection for his old friends and high regard for the music CSNY create was very apparent.

Crosby, Stills, Nash & Young at the Arlington Theatre, Santa Barbara. February 1987.
Photo: Henry Diltz

• • •

I don't know if this is a project you want to talk about now, but I understand you've been doing some recording with Crosby, Stills & Nash.

[Pause] Well, I'm doing the Crosby, Stills, Nash & Young album. And we're about halfway finished with the recording process. Five songs are basically done. They just need to be mixed.

We started off with Stills and I recording together for two weeks. Then David and Graham came up, and we've worked now for two weeks with them. And, during that period, we've got five complete records, which is a good thing.

Sounds like it's more productive than previous CSNY recording attempts.

Yeah. It's very productive and it's been very good. I think that the music really sounds magnificent. I think that the harmonies and everything are as electric as…they're more electric than they ever were before. There's more happening…

Now that David's in good shape…

275

Saying David is in good shape is pushing it. David's not strung out. He's not addicted to drugs and is very alive. Emotionally, he's living life to the fullest. He's going through every little thing that happens, and feeling everything, to great extremes, after having not felt anything for ten years. So, he's very much alive and I really love him for being strong enough to do what he's done. But the job's not over yet.

Looking at CSNY as an entity now, how is it different from when you were with the band in '69 and '70?

The difference now is…it's more CSNY than it ever was. I was just sort of an add-on before. Now I'm the driving force in the band. And basically, that says it. But I don't think we've reached our true potential yet.

Several years ago, you commented that CSN had become like the Beach Boys, that the band was just stuck in a groove and wasn't progressing.

Well, that's true. But now they've got new songs. Graham is writing some great songs, David has some great ones, and Stephen also has some great songs. The energy is…in the studio it's really great. Live? I don't know what it would be like. If CSNY was to go on the road today, it would be an inconsistent high. It wouldn't be a consistently great thing every night. So I'm hoping that, given time, it will reach a place where everyone can fully give everything that they have, that the band will reach its potential and truly live up to what people expect of us. That'll be when I go on the road with them.

This CSNY potential you speak of, wasn't that reached the first time around back in 1969?

On stage, but not on records. Except maybe on "Ohio" and maybe "Almost Cut My Hair" and a few things like that, where I felt like I was truly part of the band. But of all of the *Déjà Vu* stuff, I only played on four songs. I wasn't even on "Teach Your Children." I wasn't even on, what's the other one? "Carry On," There are several songs that I wasn't on, where I wasn't even there. So *Déjà Vu* was like CSN with me added on, me singing a couple of my songs with them singing with me. But that's not CSNY.

There's never really been a CSNY studio album. What we're doing now is more a CSNY studio album than anything that has ever happened. And I really believe that it's a great record. I don't know how long it's going to take to finish, but we're dedicated to finishing it.

CSNY is a different thing from CSN. CSN will probably be on the road this summer. And I'll be out with the Bluenotes. But I'm dedicated to doing this [CSNY] record, then some day in the future doing a tour with CSNY when it is capable of being strong and consistently aware and on top of it. That'll take work.

I know you want to avoid having CSNY go out just as a nostalgia act.

Well, it always will be that. There's no way around it. But if nostalgia is what people want, there's a healthy nostalgia and an unhealthy nostalgia. The worst kind of nostalgia is when musicians stand up there and are a

Crosby, Stills, Nash & Young. 1988. Photo: Henry Diltz

shadow of their former selves. And all of the people that loved them so much start to think that they are only a shadow of their former selves. And the whole audience goes home with this feeling like their life is over, as if they're just sort of marking time until they die, like those guys they just saw on stage. I don't want to do that to people. I mean, people believe in CSNY. When they see CSNY, even if it is a nostalgia trip, I want them to believe that their life is worth living, and that the rest of their life is going to be better than the first part. I want people to feel an energy from the band that makes you feel great and makes you feel like these guys really believe and are strong and are alive and value their lives and their bodies and the way they are and everything. Not that we're capable of actually transferring energy, but people will see the good things in themselves and get strength from themselves out of seeing how strong we are and how sharp we are, and how we are still creating, and how everybody is still a hundred percent and everything is there. But if we were to go out now and it wasn't happening and the audience could see, "Hey, the sparks aren't flying tonight. The guys look a little sleepy. I wonder what they did this afternoon to be like this tonight? Wow, did you see that?" I don't want any part of that kind of show and I will not be part of it.

I remember being in the crowd at the Oakland Coliseum in 1974. When CSNY played "Don't Be Denied" and "Pushed It Over the End," there was definitely some kind of energy there. You could feel it.

There were good moments on that tour. There really were. That was before Crosby was fucked up and everybody else in the band was very strong. I mean, the band wasn't really a hundred percent clean, but they were still young enough so that whatever they may have been doing wrong wasn't screwing them up so much that the initial feeling was gone. You see, when you reach a certain age, you have to stop doing abusive things to yourself or you really are only a shadow of your former self, just turning pages in a book, hoping that there won't be any new words on them. But at some point the body gives out and can't continue at the same level unless you step back and rebuild and stop doing all the things that hurt you, so that you can continue to create and rise higher, not just tread water. That's my whole thing now. I'm really dedicated to that awareness of living.

• • •

A Louisiana Encore for
Stephen Stills

BY Steve Rush
New Orleans
(LA) Times-Picayune
June 24, 1988

While Stephen Stills' early roots reach into several different regions—primarily Texas, Illinois, Louisiana, Florida and Central America—he has acknowledged that his musical career began in New Orleans. With a new CSNY album nearing completion, Stills flew into the Big Easy to take part in a benefit concert in June of 1988. This article by *Times-Picayune* reporter Steve Rush included insights into Stills' formative years in Louisiana as well as very candid comments about CSNY and his relationship with Neil Young.

Stephen Stills on stage with keyboardist/vocalist Michael Finnigan.
Photo: Roger Barone

With a daughter only a week old, it's fitting that Stephen Stills will return this weekend to the city he says was his musical cradle. Stills, who lived in Covington as a boy and performed at clubs in the French Quarter before hitting it big with Buffalo Springfield in the mid-1960s and later with Crosby, Stills, Nash & Young, will appear Saturday at a "Raisin' the Roof" benefit concert for the Cabildo restoration. The show, which will include Allen Toussaint and the New Orleans jazz fusion group Woodenhead, will be at Riverwalk's Spanish Plaza.

"I started my career in New Orleans," Stills said in a wide-ranging interview this week. "It was about that time that I was starting to think, 'Well, maybe I'm actually good enough at this to actually try it.' I played a couple of clubs on Bourbon Street, around the Quarter, and basically just sort of hacked around. Did a little bartending. I spent a lot of time at the old Cosimo's. And I was in attendance when they had the funeral for the Bourbon House, which dates me. Anybody that's been around the city for awhile is going to know how long ago that was. I'm just a typical Louisiana swamp rat, you know. When I was a little kid we were living across the lake in Covington. I learned how to fish on the Bogue Falaya River. The city's real special to me. I spent some formative times there at a couple of different points in my life. Of course, the music was just a phenomenal influence on me."

Giving something back

Stills said that when he was approached about playing the Cabildo benefit, "I didn't have to be asked more than once. I would always show up for something for the city. It's unfortunate that it comes during tragic circumstances, but I have waited a long time to be able to come and give something back to the city. And I'm gonna be there with bells on." He said he was crushed when he heard of the May 11 blaze. "Knowing New Orleans, I have this feeling that everyone might have been a little surprised at the international news," he said, "because the people in New Orleans have a tendency to either make too much of it or take it a little bit for granted. But the Cabildo is a national treasure. I'd walk by it on my way to work every day; sometimes I'd stroll in; it was just part of your heritage. I had an apartment catty-corner to it for a time. We're real lucky that it didn't get down into the lower floors. From what I can ascertain the fire department people were real quick and did a fantastic job." At 43, Stills sounds excited to be entering a new phase of his life, personally and professionally. He has his new daughter, Eleanor Mary, a new home in Beverly Hills, and CSNY has recorded a new album to be released in September.

After success, solos

The band [CSNY] achieved phenomenal success in the early '70s after two studio albums (the first without Neil Young), but splintered into a succession of solo projects. While Stills, Graham Nash and David Crosby have reunited off and on in the past decade for recordings and concert tours, this will be the first studio album to bring all four together since the landmark *Déjà Vu*. "We recorded it up at Neil Young's ranch in California, and we're into the last week of mixing," Stills said. "We get back to some basic methods. I think it's going to be called 'SYNC the Ranch,' SYNC for Stills, Young,

Nash and Crosby. It's time for a change." At a time when rock bands and sounds come and go overnight, the pure vocal harmonies of Crosby, Stills & Nash have endured critically and commercially, and Stills tried to put his finger on some of the reasons. "With David, Graham and I you have three very unique-sounding voices and everybody is pretty much an original," he said. "I'm a Southern-born and -bred musician and I've been through the kind of discipline that any musician who plays New Orleans gets...there's not a lot of room for amateurs there. I think that's why a lot of pop groups don't really fly in the city; you don't hear about the big Gotterdammerung concerts happening in the Superdome. Because New Orleans people, man, this is us. We do this, we hear the best all the time. And they're playing to real music people, so all that fluff just don't fly. David Crosby is an old folkie, you know, drifting around all over, and Graham Nash is the same kind of an original from the north of England with a very easy-to-recognize and well-developed voice, as all three of us do, the combination of it makes a sound that is a paradigm example of the whole being greater than the sum of the parts. And we've managed to keep our ability to sing and our musicality foremost, more important than the celebrity part of it, which I really loathe even talking about. We are musicians first of all. The rest of it is an accident and a game, and we do it as best we can, and suffer the consequences of celebrity."

Putting rumors to rest

Stills was eager to put to rest stories that have circulated in the past of rifts between him and Neil Young, and said the press blew any such conflicts way out of proportion. "Particularly since the Rupert Murdoch influence on the American journalistic profession," he said. "I mean, they just sort of warmed up on us, on people like us. But this whole element of gossip journalism has become de rigueur. You've got a couple of ordinary people who are interesting and intelligent but nevertheless the thing that makes them interesting and worthy of comment is the power of their music. And that gets maybe third paragraph. But the lead now is how I've been fighting with Neil Young and how long we've been fighting. But as far as our interrelation, that interaction, there's always gonna be sparks when there are intensely creative people. Sort of like brothers, particularly with a bunch that's been together as long as we have. I mean, Neil has been waiting for several years to find the right time to come back into this group. And actually he's only now truly asserting himself within the group, as he always should have and as he did on the road and as we did together in the Buffalo Springfield. You've got to remember that Neil Young and I started that band in 1965, and that was the foundation of the whole program. And that's like a couple of brothers."

A home to return to

"We devised the name Crosby, Stills, Nash & Young not to pretend we were Merrill Lynch, Pierce, Fenner and Smith, but to allow everyone the latitude to go off and pursue individual careers and always have this home to come back to. So all the fussing and all the silliness that went on when we were kids is the kind of silliness that goes on when you're kids, you know. And we suffered the consequences of becoming very, very successful very early on, in our early and mid-20s. And I'm here to tell you that that'll crack your brains. Now that we've been around the block a couple of times we're trying to get our minds right. And this process that we've been through with this latest album has really shown everybody why we made a commitment to each other years ago. There's much more professional musicianship involved here than celebrity or being a pop star or any of that."

Stills was reticent to talk about Crosby, whose problems with drugs and the law have been much-publicized in the past couple of years. "David's recovery and what he went through is a matter of public record," Stills said. "I am not going to share my insights on it, because it's personal, he's family and I don't think anyone is served by what I think of it. David will explain it, David will address it and he will do so just wonderfully; he can speak very much for himself. I know what I went through with him; I know what we all went through with him and saw the whole procedure occur. But I want to give him the opportunity to come forth about what he's been through and how he has contended with it and how much more he has to do. And God bless him. I mean, that's a strong man; I'll tell you what, that is a strong man."

CROSBY, STILLS & NASH: DÉJÀ VU ALL OVER AGAIN

BY CHUCK CRISAFULLI
Los Angeles Times
July 24, 1994

With the 25th anniversary of the Woodstock Music and Art Fair at hand, CSN (minus Y) decided to take part in "Woodstock '94." In the midst of recording a Glyn Johns-produced studio album as a trio in Burbank, California, the musicians talked to Los Angeles-based writer Chuck Crisafulli about their music, lives, and feelings related to returning to Woodstock.

Graham Nash and David Crosby at the original Woodstock. August 1969. Photo: Henry Diltz

W hen David Crosby, Stephen Stills and Graham Nash went on stage at Woodstock in 1969, it was only their second show together. This year the band celebrates a quarter-century of music-making with an album, a tour and, fittingly, a performance at "Woodstock '94," which will be Aug. 13 and 14 in Upstate New York.

But if these three '60s survivors are supposed to present themselves as solemn elder statesman of the Woodstock Nation, they aren't playing the part very well.

Crosby, Stills & Nash are in a Burbank recording studio working on the final track for their first album together in four years.

Considering the trio's ties to Woodstock, their respective backgrounds with the Byrds, Buffalo Springfield and the Hollies, and their fitful relationship with Neil Young, they represent an enormous chunk of rock 'n' roll history.

But the mood in the room is not one of dignified reflection—and there's no talk of historical significance. Instead, food fights are narrowly avoided, O.J. jokes are circulated and spreading waistlines are made fun of.

Stephen Stills at the original Woodstock. August 1969. Photo: Henry Diltz.

The band so famous for its heady harmonies and shifting grudges is, in short, having a hoot.

"Our general rule is, 'If it ain't fun, we ain't going,'" says Stills, 49. "We enjoy laughing too much. We can't think of ourselves as a big deal. Not in here, anyway. We poke fun at each other relentlessly. And after all this time, it's still not as much fun to make music if the other two aren't around."

The music at hand is a Stills composition titled "Only Waiting for You." The group thought it had completed its album, *After the Storm*, during recording sessions with producer Glyn Johns, whose credits—from the Rolling Stones and the Who to Eric Clapton and the Eagles—represent another chunk of rock history. But two weeks into their current tour, Stills put together what may be the record's strongest track. Instead of taking a weekend tour break, the band has returned to the studio with longtime CSN keyboardist/vocalist Michael Finnigan and are yukking it up.

"We sound like church geeks," complains Crosby, 52, after hearing a playback of the song. He's at a microphone with Nash and Finnigan saying that the "ooohs" they're singing over Stills' lead are too sweet.

The part is changed to "aah" on a second take, but the attack is too harsh for Stills' taste.

"Good God," Stills grumbles in the control room, "not so much Bruce Lee."

"Well, it's hard competing with Mr. 'Star Search' Voice here," says Finnigan, eyeing Crosby.

When it looks as if a musical impasse is nearing, Nash diplomatically works out a part his bandmates are happy with. On the final take, the blend is just right. And when Nash bends his note in counterpoint to Crosby's, there it is: the shimmering mix of voices the group is famous for.

Stills' smoky baritone is now mostly grit and gravel, and his partners' harmonies aren't as pristine as they were back in the "Suite: Judy Blue Eyes" days of the late '60s, but the gracefully spirited union of their talents is still powerful and affecting. The new song has sprung to life.

Later, away from the mike, Crosby flashes a mischievous grin. "Man, these were supposed to be vacation days for us. But Stephen had to go and write the single after we finished the album—the dip."

"Actually this is not unusual at all," Nash, 52, points out. "The same thing happened on [the 1970 album] *Déjà Vu*. We didn't quite have an opener for that one. We said, 'When you tear the shrink wrap off the LP, what's the first thing you want to hear?'

"We told Stephen we didn't have it. The next day he came in and said, 'What about this?' and played 'Carry On.' David and I got a bit wide-eyed and said: 'OK, Stephen. I think we hear it now. Thanks very much.'"

Crosby, Stills & Nash were among the first collections of rock 'n' roll notables to be dubbed a supergroup. But, as each member emphasizes in separate interviews, their intention in getting together all those years ago was to be more of an *anti-group*.

"The reason we used our own names when we started the band was because we also wanted to pursue individual careers as well," explains Crosby. "We didn't like being locked into roles the way we were in Buffalo Springfield and the Byrds and the Hollies.

"We've always pursued other projects, and we sing on other people's records all the time. It's a tremendously healthy way to do things because you get a chance for some musical cross-pollination and you learn something new. And when we're ready, we bring it all back to CSN."

The three met through Cass Elliot of the Mamas and the Papas. When they first sang together—in Elliot's kitchen or in Joni Mitchell's living room, depending on who's telling the story—the sound they made eased their fears about collaborative work. All had bad tastes in their mouths regarding previous affiliations: Crosby had splintered from the Byrds acrimoniously, Nash had tired of the Hollies' pop direction, and Stills was bitter over the breakup of Buffalo Springfield.

Nash (who believes it was at Mitchell's house) recalls that the first song they worked on was "You Don't Have to Cry," which appeared on the trio's debut album.

"David and Stephen had worked out the song, and after I heard it a couple of times, I came up with a part to fit against theirs," he says, sitting on a patio during a break in the recording session. "Halfway through it, we burst out laughing. Because as much as we were bored with groups at the time, and as much as we [each] didn't want to be in anything remotely resembling the band we had been in, we realized that we were going to have to spend some time together."

Their first album, 1969's *Crosby, Stills & Nash*, was something of a last prayer for the '60s counterculture. The fluid, folky grooves of the music and the wizened idealism of songs such as "Wooden Ships" and "Long Time Gone" seemed a perfect soundtrack for the Woodstock summer. The album made it to No. 6 on the pop charts, and Nash's upbeat "Marrakesh Express" single made the Top 40.

The group quickly added Neil Young, who had played with Stills in Buffalo Springfield, and after some particularly volatile recording sessions, the foursome released *Déjà Vu* in 1970. That record went to No. 1, partly on the strength of the group's first Top 20 single, the Joni Mitchell-penned "Woodstock."

Nash's gentle Aquarius Age anthem "Teach Your Children" was released as a second single. The song was headed for the Top 10, but when four student protesters were killed by National Guardsmen at Kent State University, the band quickly recorded and released Young's angry response to the deaths. CSNY's "Ohio" made it to the Top 20 and knocked "Teach Your Children" off the charts.

There also have been some memorable lowlights over the years. The band is closely associated with Woodstock, but they also played with the Rolling Stones, Jefferson Airplane and others at the ill-fated Altamont show in California. A fan was stabbed to death during a melee in front of the stage.

The lowest point came in 1985 when, after several years of drug addiction, Crosby was incarcerated for nearly a year in Texas on drug and weapons violations.

"It was a terrible time, because I had stopped writing," Crosby says now. "And I'm not good for much of anything in this world if I'm not making music. I'm fortunate that Stephen and Nash stood by me, and I'm writing more than ever now. I've probably only made a couple of smart decisions in my life. One was marrying my wife [the former Jan Dance, in 1987], and the other was getting sober."

Since *Déjà Vu* there have been three more Crosby, Stills & Nash albums: *CSN* in 1977 and *Daylight Again* in 1982, both of which made the Top 10, and 1990's *Live It Up*, which didn't crack the Top 50.

Crosby, Stills & Nash at Woodstock '94, Saugerties, New York. August 1994. Photo: Henry Diltz

But it is misleading to measure the trio's contributions in terms of official CSN albums. Through the years there have also been two more CSNY albums, several Crosby-Nash packages, a Stills-Young collection and numerous solo projects.

Although the media has often written about CSN in terms of breakups and reunions, Crosby sees their efforts as part of a continuing stream.

"Breakups and reunions are more dramatic, but it's a bunch of crap," Crosby says with a laugh. "We're doing what we intended to do when we started. One of the reasons I don't think much about this being our 25th-anniversary tour is that we've never really stopped, except for the year that I was in the joint. One way or another, we've worked together every year since we started."

The band opened its current five-month North American tour in June with a rare club show, at L.A.'s House of Blues. It will include shows Oct. 17 and 18 at the Universal Amphitheatre.

Asked whether there was any talk of bringing in erstwhile cohort Young for the new record, Crosby grins.

"Let's put it this way," he says. "You don't bring Neil Young anyplace. 'Neil, over here please' just doesn't apply. It's never worked that way. And, frankly, I love the guy, but he needs us like a stag needs a hatrack. Once in a while, when we really need to pull out the horsepower, we'll get together.

291

"We did it at Bill Graham's wake [in 1991], and it was one of the best afternoons we've had in many years. And friends of mine who are totally honest with me—Phil Lesh and Jerry Garcia from the [Grateful] Dead and Robin Williams—heard that and said, 'That's the real stuff. What's the matter with you guys? Why don't you do that?'"

That's the question that producer Johns forced the group to confront as they made *After the Storm*, which will be released Aug. 16. CSN had always produced their own work, but, because they were unhappy with the sound of their last couple of albums, they brought in Johns in hopes of recapturing some of the magic.

"I set out to make a record that was true to the sound that excited all of us who loved Crosby, Stills & Nash at the beginning," Johns says.

The group says their newest songs do well among the old favorites in their concert sets. All three wrote for the album, and lyrically the material continues the familiar CSN weave of self-examination, romantic intrigue and political consciousness. The record also features a stark reading of the Beatles' "In My Life."

Adds Johns, "Bands that have been around as long as they have naturally try to change with the times and adapt what they do. But I felt now would be a great time to have a record that related a little more to what they used to be. That's what I set out to achieve, and they readily climbed on board."

The group wasn't so eager to return to Woodstock, though. They were ready to record and ready to tour, but they didn't see much point in playing at something they saw as an attempt to cash in on nostalgia.

But as the bill began to fill up with acts such as Aerosmith, Nine Inch Nails, Cypress Hill and the Red Hot Chili Peppers, CSN decided they could stop worrying about the day's cultural significance and simply enjoy the show.

Crosby holds out hope that some of that original spirit will surface even at this tightly scheduled, highly organized '90s-era event.

"Old unreconstructed hippie that I am, I've been trying to cause as much trouble as I can," he says, smiling. "I'm loudly predicting that at this carefully managed 250,000-people event, 2.8 million people will show up, and I'm hoping it becomes a self-fulfilling prophecy.

"If every Grateful Dead fan in the country packs up their tie-dye and gets there, nobody would be happier than me. I'd love to see a 10-mile-long tailgate party on the New York Thruway. It'd be nice to think that there are still some things that aren't totally manageable."

Nash says that despite the trip back to Woodstock, CSN remains intently focused on its future and the music to come.

"I suppose we could spend time dwelling on how meaningful we are, and how important the last 25 years are, but we don't. We're lucky to take it a day at a time. We can't continually look into the past, because that's not who we are anymore.

"We've all grown as musicians, and we've expanded as people." He rests a hand on his midsection and cocks an eyebrow. "Please smile when you say we've expanded."

Stills says he is simply looking forward to a weekend of good music and better accommodations than they had 25 years ago.

"Of course we had mixed feelings about going back to Woodstock," he says, "but we're going to have fun with it. We just want to arrive early and get a good parking space. We've got a much nicer tour bus this time around, and as long as I'm on the bus, I know I'll be comfortable."

STEPHEN STILLS

BY PARKE PUTERBAUGH
Posted on the Rock and Roll Hall
of Fame and Museum Web site
May 1997

Veteran journalist Parke Puterbaugh chatted with Stephen Stills a week before the musician was inducted into the Rock and Roll Hall of Fame as a member of Crosby, Stills & Nash and Buffalo Springfield on May 6, 1997. Puterbaugh elicited a number of fresh views from Stills on various aspects of his his music and career. This interview was originally posted on the Rock and Roll Hall of Fame and Museum Web site.

Stephen Stills at home with his White Falcon and other Gretsch guitars. Beverly Hills. 1997. Photo: Henry Diltz

*A*s a member of both Buffalo Springfield and Crosby, Stills & Nash, Stephen Stills is the first musician to be inducted into the Rock and Roll Hall of Fame twice in a single year. One of the pivotal musical figures of the rock and roll era, singer/songwriter/guitarist Stills formed Buffalo Springfield with Neil Young, Richie Furay, Dewey Martin and Bruce Palmer in Los Angeles in

297

1966. Their biggest hit was Stills' folk-rock protest song "For What It's Worth," but the group's three far-ranging, eclectic albums left a huge legacy in terms of defining the various styles rock and roll could encompass: folk, rock, country, pop, R&B, orchestrated, avant-garde and more. When the group fell apart at the end of the decade, Stills teamed up with David Crosby (late of the Byrds) and Graham Nash (late of the Hollies) to form Crosby, Stills & Nash, whose harmony-rich, socially conscious music has been part of the musical landscape for nearly thirty years. Reached on the road during a recent CSN tour, Stills talked freely about his musical associations and feelings on being the first dually inducted rock and roller.

I think it's unprecedented in the history of these things that anyone has gotten into the Rock and Roll Hall of Fame twice in the same year.

I'm tickled pink to be part of this, and you could never have convinced me that they'd both happen in the same year. I thought they would cancel each other out, you know? I thought half the voters would vote for Buffalo Springfield, half would vote for Crosby, Stills & Nash, and it wouldn't be enough to get either one in. Now that they're both in, I'm just going to say thank you and get off the stage before they figure out I shouldn't be there! [laughs] It's cool with me. You're going to watch one bedazzled kid on his diplomatic best because he has two bands to make sure everybody gets their props. We're really looking forward to being there, and, like I said, I'm flattered beyond measure. I'm just hoping Neil shows up with a guitar.

Of course, David will now be in twice, with the Byrds and Crosby, Stills & Nash. I was thinking that when Graham gets in with the Hollies, it will be a hat trick for you guys.

Robert Hilburn asked me who I thought should get in, and he surprised me so bad I kind of went, "Uh...." So then when the *New York Times* guy asked, I finally remembered to say, "The Hollies, and then the whole group will be happy."

I always have viewed the Buffalo Springfield as the great American rock band, in that you touched on so many different kinds of music that it was really a sort of melting pot.

Well, the family tree alone...Richie went on to another great band [Poco]. David was almost an honorary member of the Buffalo Springfield. So it's all this potpourri of guys who were hanging around Southern California.

Who do you consider Buffalo Springfield's official bassist? In terms of the definitive lineup, is it Bruce Palmer or Jim Messina?

Bruce Palmer, absolutely. I hope that the Hall of Fame was able to contact and notify him. It could be that Messina should be part of it, too.

CSN at Kent State University, Ohio. May 4, 1997. Photo: Dave Zimmer

Basically, Neil's been on top of all that. I've been on the road, so I've been kind of out of pocket for those decisions, especially the really ticklish diplomatic ones. It's like *The Razor's Edge*; it's a lose-lose situation. To be fair, I have no idea what to do. I think Jimmy should probably be part of it, because he produced one record and then became the bass player.

Is Dewey Martin still around?

Yeah, he's around. He's all excited and thrilled about it and calls everyone regularly.

Where's the Springfield boxed set that's been rumored to be in the making for years?

Well, Neil was working on it. I've been house-hunting and on the road and haven't really had a chance to get up there [to work on it with him]. He had it all laid out, and it was really beautiful. We've just kept saying, "Next week I'll be sure to come; just call me and we'll make finalized plans" and all that stuff.

Have you communicated with him about this event? Do you guys have anything up your sleeve?

We were going to rehearse Buffalo Springfield, but Neil couldn't get everybody together to make sure they could get there for a day of rehearsal and he kind of got cold feet, so I think he's just going to come in and get his award and that's it. That's the last I heard from Elliot Roberts [Young's manager]. That's what I've been told.

Anything can happen at these events.

Exactly. If you turn him and me loose, there's no telling what could happen.

I last saw you two together onstage during the Stills-Young Band tour in 1976. Have you and Neil had much of a chance to jam around since then?

Yeah, we've rehearsed the Springfield a couple of times, and we've done some work at my house. But we haven't been onstage together, and I think it would really be deliciously fun.

Back on the cover of the first Buffalo Springfield album, there's a line to the effect that "Steve is the leader, but we all are." What did that mean? What was it like trying to...

...lead with everybody being the leader? Exactly what you might think it would be! [laughs] But it worked out. We basically assimilated everybody's ideas, and it was just wonderful.

How do you think a band like Buffalo Springfield would fare in today's musical climate?

The thought of tattoos and body mutilation scares me. It's actually nothing I want to have anything to do with. But who knows? People keep discovering this band, and I always hear about young groups doing covers. It's hard to remember being that young and that smart and stupid at the same time.

Who did you write the Buffalo Springfield song "Rock and Roll Woman" about? Did you have a particular person in mind?

I'll never tell. A lady needs to have her secrets!

I saw Crosby, Stills & Nash a couple summers ago and was very impressed with the way you all sounded and looked. You, in particularly, seemed to be pretty fit.

Yeah, that was the beginning of it, and I really lost a lot of weight the next few months. This year has been a lot of sitting around the house and house hunting and stupid things, so I've slipped a bit, but not much. My size 42 tuxedo still fits me!

What was the segue between Buffalo Springfield and Crosby, Stills & Nash? Was there anything in between for you?

That's when I met Jimi Hendrix. We did some things together, some of which have seen the light of day and some of which we're going to unearth at some point. Ahmet [Ertegun] gave me leeway to go into the studio, so I was fiddling around deciding what to do next. David and I were hanging around, then Graham came along. Cass Elliot [of the Mamas and the Papas] sort of made it happen. She was the empress: "I dub thee a trio!" She said, "You want a three-part harmony. You should come over and meet this guy [Nash]. Just leave it to me." So Crosby calls me up and says, "We have to go

300

to Cass'. Demands that we come." That's where we sang for the first time and the rest, as we say, is history.

The first CSN record came out in '69. It really started to foreshadow a lot of things that began to happen in the early '70s with more acoustic music, what now gets called "unplugged."

Indeed. Actually, we did "Unplugged" once, and I was so sick I couldn't talk. I couldn't get anybody to realize it was really stupid to do this when I was sick. So we did not do that well, and it should have been one of our finer moments. I dunno. We seem to be destined to do all of our great shows in places like Manikota, Minnesota.

You guys were unplugged long before that term was coined.

The best combination was when we did some shows without the rhythm section. I played electric guitar and Crosby and Nash played acoustics. That really worked out cool. I like what we got going now. We've got the best fans we've ever had, and everybody's really gentlemanly and friends. We're having a delightful good time.

How's David getting along?

He's great. Of course, if there's a bug going around, he gets it worse than anybody. Most of us can shake it off with vitamin C. David's a little more complicated than that. But he's in fine fettle and good attitude and has a great take on things. We've all got really nice, good new songs to bring to the table for our shows.

What's on the recording horizon? Anything in the works?

As it comes, you know. When we've got a couple, we go in. If we don't have anything to do, we don't sit there and waste a lot of money. We just get 'em going as they appear, and when it's done, it's done.

CROSBY PLAYS HIS HEART

BY JOEL SELVIN
San Francisco Chronicle
August 29, 1997

David Crosby was tested once again in the mid '90s when he was diagnosed with Hepatitis C and had to undergo a liver transplant. He and his wife Jan also welcomed a baby boy, Django, into the world and he reunited with a son, James Raymond, whom he had fathered and put up for adoption in the late '60s. Crosby talked about the latest chapter of his life with *San Francisco Chronicle* pop music critic Joel Selvin.

Django, Jan and David Crosby. 1997. Photo: Dave Zimmer

D avid Crosby was dying. His wife was pregnant. And the son he gave up for adoption more than 30 years earlier discovered who his father was.

"When he found out—not to put too fine a point on it—I was dying," said Crosby, who underwent a liver transplant in November 1994; a few months later his wife, Jan, gave birth to their son, Django.

Crosby has spent the last few weeks in a Santa Monica recording studio making what he thinks is some of his best music ever. Among his collaborators is his long-lost son, James Raymond, who has been a professional musician himself for nearly 20 years. Along with guitarist Jeff Pevar, they are the Crosby-Pevar-Raymond Band. In the way his other band, Crosby, Stills & Nash, reduces to the initials CSN, Crosby calls this group CPR.

"Music to restart your heart isn't a bad idea," he said. The band will appear tomorrow at Wavy Gravy's annual fundraiser, the Hog Farm's "No Dog" Pignic at Black Oak Ranch, outside Laytonville off Highway 101.

CPR: Jeff Pevar, David Crosby and James Raymond. 1998. Photo: Henry Diltz

Raymond, 34, began his search for his biological parents when he was getting married a few years ago. "When I first saw his name on some paper, I thought it's some other guy named David Crosby," said Raymond.

Raymond happened to meet keyboardist Mike Finnigan, Crosby's longtime musical associate, who encouraged him to contact Crosby. At the same time, Raymond's adoptive parents, without his knowledge, sent Crosby a letter. After an initial phone call, father and son arranged a meeting at a coffee shop near the UCLA campus.

"I was wrought up with emotion," said Crosby, 56. "We had to go outside to talk. I was on the verge of tears because I felt like I went AWOL on this kid and I'd been beating myself up about it for 30 years."

But, according to Crosby, the first thing his son wanted to tell him was that his life had been wonderful and his adoptive parents loved him well. "It was as if he was reading my mind," said Crosby, "and soothing me in places where I felt I hadn't done the right thing."

Crosby, inducted into the Rock and Roll Hall of Fame in 1991 as a member of the Byrds, didn't mention the child he gave up in his otherwise candid 500-page 1988 autobiography.

Raymond, who said he knew Crosby's music mainly from the radio, plays keyboards and has worked as a journeyman musician in Los Angeles for many years, playing recording sessions and backing touring musicians.

He recently played in the backup band for the Spice Girls' U.S. television appearances.

The day after he met his biological father, his own daughter was born.

"He's more like a brother than a son," said Crosby. "We're raising these kids together. Our wives love each other."

Crosby, who preferred not to talk about Raymond's mother, said he and Raymond have been writing fabulous music together. "It's a fountain of songs," he said. "I've written four, five or six of the best songs I've ever written in the past six months. I gave him a set of words to 'Morrison' and it came back sounding like a Steely Dan demo. It's the most growth I've felt, the most fun I've had since the *Wind on the Water* period with Nash or the original record with CSN."

Raymond echoed those sentiments. "I'm getting to make music with one of the greatest songwriters of our time," he said.

But Crosby, a large-hearted spirit whose ebullience can sometimes make him seem like an overgrown puppy, is beside himself with how his life is going since his brush with death.

"I'm not complaining," he said. "A, I didn't die. B, I have the greatest little son. And C, James is like a bolt of lightning from the sky. Whoever's running this thing, thanks! Life is good."

TALK TALK: GRAHAM NASH

BY BILL DEYOUNG
Goldmine
June 19, 1998

The year 1998 found CSN working occasionally as a trio, CPR (Crosby-Pevar-Raymond) recording and touring, the Stephen Stills Band hitting the club and casino circuit, Young recording some of the songs that would ultimately become part of another solo album, *Silver and Gold*, and Nash pursing a variety of projects on his own. Writer Bill DeYoung, in the *Goldmine* magazine column, "Talk Talk," portrayed Nash as the keeper of the flame, the guiding force. He talked about the release of a classic 1971 Crosby and Nash concert on CD, working with Crosby and Stills, and why more CSNY rarities were not included on the CSN boxed set. Nash emerged, once again, as a man who gets things done.

Graham Nash. Photo: Henry Diltz

Nearly 30 years into his partnership with David Crosby and Stephen Stills, Graham Nash has become the keeper of the flame, the bearer of the torch, the one who cares enough to make sure things are done properly. Maybe Nash's name should've been the one in the middle, because he's been keeping Crosby and Stills from killing one another for years now. He certainly helped steer Crosby away from a reckless suicide.

The one-time member of the Hollies has been Crosby's Siamese twin and most vocal cheerleader since the days of "Guinnevere" and "Long Time Gone," and he staunchly stood by his cohort when everyone else had run away screaming because of Crosby's rampant and destructive drug abuse. When Crosby was released from a Texas prison in 1986, Nash's house—a very, very, very fine house—was the first place he went.

Nash's high harmonies and sweet, simplistic songs have always offered the perfect Yin to Crosby's dark, complex Yang—and they've recorded and performed as a duo since 1971, after *Crosby, Stills & Nash* and *Déjà Vu* had already made household names of the trio (and, of course, with addition of Neil Young, the quartet).

Recently, Nash pulled together *Another Stoney Evening* from tapes of a '71 Crosby-Nash show at the Dorothy Chandler Pavilion in Los Angeles, and its exotic, quixotic songcraft serves as a reminder of just how brilliant—how damn moving—they were in their salad days. Released on the independent Grateful Dead Records, it's intended as the first in a series.

Of course, Crosby, Stills & Nash as a group are still together and still doing decent box office, just as there are still the occasional Crosby-Nash concerts.

Nash and his wife Susan, married 21 years, have three children—and yet the legacy is also Graham's baby. He's the one who added the extra tracks to the CD reissue of *4 Way Street*, and he assembled *CSN*, the four-disc box set, in 1994 (over the objections, as you're about to read, of Young and his manager, the estimable Elliot Roberts).

Since 1989, Nash and a partner have operated Nash Editions, a digital fine art press that distributes prints by artists including David Hockney, Francesco Clemente and Jamie Wyeth. And *LifeSighs*, his acclaimed one-man stage show, will soon make a reappearance in several major cities.

Graham and Susan have homes in California and Hawaii. Annual Christmas guests at the couple's island home included drummer Russ Kunkel and his wife, Nicolette Larson.

Graham was one of the visitors in Nicolette's hospital room the day she died last November. "She was only in the hospital a week," he says sadly. "It was massive liver failure, that put her in a coma, and that gave her a brain hemorrhage. A terrible thing."

Not surprisingly, Nash was the man behind two February concerts in Santa Monica, benefits for the UCLA Children's Hospital, with a special pediatric endowment fund set up in Larson's name.

Along with Jackson Browne, Linda Ronstadt. Bonnie Raitt and others, the bill included Crosby, Stills & Nash, as harmonious as ever even though Neil Young, who'd promised to attend, was a no-show.

The beat goes on.

Tell me about *Another Stoney Evening*. I, for one, thought it was great to go back there.

When I was pulling together the box set several years ago, I took the opportunity to get all our tapes archived professionally. I went into everybody's tape vaults and put 'em all in chronological order, and put 'em all into a database. So I see there the multi-tracks for the Dorothy Chandler show. And I know that the bootleg called *A Very Stoney Evening* was supposed to be the Dorothy Chandler show. I check it out—it's not the same show. So I go "Shit! Where did that come from?" It was obviously an audience tape.

Well, we still haven't found the multi-tracks—we think it was one of our shows at Berkeley—and I said, why don't we just bootleg ourselves? When we listened to the multi-tracks, it was a great show. And I remember it being a great show. Because David was very sick that night. He had a temperature of, like, 105 or something really out there. He was going to cancel the show and I said, "We can't cancel the show, it's L.A., it's our gig." So we did the show, but he was pretty spacey, and we were very high at the time, also.

Why is it out on Grateful Dead Records?

In the meantime, Crosby, Stills & Nash have left Atlantic because we are extremely upset that they're taking no notice of us, and not servicing us, and not putting any energy into CSN, who have made them millions and millions of dollars over the years. And I understand the new kid on the block theory, cause we were there at one point. But I also understand people selling millions of records in their latter life as recording artists.

We'd left Atlantic, and we were looking for alternative ways of marketing our music—checking into the net, mail-order, direct response and all those other ways of making sales. And Stephen Barncard, who mixed it with me, said why are we reinventing the wheel here? He said that Grateful Dead Records had a database of 30,000 loyal Deadhead fans, and they would love to do it. So we did—and it was the first piece of non-Dead material that Grateful Dead Records have put out, and they've been very good so far.

In those days, what did you get out of a Crosby-Nash show that you didn't get from the other thing?

The ability to make a left turn whenever I wanted. You gotta understand, with Crosby, sometimes he appears very spaced to people, but he's unbelievably focused. So if I say, "Hey David, you want to do 'Triad'?" he'll give it a shot. He's got great courage and so do I. Two years ago, we did a show at Westbury Music Fair back east, and we asked them "OK! What do you want us to play?" And we did the entire two-and-a-half-hour show from requests.

Crosby and I never stayed to the hits, which is probably one of the charming things about Crosby-Nash: You never really knew what to expect.

What do you and Crosby give to each other that others can't?

I think what I provide for him is stability and accuracy. I am so linked, psychically, with David, that if we're in the middle of a song and I know that he's gonna fuck up the next line, I can make the same mistake so it comes out correct to the audience. I've done that so many times, and he looks at me with his walrus smile and I know that that's very valuable to David.

What he gives to me is an unbelievably unique musical framework. There's nobody I know that plays music like David. It's completely foreign to me. I can't play those jazz chords. That's not me; I'm much more simple than that.

He's been straight a long time now. Are there days when you, his friend, can't even remember what he was like during the worst period?

I have this ability to take everybody as "How are you today?" And he's been clean and straight for 11, 12 years, and that's how I remember him now. I mean, why would I want to go there? It's so painful. Why would I want to pull those negative images and keep them in my mind?

If I want to, I can remember every fucking moment of his madness. But I don't want to do that. I'd rather see him as he is now, strong, trying his best, still exploring musical avenues that baffle me.

What about his liver transplant? Were you amazed that he came out of it in full vigor?

No, I knew he would. He's a Leo, and he must be on his 12th life. He's a hard fucker to kill, this guy. [Laughing] God knows he's tried.

We're approaching the 30th anniversary of CSN. Are you suprised to still be doing it after so long?

Frankly, yes. It was such an amazing sound right off the bat that I knew that when you put that kind of sound with the kinds of songs we had then, if that was the tip of the iceberg it was going to go on for a few years. But 30? I don't think so.

It's no secret that there's no love lost between Crosby and Stills. What's your relationship like with Stills?

I'm a little more compassionate with Stephen than David is. I know all our weaknesses, and all our strengths. And what I do is try and concentrate on the strengths.

It's true, David and Stephen have butted heads many, many times. I'm the kind of person that wants to smooth out everything because we've got a job to do. And I know that some of that tension adds to the music; I also know that once it goes over the edge, then no music gets made.

That's why I wrote "Wasted on the Way." We've made a lot of music in 30 years, but there's a tremendous amount of music that never got made. How about the *Human Highway* album? Never got made. It was fucking great; we knew exactly what the 10 tracks were. I'm looking at the fucking cover right now, hanging on my wall.

The point being that yes, tension gets in the way, but I don't want it to stop forward motion.

Since sales aren't there for CSN, and haven't been the issue for some time, wouldn't it have been easier to say "Let's just do Crosby-Nash, have fun, and not have this other thing to worry about?"

Yeah, it's true, but think about what you're saying. There'd be no CSN sound again. And that's painful to me. I can't accept that.

I'm a pretty logical man. So I go "Well, maybe we're not doing it any more." But the *After the Storm* record, I thought that deserved a better shot than Atlantic gave it. So if the record company isn't putting any effort into it, I can't take all the blame.

So maybe if it's not paying the rent we should just do what we want. But I want to do CSN. Because it's an incredibly special sound.

Yes, I want to do Crosby-Nash too, because that is very special in its own way, too. But I don't want to kill CSN.

Do you have to talk Crosby into it: "Let's hook up with Stills again?"

Yeah. It's not David's favorite thing. I'll be honest with you. But once the opening bars of whatever the first song is, David's off his trip. And he's getting into it, because music takes over.

I've seen Crosby feeling so shitty 10 minutes before a show—liver bothering him, got a cold, can't do it, fuck, man…and the opening bars happen, and he's right there. And for two and a half hours he's forgotten his trip with Stephen, and he's forgotten the fact that he's not feeling great. And he's flying.

Does it bother you that you're not selling records in today's market?

It does, because I'm a communicator. And I want to sell millions of records, not for the monetary gain, but for the fact that people are listening to our music and being helped by our music. And that's my biggest pain here.

The first duo album, *Graham Nash/David Crosby* on Atlantic, came out briefly on CD a year or two ago.

No, they pressed it, but it never got out. That was one of the backbreakers for us. That was heartbreaking that they would've had CDs…David phoned Atlantic and found out that they had pressed them and not serviced them, and we went fucking crazy.

That was the point where we decided that they didn't give a fuck about us. Because, if they can press a record and not give a shit, that's a great indicator of how they feel about us.

Wasn't there some sort of difficulty getting Neil's stuff for the CSN box set?

Well, what happens with Neil is that you get caught between the good cop/bad cop thing between him and Elliot. I talk to Neil, and Neil's totally into it, I can use anything I want—great. I'll be discreet and use only great stuff. And Elliot calls me and says, "No, man, you can only use seven things."

I said, "I'm not gonna play your fucked game. When you put your box set out, you can use anything that you want." Because I gotta tell you, they were fucking with history. And they have no right to do that. We did all that work with Neil, we should've been able to use whatever the fuck we wanted. Because we were making an historical document. I wanted to put "Pushed It Over the End" on so bad. And I'll never forgive Neil or Elliot for that, and you can fuckin' print that in headlines if you want. Because I'm pissed with them.

This wasn't "Let me use as many Neil songs [as possible], cause we'll sell more records." It was nowhere near that. I wanted to represent what music CSN and CSNY had done in their careers.

Have you spoken with Neil about it since it happened?

No. But I won't play that game.

Oh. I did talk to Neil, and I said, "I didn't like that game, but as far as I'm concerned, when you want to come to us and seek permission, you can use anything you want." For the historical document that Neil is preparing.

I didn't say, "Well, you wouldn't let us, so we're not gonna let you…" I don't give a fuck about that, because this is history.

So is the CSN box set therefore flawed to you?

It is flawed, yes.

Didn't "Pushed It Over the End" come out somewhere in '74?

There's a live "Pushed It Over the End" with studio overdubbed vocals. I believe it came out in Italy, if my memory serves me right.

Tell me about your stage show *LifeSighs*.

I spent five years putting it together. I did six shows in Philadelphia, and then everybody wanted to rock 'n' roll for a couple of years, so I kind of had to abandon it. But I'm not finished with it, because it was a very satisfying piece to do, to have technically pulled off what I did was amazingly satisfying to me.

Basically, I'd go out there with my guitar and my piano, and a 30-foot by 17-foot high definition screen, and a wireless mouse, and I would start talking. And I would use my life as I use my songs. Everybody's been through what I've been through.

I'd go through the important parts of my life, the decisions in my life that brought me to that very performance. And I'd let them know that whatever you did out there in your life, every decision you've ever made in your life, brought you to this performance tonight. And let's go on this journey. My life is the same as your life, and you're gonna find very similar things here.

Do you plan on doing this again?

It will come up again. Right now, I'm trying to negotiate, and I'm getting good results, with the Museum of Modern Art in New York and in San Francisco.

What happens to CSN now, recording-wise?

Well, we're entertaining some very interesting offers. Because, quite frankly, I'd rather be with a small company that was clamoring for us, that's thrilled to have us, than a big company that doesn't give a shit.

CSNY: Déjà Vu All Over Again

BY JOEL SELVIN
San Francisco Chronicle
October 9, 1999

In 1999, Neil Young dropped into a CSN recording session in progress, decided to stay and a CSNY project evolved. With a new studio album complete and a North American Tour mapped out, CSNY was ready to meet the press in October of that year. Even though Graham Nash had broken both legs in a recent boating accident, he and his fellow bandmates were loose and jovial. *San Francisco Chronicle* writer Joel Selvin prompted a number of memorable remarks from the musicians as CSNY held court in the St. Francis Hotel in San Francisco.

Crosby, Stills, Nash & Young take a break outside Conway Studios, Los Angeles, during the recording of *Looking Forward*. 1999. Photo: Henry Diltz

"CSNY2K" is coming. The title for the 41-city Crosby, Stills, Nash & Young tour that starts in January may seem obvious, but it did give the band members an opportunity to crack jokes about possible T-shirt slogans.

"CSNY2K—Ask Your Parents," suggested Neil Young.

"CSNY2K—You're Not Ready," said David Crosby.

The four horsemen ride again. On October 26, CSNY will release a new album, *Looking Forward*, an event that happens about as often as a solar eclipse. Tours are even rarer. Their last tour 25 years ago invented the stadium rock concert, an epochal enterprise that was the biggest-grossing tour at that point in history. The new tour dates, including the Bay Area, will be announced Tuesday.

All four rockers—Young is 53, Stills 54, Nash 57 and Crosby 58—spent the better part of the last two days in the General MacArthur Suite at the St. Francis Hotel, meeting the press two at a time, seated throne-like behind a coffee table covered with plants and candles. Graham Nash, originally not expected to attend, was cheerful as usual, despite having broken both his legs in a boating accident three weeks ago in Hanalei Bay on Kauai, where he lives.

"I'm OK from the knees up," he said.

The reunion album was born when Young and Stephen Stills were working together on a box set for their old band Buffalo Springfield, which predates CSNY. Stills asked Young to play on one of his songs that Crosby, Stills & Nash were recording.

"We didn't plan it," said Crosby. "We didn't talk about it, think about it or do it. We didn't focus on anything except the music that was in front of us. If we do that, it works like a charm."

"Those were good days," agreed Young. "We never talked about doing a CSNY album. It was just obvious that we were.

"I came down," Young continued, "I was just visiting, and the tunes were real good. They were making a record. They started it because they wanted to—not because the label told them it was time or anything like that—and that's a great reason to do it. I could hear that from the first note."

Crosby, Stills & Nash didn't have a record contract and were financing the sessions themselves. The trio, whose first album was released in 1969, has been working steadily since Crosby was released from a Texas jail in 1986, where he served a year on drug charges. While the group remains a concert attraction, its infrequent latter-day recordings have largely been lackluster affairs widely ignored by the public.

With Young on board, the band's commercial prospects brighten considerably. Alone among the four, Young has long established himself as a solo artist, and the Crosby, Stills, Nash & Young configuration echoes the band's glory days in 1970 when the first CSNY album, *Déjà Vu*, was No. 1 and songs like "Teach Your Children," "Ohio" and "Our House" were everywhere. Their 1988 reunion, *American Dream*, is not as well remembered.

"We get together whenever we feel like it," said Young. "Obviously it doesn't happen all that often—this is our third record. We're on a roll."

To select the 12 songs that appear on *Looking Forward*, the group posted a list of all the songs recorded, and each musician put a check mark beside songs he wanted to include. On the first pass, they chose nine songs unanimously. "The next part took a month," said Stills.

Although the album contains only new originals, the group experimented recording some old songs—"Turn Turn Turn" from Crosby's old group, the Byrds, and the Springfield oldie, "Rock and Roll Woman," with Joe Walsh on guitar.

"We did an old song of mine called 'White Line,'" said Young, "one that I don't recall releasing at all. We did a great version, too. Then the engineer said he also liked the one I did on *Ragged Glory*. I was shocked. Senior moment No. 58."

"See how much we like you?" said Crosby. "We didn't even rag on you."

The fellows were getting a little giddy after all the questions and cameras. Crosby was apparently still thinking T-shirts when an interviewer asked what he hopes fans will come away from the concerts with.

"Smiles," said Crosby. "And merchandise."

FOUR PLAY: CROSBY, STILLS, NASH & YOUNG

BY GARY GRAFF
Guitar World
February 2000

Of all of the CSNY interviews and articles that came out in the wake of the release of the group's 1999 album, *Looking Forward*, and subsequent CSNY2K tour, this piece by *Guitar World* contributing editor Gary Graff was my favorite. It captured the essence of the four musicians equally. Focusing primarily on the present and recent past, with just enough historical perspective, Graff got each of the guys talking and sharing thoughts about a great range of topics of pertinence and passion.

Stephen Stills and Neil Young at the Palace, Auburn Hills, Michigan.
Photo: Tony Bittick

The shades are drawn. The candles are lit. Platters of food are ready in the hallway, next to tables laden with bottles of soft drinks and juice. Artwork from the new album—their first in 11 years—has been taped onto the walls.

And in the suite at New York City's posh Hotel Pierre, David Crosby, Stephen Stills and Graham Nash are having a grand time talking about the way Neil Young plays the guitar.

"I read a great quote from you, Stephen," says Nash, who's in a wheelchair due to a boating accident that badly broke both of his legs. "It said, 'Well, you know, my guitar playing is a little more toward Eric Clapton and Jeff Beck, whereas Neil, he's got that spear-in-the-back dance.'"

325

The "spear-in-the-back dance"?

"You just have to see it," explains Stills. "You have to experience it. It's a whole experience."

"It's tribal, baby, tribal," adds Nash.

"I don't mean to say the spear-in-the-back thing implies a certain awkwardness or lack of grace," says Stills, elaborating on the subject. "It's the whole unique thing of being Neil, which is like a universe unto itself and of which I am proud to be a satellite."

Crosby, perhaps sensing that all of this may be drifting toward the other side of irreverence—particularly with Young in a chair just a few feet away, rolling his eyes—steps in to bring some perspective to the conversation.

"Neil conveys a lot of energy and a lot of intensity," he explains. "And like everything else he does, he doesn't do it like anybody else. But he does convey it. You'll see; it's easier to see it than talk about it."

All eyes turn to Young, who is sitting in a chair with his legs crossed under him. "It's the way I play guitar," he says with a shrug. "You have to be there."

We are there. Again. During the past year and a half, the planets have aligned, the circumstances have coincided and the egos have sublimated enough to allow for one of the periodic reunions of Crosby, Stills, Nash & Young. The supergroup that became one of the defining points for the Woodstock generation, CSNY are back in action with the optimistically titled *Looking Forward* (Warner Bros.), their first album since 1988's *American Dream* (Atlantic) and only the third studio project of the quartet's association. On January 24, 2000, the group hits the road for the first time since 1974, launching the "CSNY2K" tour in suburban Detroit, a three-month arena jaunt that will command up to $200 for the premium seats.

How they came to this point in time is a tale of early successes and squandered opportunities, of public fights and private reconciliations, of drug arrests and rehabilitation, both physical and spiritual. From the beginning, there was an air of restlessness to the group. When Crosby, Stills & Nash first came together in 1969, they were a trio of disgruntled musicians who had each made a name for himself in a previous band: Stills with the Buffalo Springfield, Crosby with the Byrds and Nash with the Hollies. Each had left his respective band, searching for new musical adventures. Introduced either by Mama Cass Elliot or Joni Mitchell (nobody seems to remember, or agree), they forged a trio with a formidable musical pedigree which manifested itself in the group's landmark 1969 album. Titled simply *Crosby, Stills & Nash*, the record grabbed the rock world with its homogeneous vocal blend, Stills' nimble guitar work and songs heavy with meaning, both romantic ("Suite: Judy Blue Eyes") and political (the anti-war "Wooden Ships").

Wanting to bolster their live presentation, the trio approached Neil Young, who had been Stills' bandmate in the Buffalo Springfield. Young agreed to come aboard—but only on the condition that he could join as a full-time creative partner. Their second gig was at the original Woodstock festival in 1969, a fitting launch for what was to be one of the most celebrated and turbulent collaborations in rock and roll's pantheon.

There's no question CSNY had the musical goods. Whether it was the timeless sentiments of campfire singalongs like "Our House" and "Teach Your Children," the hippie aesthetic of "Carry On" or the group's own particular brand of raging against the machine via the pointed social commentary of "Almost Cut My Hair" and "Ohio," the quartet did it with style, taste and some of the most exquisite harmonies ever to grace rock and roll. And if its albums seemed a bit, well, tame, the group's concerts—as captured on 1971's live *4 Way Street*—showed that it could get a little fierce, as evidenced by extended versions of "Carry On" and Young's "Southern Man."

But these were volatile, combustible, creative, control-freak personalities, which meant the next 30 years were marked by rumors more than actual reunions, a paucity of product and enough trials and tribulations to fill a month's worth of *Behind the Music* episodes. Of course, none of that has hurt the group's mystique, and the undercurrent of drama has made their occasional appearances, such as the 1985 Live Aid concert in Philadelphia and the 1990 benefit concert for former drummer Dallas Taylor, that much more special.

This time, however, they're playing for keeps. With the release of *Looking Forward,* CSNY is beginning the 21st century as a friendly, affable, music-making entity, keenly aware of the time they have wasted on the way and hopeful that the album and tour are the first steps in a continuing collaboration rather than just more blips on the timeline.

"There's a lot of unfinished business," says Young. "I don't think we really reached our potential, and so we have a lot of things to show and a lot of things to do. This is why it's so exciting: there are things that we started doing on the record that show us the future. I mean, this band can sing like the Byrds and jam like the Dead...and hopefully we can get the audience turned on to what we're doing and have it just be a music thing."

Guitar World: The current CSNY reunion began with a journey through the past, if you will. Young had taken the lead in compiling a Buffalo Springfield box set, due for release sometime this year, and invited Stills to his compound in Northern California to hear what he'd put together.

Stephen Stills: I went up to the ranch, and Neil and I relived our childhood, literally. And we laughed and cried and had to stop and walk outside and have a brewski and calm down and go back in, 'cause we saw ourselves grow up and grow apart, the whole thing.

GW: You could hear that process on record?

Neil Young: Oh, yeah, you can definitely hear it. It's one of the saddest things you'll ever hear. It's beautifully documented, and it's chronological and there's nothing to say. It's all just there.

Stills: So I went back up the next week, and this time I brought my new Stephen Stills signature Martin acoustic, which we've been working on and driving Martin crazy with, trying to get it just right. I wanted to show it off. [*laughs*] So I took it up with me and said, "Oh, by the way, I have this song." I played it for him, and he said, "That's a really cool song." I said, "Would you like to come down to L.A. and play it with me? 'Cause we're doing a CSN record we're financing ourselves." He said, "Sure, man. I got a couple of things to do, then I'll be right there."

GW: At the time, Young was working on a new acoustic album, titled *Silver and Gold*, and he was still in the midst of putting together his long-promised retrospective box set of his own music. But he made good on his promise to Stills. He loaded two guitars and an amplifier into one of his vintage autos and drove down the California coast to the studio where Crosby, Stills & Nash were making an album independent of a major-label deal.

And what Young found there impressed him immensely.

Young: I came into the studio and discovered that they were working on a record by themselves, on their own and without the help of a record company. They had to finance it themselves, so obviously they were really into it. That's the only real good reason to play music. It gave me a good feeling all over again, that three guys who have been making music together for 30 years would still want to do it enough to finance a recording project. That's a fantastic testimony right there to why someone would want to be involved in that energy. It was all positive. And the music was really great.

Stills: Not having a record company was by design. But we also had to wait for another presidential impeachment and an unpopular war. [*laughs*]

David Crosby: It's sort of a formula with us—unpopular war, presidential impeachment, we work. Actually, there were several record companies interested in signing CSN, but we had just gotten free, by choice, from our previous record company. Atlantic just didn't seem interested in promoting our albums anymore.

Stills: And all those record companies would've had their ideas of what we should do, and that just doesn't work with this band. We're just going to be us—us right now, not us 20 years ago.

Graham Nash: I think once Neil saw our situation, and when he heard the music we were making, he found it much more enticing.

CSNY2K Tour: Stephen Stills, Neil Young, Graham Nash and David Crosby. First Union Center, Philadelphia. March 5, 2000. Photo: Roger Barone

Young: The first thing I heard was [Nash's] "Heartland." Then Stephen and I played on it. We actually played off each other and found some great parts. And away we went.

Nash: He's no fool. When I played him "Heartland," which at the time was a rough two-track demo I made for Crosby, he wanted a piece of that. He said, "I love that fucking song. Lemme sing on it. Lemme play on it. I've got ideas." That's how it all starts. It's all music driven.

Young: And it was just one song after another, one song at a time. We were never saying, "What are we doing?" We just took it one day at a time, until we went through the whole thing.

Crosby: I think we found the "key" to making this group work. We just didn't talk about what was going to happen or who was gonna do what or where it was all going. We didn't even talk about whether it was going to be a record or not. We didn't project. We didn't have expectations, which are real dangerous things because they hedge you in. What felt good was to just do the music that was on our plate at that second and stay focused on it. And doing that kept the right vibe going. I don't know how to explain it better than that.

Young: After I finished focusing on what they had, I brought some of my tunes down. I said, "They're yours. Go ahead and take the best ones that you think we can do the best job on, and we'll put those out and see what happens…one at a time."

Nash: It wasn't like he was hiding anything or keeping the best songs for his solo album or his box set. He just said, "Choose whatever you want." That showed great trust and a great commitment to doing a great piece of work.

GW: There are, of course, skeptics buzzing all around the periphery of the new CSNY lovefest, and you really can't blame them. After all, barely a month went by during the early seventies without some rumor of CSNY activity, even as the four pursued solo or duo endeavors. And while the album has been released and the tour appears to be a reality, it's hard to forget the harsh words, false starts and unfulfilled promises that litter the landscape of the past three decades.

"The four of us together is like juggling four bottles of nitroglycerin," Crosby said when *American Dream* was released more than a decade ago. "Yeah," responded Nash, "if you drop one, everything goes up in smoke."

But now, Nash says, "We're more than friends. We're brothers. And, unfortunately, brothers fight occasionally. But it's been 30 years; something's going on."

Ultimately, CSNY would like us to forget all the bad stuff. An album title like *Looking Forward*—named after one of the five songs Young contributed to the project—doesn't exactly invite an examination of the past. And when the topic comes up, Crosby shakes his head and says, "No, no, no, let's not go there."

But they do nevertheless.

Crosby: We've sort of made a policy of not issuing ultimatums. We have a system of working things out when we disagree—because we do disagree.

Nash: One of the main differences between then and now is that if anyone has an idea, we will chase that idea until it either works or it doesn't work. Previously we would have discounted ideas, and that's where you get into trouble, because we're each extremely good at making records. We've been doing this for 30 or 40 years, so we should be listened to. Everyone who makes their suggestions should feel that at least we tried, and that's all you can ask.

Stills: There was a lot more listening going on than ever before. There were no agendas, no tricks. One of the things we realized fairly early on in this project was that some of the ridiculous little kid games we used to play with each other—the ones that would make each of us mad and end up crashing the sessions—were really hysterically funny.

Young: It used to be if Stephen was singing flat or something, David would get on Stephen's case. And Graham and David, being better than Stephen, let him know that, "Hey, we're faster than you and this is fucked.

Why aren't you ready?" Now they realize everybody has their own speed, and that it's worth waiting for Stephen to get the part right. And with me it's even worse, 'cause I take longer than Stephen.

Nash: Once we all had the patience to wait, that process actually got faster. I remember when we were doing a song of David's that didn't make it onto this record, me and Neil did the vocals in a couple of takes. And they had quite a complicated harmonic structure.

Crosby: The key thing is what Neil said: let things happen at their own rate.

Nash: I hate when these personal things get in the way. The other guys realize that I want it all, I want all the best music, and I want it now. We're in a situation where we can make great music together, and I hate to have other things interfere with it.

GW: Drugs and alcohol, of course, have played a significant part in CSNY's turmoil over the years. Stills' and Crosby's habits, in particular, have been widely reported, and in Crosby's case resulted in his incarceration in 1985 and necessitated a liver transplant in 1994. Now the group present themselves as sober and in control, the only discernible problem being Stills' residual hearing loss that occasionally requires his bandmates to repeat comments and questions to him from close range.

Crosby: I probably have partied harder than anybody in the world. But 18 years clean has worked for me as a very good change, and I like it a lot. I can remember where I'm singing. I can remember who I'm singing to. I can function.

Young: He can actually sing.

Crosby: Yes, and all those things are good.

Stills: One of the things that occurs to me every time I see a TV show about some band, not one of these people say they really had a great time walking onstage all torn up. I have not heard one band say that was a cool thing to do.

Nash: And then there's Keith Richards…[*everyone laughs*]

Crosby: When you're young, you feel like you're bulletproof and 12-feet tall and will live forever. Young bands, I'm sure, still do get totally wrecked and play. But I don't think you'll find anybody in the singer-songwriter milieu who still wants to be wrecked when they try to play. I don't know of any of our contemporaries that try and do it, and I know them all. What we do requires you to be really on top of it.

GW: One of the things Young is most pleased about is that *Looking Forward* has returned the group to the single-microphone vocal recording style it employed during 1969, achieving what he calls the "air blend" of the quartet's voices. "People are looking for the magic of the four of us together, and the four of us together on one microphone is the essence of the magic that people like, and that, more importantly, we like," he says.

But there's another piece of the CSNY magic that often gets short shrift, and that's the way the group's members play their guitars. There are many moments of six-string transcendence throughout CSNY's canon, starting with Stills' dazzling display on "Suite: Judy Blues Eyes," the opening track from the *Crosby, Stills & Nash* album.

And there has been fire, too, in the group's playing, from the textured duels on "Wooden Ships" to the crunchy licks of "Woodstock" and "Ohio" to the all-out jams on the extended versions of "Carry On" and Young's "Southern Man" from 1971's live *4 Way Street* set.

At one point, Stills makes the observation that "Neil and I are finally working like we did back in the Springfield days," which seems like an apt point at which to steer CSNY into a guitar discussion.

GW: How was playing in Buffalo Springfield different from the way you play for CSNY?

Young: It wasn't. We're better now, but we're doing the same thing.

Stills: We get hooked up in that "psychic highway" thing and just run with it.

Nash: These two guys were interactive before the word was invented.

Young: [Stills] plays a great guitar. I know how to support his playing. And when I feel like playing lead, he can support me. That's the way we've always been. Sometimes we both play lead at the same time. I mean, this band can space out for 45 minutes.

GW: What do you do to support what Stephen is playing?

Young: It's hard to elaborate on that. Look at Keith Richards; he's a support guitar player. He plays great lead, too, but that's not what he really does. He's a great rhythm guitar player, and he plays great chords. He's supporting a groove. When Stephen plays, I have no problem making him sound better just by finding certain things that support what he's playing.

Nash: You have to listen to what the other guy's playing, too. He's actually conversing through his guitar. You don't want to interrupt a sentence.

Crosby: They both can do it. Stephen, along with being a great guitar player, is an unbelievable rhythm player because he has an unbelievable sense of time.

Stills: That's what allows you to become a decent lead guitar player; you've got to play rhythm first. That's why Keith Richards is also one of my favorite guitar players. He just lays down a pocket that will not quit. It's always cool, and you can put a whole stadium on that rhythm guitar and the place jumps.

GW: There is a particularly fierce guitar jam on the *Looking Forward* song "No Tears Left." How did it come about?

Stills: I started recording the track at my house with a drum machine. I put on one acoustic guitar part and sang along to it. Then Graham and David sang some harmonies on it, and I had this great doubled bass part.

Then we got to the studio and put the drums on it, and the next day I put a stack of Marshalls in the studio and played through it twice, then came back the next day and played it again. It was scary, because it was loud as shit. It was just great.

Then Neil came in with the coolest idea, and it was so simple. He said, "I don't know what I want to do; just record me singing and playing guitar at the same time." When it came to the "it's my life part," he thought it needed a counter line. So he sang and played in unison, and did it four times until he had it right. He basically blazed away and got it really quick, and what he did sets off the chorus perfectly. And there's this little place in the middle where he plays…well, only Neil can play that kind of guitar. So we have this blazing spot from me and these three great little notes where Neil comes in. But that's the trick—knowing how to lay back and wait for the cool little spot to get in there and do it.

GW: What kind of discernible, noticeable improvement have you made as players?

Stills: Well, there's a particular finger move I've been trying to get for 20 years that only kicked in last year. And about five years ago, David and Graham and I did a tour that was just us with our guitars—no drums or keyboards or anything. There was nothing to hide behind, so you could hear every freaking note that I played. The result was my chops went through the roof. After about six months of it, I had been playing like I was trying to for the previous 15 years.

And, quite frankly, I've had conversations with real masters, players and singers like Tony Bennett. And they tell me there's this whole other level that happens in your fifties. You may lose a certain kind of step, for instance. I can't leap six feet in the air anymore. I can only make about three. But there's a thoughtfulness in knowing your way around the fretboard; it's like a different world. When you put the kind of energy you have now into it, there's a whole different youthfulness. So put me up against any kid band you have. I'll gladly follow them.

GW: The last time CSNY tried to show the kids a thing or two was in 1988, when they recorded *American Dream*, a less than earth-shaking effort that was prompted by Young's promise that he'd do another CSNY record if Crosby cleaned up and kicked his drug habit. But the album simply limped out at the end of that year, with no tour to support it.

"The feeling between us then was not as good as it is today," says Nash. "I don't think we had the commitment. I think we had the commitment from Neil because he promised David—but, unfortunately, it takes more than that to make a great piece of music.

"There are some great songs and great recordings on *American Dream*, and we were very proud of that record. There are also some funky songs, too—songs that maybe should not have been there. But we didn't have the long-range commitment to prepare a great piece of music and go forward with that"

CSNY has been making preparations for the *Looking Forward* tour since November. The repertoire is immense. Young's archive manager, Joel Bernstein, put together a list of 976 songs the four have had anything to do with since the mid sixties, prompting Crosby to ask Young good-naturedly, "So is he getting the lyrics together for all of those?"

The band is slated to include Booker T. and the MGs bassist Donald "Duck" Dunn and longtime colleagues Joe Vitale and Michael Finnigan on drums and keyboards, respectively. A percussionist may also be added to the lineup.

Crosby: We certainly have a couple of hundred songs that we could do. If we get a chance to rehearse for a good length of time, we'll probably have more than we need, and the show will likely change from night to night.

Nash: We want to play every song from the new record. And then we want to play a selection of songs that our fans know and love us for. As long as we can make the older songs musically interesting, and provided they still have meaning, playing our older material should be no problem. For instance, when you think about the two white supremacists in Texas who dragged that black man behind a truck, isn't "Southern Man" still appropriate today?

Young: I think our energy's going to come from delivering new songs. But the past is still valid. We want to sing songs like "Teach Your Children" because every word in it is meaningful and the people out there were moved by what the song said in the first place. So if they want to sing along, that's fantastic, but when we're singing it…we're gonna sing every word like we want our children and grandchildren to know who we are and where we all started from. There's not gonna be any jivin' around. We're gonna be presenting real music when we go out. It's really an opportunity of a lifetime; it's a chance for us to make a connection, and I think we're gonna rise to the occasion.

Crosby: Actually, I'll bet you a considerable sum that we'll play things on this tour that we haven't even written yet.

GW: The obvious question facing the group today is, where does CSNY fit into the current music scene? Some of the groups have kids who are older than members of the Backstreet Boys and 'N Sync—older than Kenny Wayne Shepherd and Jonny Lang for that matter. Can these old kids on the block still matter in the post-classic, post-grunge, perpetually metalicized and hip-hopped landscape of pop music?

Nash: We don't care. We truly do not care.

Crosby: You've got to remember that those people are aimed at a certain part of the population: 13-year-olds. We're aimed at everybody from 15 to 55. And we fill gigantic rooms with those people, and we sell tons of records to those people. So we know they're out there. And we're not in competition with any of that other stuff. We're glad it's out there. The people who enjoy it, God bless you, have fun. But there is an audience for us. There's a huge audience for us.

Stills: One of the more delightful things in my life has been that each of my children, which range from three years old to 31, gets to a certain age—about 11 or 12—when they discover our old records. And sooner or later they say, "Dad! You guys were hot!"

GW: The other question, of course, is how long can they be Crosby, Stills, Nash & Young this time around? There is a lot of optimistic talk about songs that haven't been released, songs that haven't been written yet, unfulfilled potential and unrealized visions. Hell, there's even an album title, *Looking Forward*.

But there's also a track record, a long one, of things falling apart more easily than they stay together. And there are other projects on each musician's plate: Young's *Silver and Gold* album and archival boxed set; a half-finished record by CPR, Crosby's side group; and solo material that Stills and Nash have been working on.

To their credit, the four seem deadly serious about keeping CSNY on track. Wherever they conduct interviews, a piano and guitar sit nearby; during breaks, they make a beeline for them—even Nash in his wheelchair—and tinker until it's time to be grilled again. "Everywhere we go, we're going to have music around," Young explains.

They still like to refer to CSNY as the "mothership" from which all these endeavors spring. But the truth is that the ship has been in the dock far more often than it's been in orbit, and it will be hard to accept anything different until another CSNY album and tour follow in close proximity to *Looking Forward*.

Young: We need the tunes. The new tunes gotta come. We have an occasion and we have an opportunity; we've just got to keep the door open. That's why we have the instruments around. We want to be ready. If somebody writes a song, if we get a couple of songs together, we go back in and cut 'em.

Nash: But it won't be for a record. It'll only be because the tunes exist and we want to get in and record them. I know I've already written three songs since this record was finished. And I know a couple of mine didn't make it to the *Looking Forward* record, and a couple of David's didn't and there's three of Stephen's and two of Neil's—my point being that we want to bring out another record within a year and a half of this one.

Stills: I have three-quarters of a solo album in the can…and when I get enough for a whole album, I'll put it out. In the meantime, every time I come up with a new song and these guys decide they want it, all they have to do is say, "We'll have that."

Crosby: Yeah, the other stuff still goes on. But this is pretty special. I think this takes the cake.

BAND OF BROTHERS

BY GARY GRAFF
The Oakland Press
February 3, 2002

In the two years since the CSNY2K tour ended, much had happened—in the world of CSNY and the world at large. CSN and CPR continued to tour while Young was on the road with "friends and relatives," subsequently released as *Road Rock, Vol. 1*, a live album and DVD that chronicled Young's latest solo phase. Another turn around the wheel for CSNY was uncertain. Then the terrorist attacks occurred in the U.S. on September 11, 2001. In the time following that international tragedy, the process of healing took many shapes and forms. When Neil Young initiated talk of another CSNY tour, his compadres agreed that it was time to get back on the road. Gary Graff spoke with Graham Nash and Neil Young a few days before the group's Tour of America began in Detroit, discussing the motivations, energy and emotions that inspired this coming together.

CSNY Tour of America 2002: Stephen Stills, Graham Nash, Neil Young and David Crosby jam. Photo: Buzz Person.

L ast fall, in the wake of the September 11 terrorist attacks, Neil Young told his occasional sometimes bandmates David Crosby, Stephen Stills and Graham Nash that it was time for them to carry on again. And the other three agreed.

"We got a call from Neil, who was talking about that maybe it's a good time to go out and play some music for the folks," Nash says in recalling the genesis for the latest reunion of the late '60s supergroup, which has only recorded and toured together a handful of times and whose 2000 outing was the group's first in 26 years.

Going out again, Nash says, "seemed to make sense to us. It was a little earlier than we had kind of planned in our lives, but, y'know…so what?"

CSNY kicks off a three-month tour on Wednesday at the Palace of Auburn Hills—where it also began its 2000 reunion tour—and will criss-cross the country for the next three months, wrapping up in late April.

Unlike the 2000 trek—which played for 551,000 fans in 35 cities, gross-ing $42 million in ticket sales to support the 1999 CSNY album, *Looking*

339

Forward—there will be no fresh release to accompany this tour. CSNY taped all of the shows during the 2000 tour and was expected to release a live album from it, but those plans were scuttled. Stills explains that, "There's some real good stuff on [the tapes], but I think we need another [tour] under our belts." However, both Young and Nash will release albums—*Are You Passionate?* and *Songs for Survivors*, respectively—while the group is on the road, though release dates for each have yet to be determined.

Nash says that during rehearsals in Los Angeles and, this week, in Saginaw, the group has worked on several songs from Young's album—including "Let's Roll," which was inspired by the words of Todd Beamer, one of the passengers on United Airlines Flight 93, who attacked terrorists who hijacked the aircraft, reportedly with plans to crash it in Washington, D.C. It should dovetail nicely, he says, with other politically charged and socially conscious pieces in the CSNY canon, including "Daylight Again," "Find the Cost of Freedom" and "Military Madness."

"We're just reflecting on the times, which is what we've always done," explains Nash, 60, who was in Denver on tour with Crosby and Stills on September 11. "I think we've always represented relevance to ourselves. We go through this crazy life and we make comments on it, and we've been doing that all our lives. This time is no different. I think that the shows might bring some solace to people, to see a good rock 'n' roll show."

Young concurs, "It just felt like a good time for CSNY to go out and play. CSNY's been around for a long time. People of our generation, I think, might get some kind of feeling of comfort or something from coming to a show of ours and seeing that we're still here and everybody's still here and we're still doing what we do."

CSNY will be accompanied on the tour by keyboardist Booker T. Jones and bassist Donald "Duck" Dunn—half of the acclaimed R&B ensemble Booker T. and the MGs—and drummer Steve "Smokey" Potts. All three musicians perform on Young's new album, and Nash acknowledges that Young is the man in charge of things these days.

"The man's a genius," Nash says. "We all have our roles to play; it's just that Neil is taking the reins this time, and that's fine with all of us. I'll follow anyone who's right. If you're not right, I go 'Wait a second,' but Neil has been right a tremendous amount of the time. His instincts as a musician are wonderful; as a musician he lives in the moment, and I'm perfectly willing to follow him right into the moment."

Young, however, deflects the mantle of leadership. "I don't run it—I don't want that responsibility!" he says with a laugh. "The reason I play with CSN is because…I don't have to sing every song, because I like playing with them. I like being with guys I've known for 30 years that have gone through so much with me. It's a rewarding experience. It's fun to look around and see those guys."

340

Fans certainly feel the same way—especially if it makes CSNY active on a more regular basis. The quartet formed during 1969, when Young joined former Buffalo Springfield bandmate Stills, ex-Byrd Crosby and ex-Hollies member Nash—who had already released one album as a trio. The quartet's second public performance was at the first Woodstock festival.

But in 33 years CSNY has managed just three studio albums, a live recording and some best-of sets—while still managing to come up with a durable catalog of songs that mixes introspective such as "Our House," "Teach Your Children" and "Suite: Judy Blue Eyes" with protest anthems like "Ohio," "Carry On" and "Almost Cut My Hair." Over the years, the quartet has been hampered by fits of creative and personal pique, ego battles, substance abuse problems and other tribulations.

Now, however, Nash says most of those have given way to a more mature appreciation for what they're able to achieve together. "I think it's just getting a little smarter, getting a little more appreciation of our families and our friends and our bandmates," he says. "And that is great, because there's more energy for performing and less energy for dealing in mindless details, which have always caused problems in the past. We're more than friends; we're brothers. And, unfortunately, brothers fight on occasion. But it's been more than 30 years now, so something's going on, you know?"

Déjà Vu for CSNY

Neil Young leads veteran
supergroup on hard-rocking
tour heading for Bay Area

BY JOEL SELVIN
San Francisco Chronicle
April 2, 2002

By the time the CSNY Tour of America pulled into New York City for two nights at Madison Square Garden, *San Francisco Chronicle* writer Joel Selvin was there. What he observed was a band shifting into a higher gear, not coasting, with Neil Young leading the charge.

CSNY Tour of America 2002: Graham Nash, Stephen Stills, Neil Young, David Crosby. Photo: Buzz Person

C rosby, Stills, Nash & Young made it to Indianapolis before uncorking a show they considered satisfactory. "The first five shows were rehearsals," said Graham Nash. The next stop was Madison Square Garden.

With little fanfare, no new album and a relatively short two-year wait since the four horsemen's previous tour—which came 26 years after the one before that—the quartet cruised into New York in February, almost six months after the world changed forever. Neil Young's hard-rocking take on Flight 93, "Let's Roll," had climbed all the way to the top five, more than a month ahead of the April 9 release of his new solo album, *Are You Passionate?*

According to David Crosby, he, Stephen Stills and Graham Nash make 10 times what they do on their own when they add Young. The entire 40-date tour is sold out, with a $250 top ticket price. Two nights at the Garden will rake in about $4 million. Young supplied the backup band, the road crew, the set list. It's his group.

"This is Crosby, Stills, Nash & Young," said musical director Booker T. Jones. "That's a very large ampersand."

345

But Young is nowhere to be seen as the three others conduct a round of TV, radio and press interviews the afternoon of the first show in adjoining suites at the tony Carlyle Hotel. Young does not do interviews. The others don't mind. They're happy just to make music with him.

"He understands that's what he was put here for," said Crosby, "so he doesn't waste his time doing anything else."

Crosby, 60, is seven years past his liver transplant ("The longest I've heard of is a woman who has 11 years," he said) and exudes the radiant joy of a man whose life has been spared. His wife, Jan, and their 6-year-old son, Django, stop by on their way to see dinosaurs at the American Museum of Natural History, like any other tourists in New York.

Nash, also 60, one of rock's great gentlemen, lives on idyllic Hanalei Bay in Kauai with his wife, Susan. They were joined in New York by their grown son, Will, who flew in from Los Angeles, where he is working as a trainee at a hedge fund.

Stills, 57, on the road with his wife, Kristen, has his studio team doing final mixes on a solo album he's spent 10 years recording. No major labels are in hot pursuit.

Although Crosby, Stills & Nash still qualify as a concert attraction, the only member with a viable solo career is Young.

After a year's worth of starts and stops, Young finally finished recording his new album with Booker T. Jones, his associate from Booker T. and the MGs, bassist Duck Dunn, and another Memphis musician, drummer Steve Potts. Instead of heading off on a solo tour to support the release (which he will do in September), he rounded up the three others and started a full-scale CSNY tour.

A live album and concert DVD will be made at the end of the tour. According to his long-standing manager, Elliot Roberts, Young enjoys being the guitar player in the band, backing up the other fellows, and not having to shoulder the concert's entire load. "And why not be well paid for it?" said Roberts.

September 11 is very much on everyone's minds. Nash has a new song—one of nine new ones the quartet is playing at the shows—called "Half Your Angels," originally written with the Oklahoma City bombing in mind, that he will play that night at the Garden before, undoubtedly, many people who lost loved ones—the angels of the song's title—at the World Trade Center.

At a sound check before the show, the back wall of the arena, immediately behind the stage, was covered with flyers for missing people, pages from the Bible, handwritten notes to the lost. The four musicians tried out an *a cappella* version of "America the Beautiful."

That night, the show opened with Stills singing "Carry On," from the quartet's 1970 debut, followed by Young, somewhat tentative, offering a new song from his forthcoming album, "Goin' Home." The first set ended an hour later with Stills and Young trading guitar solos on "Cinnamon Girl" like knights crossing swords. The second set began with a lengthy acoustic segment filled with audience favorites like Crosby's "Guinnevere," Stills' "Suite: Judy Blue Eyes" and Nash's "Our House."

Nash seated himself behind Young's antique pump organ, a standard part of his stage shows for years, and played some flowing, oozing chords. When the distinct beep-beep-beep of a cell phone was added on top, a shiver ran through the capacity crowd, as Young jumped on the guitar riff that introduced "Let's Roll," his stark, lean portrait of the events on the doomed hijacked flight that crashed in Pennsylvania.

From that point, the show turned, driving toward an emotional finish with Crosby's "Long Time Gone," a song inspired by the Robert F. Kennedy assassination, followed by Joni Mitchell's "Woodstock," the chorus line "got to get back to the garden" taking on multilayered meanings. Young punched the show to a close with a take-no-prisoners accounting of "Rockin' in the Free World," Stills and Young going toe to toe on guitars, as the New York crowd stood and cheered through the song's entire finale.

Backstage in his dimly lit dressing room, after accepting the good wishes of Manhattan first-nighters including Bette Midler, Young waxed ecstatic about the performance.

"It's the Springfield thing," he said, "me and Stephen. That's what people remember from the Springfield. It's an archaeological dig, but we're excavating."

At the next afternoon's sound check, Young and Stills test-drove the Buffalo Springfield 1966 hit "For What It's Worth," using a revamped arrangement borrowed from the CSN songbook ("How old is that song?" said Stills. "Let's just say the continents were closer.") Young dug around, trying to find CSNY's inner Springfield.

Dinnertime backstage is a family scene. Booker T.'s wife, Nan Jones, brought their three kids, out of school on winter break, from Marin County. Ben Young, Neil's disabled 23-year-old son who inspired the annual Bridge School benefits that his wife, Pegi, produces, wheeled into the catering area with another batch of youths. His teenage sister, Amber, reacquainted herself with Booker and Nan's teenage daughter, Olivia; they knew each other from the 1993 tour where Young used Booker T. and the MGs as his backup band. One of the new songs Young performed at the Garden, "You're My Girl," is about his daughter. ("And your daughter, too," he told the crowd.)

Filmmaker Jim Jarmusch, who has worked with Young on several films, including the 1997 concert documentary *Year of the Horse*, joined the dinner table conversation, congratulating Young on the new album. "It's Motown with coloring outside the lines," he said.

"Tonight's the test," Young said. "You've got to be able to put two good ones together."

Four hours later, Young wrung the last, reverb-soaked, echoing note out of his guitar, staggering and careening around the stage as if he didn't know where he was. Nash, who performed barefoot and spent considerable time dodging Young's lurches, draped an American flag over his shoulders and pranced around, hands aloft. Everybody was all smiles onstage. The crowd was chanting "U.S.A....U.S.A....U.S.A."

Clearly, the test had been passed.

LOOKING FORWARD:
DAVID CROSBY MUSES ON POLITICS, LIFE AND MUSIC

BY IAN D'GIFF
Musictoday.com
March 2002

David Crosby, appropriately enough, has the last word in this collection of writings. Ian D'Giff conducted a wonderful interview that was posted on Musictoday.com in March 2002. When Crosby, CSNY's heart and soul, answers D'Giff's final question, it feels like there's nothing left to add. Take it home, Croz.

David Crosby. Photo: Tony Bittick

*D*avid Crosby is one lucky man. Forget about the fact that he's a two-time inductee into the Rock and Roll Hall of Fame (as a founding member of both the Byrds and Crosby, Stills & Nash), David Crosby is just lucky to be alive. Here's a guy who kicked hard drugs while in prison, survived a devastating motorcycle accident, battled the IRS, and lost his home to an earthquake. Then he goes and gets a life-saving liver transplant and twice becomes a father within the span of a year. A musical revolutionary of the highest caliber, Crosby is currently on the road with the same band that turned in what many consider the definitive performance of the original Woodstock Festival, Crosby, Stills, Nash & Young. Crosby recently took a break from the supergroup's busy "Tour of America" to speak about his life, his loves, the state of the Union, the state of the band, and just how lucky he truly is.

Tell us a little bit about the "Tour of America" and its relationship to September 11th.

Well, you know, we wanted to tour anyway, but Neil felt, and I think he may be right, that people really wanted to see us. My personal feeling is that when people go through something really, really awful like that, there's a period of shock. The country went into shock for a little while, just because we really couldn't accept that much pain all at one time. Then there's a period of mourning, when you really do accept what the loss was and how bad it was. Then there's a period when people really want to hold out their hands to each other and feel unity within their community and family and country with their peers. We have always felt that music is a healing thing. I'm sure that it is, and there is no question that it helps unity happen. We all felt that we had entered that time and this would be a positive force. And, you know, that's who we are and what we do.

Let's dive a bit deeper into the concept of music as a healing agent.

I don't think there's any question that it is. I'd be hard pressed to tell you how, but I don't think there's any question that it does help human beings feel better. That "each man is an island" thing is true, but music is a bridge and it bridges that gap wonderfully well and it allows us to reach out to each other. I think that's a tremendous healing force. If you face tough times alone, it's completely different than if you face tough times with the support and love of people around you.

Speaking for my generation, I'm thirty now, we've never lived through anything like this before and there seems to be this overwhelming vibe of uncertainty with regards to the future. I think many of us are looking at you guys, as representatives of the original Woodstock generation, for guidance and reassurance that we can pull through this and things will, in fact, get better.

Well, if that's the case, I'd be proud to accept the job. There is ongoingness; there is a future; and there is, usually almost always, a way to make things better. We believe that. Now maybe our optimism is a little naïve, I don't know. To me it fits; it fits the world and it fits me. I think that our belief in our country and our belief in our principles are valid. I think that we're a great country of great people and I believe in us. I think that, yes, this kind of event where terrorists killed thousands of people in one shot is a real body blow—this really hurt us. I think if you hadn't been through a war, if you hadn't been through any tough times, it would smack you in the face. I think it did that to all of the people under thirty in this country. I would put it to you this way: I think we've been living in a kind of idyllic bubble. "This is America, this doesn't happen here." Well, the truth is, we've kind of joined the rest of the world. Now we know what it's like to be an Israeli—you go to the market everyday and some days you don't make it.

Neil Young and David Crosby. Chicago. February 17, 2002. Photo: Tony Bittick

Neil Young: when he enters the fold of CSN, something incredibly special happens. Can you verbalize it?

It's like putting nitroglycerin in the mix. [laughs] Neil is like an elemental force. Neil is like asking the tide to join your band or, more aptly, asking a hurricane to join your band. He's an immense and turbulent elemental force. He's a brilliant songwriter and a brilliant guitar player and a great singer; he's just an amazing man and he's very committed to making the best music he can make. He's a very exacting taskmaster; he really, really works at it hard. So, when you put two guitar players of the quality of him and Stephen Stills up next to each other, you're going to get explosions, there is no way around it. It's like putting fire and gasoline in the same container— it's gonna go off.

353

I read that during the *Looking Forward* sessions, it was Neil who really simplified things a bit by getting the four of you stand around and perform on one mic.

Well, that's something that we had done back in our early days a lot, and he encouraged us to do it again. Just as he's demanding, he's also supportive. He's a tremendously gifted guy, in terms of what music is doing in a room, and his analysis of things is usually very, very, very clear and very insightful. I like working with him. I love working with Crosby, Stills & Nash—just the three of us—too; it's a completely different band.

Let's talk about the relationship between musicians and sociopolitical activism. Do you feel that there is an inherent responsibility to address certain issues and situations through song?

Our job is primarily to entertain you, to help you feel things, to crystallize feelings for you, and also to just make you boogie. I think other parts of our job are as the troubadour—the teller of tales from far away places so you're aware of things that you might not have been—and also as the town crier: "It's eleven-thirty and all's well," or, "It's twelve-fifteen and it's not so damn good." "Something is lurking over here that doesn't make any sense, somebody shine some light on this." I think we do all those jobs and I think we're doing them pretty well. I think part of our job is to reflect our times and to reflect the people that we come from and show them to the rest of the world and to ourselves. Hopefully, we can do that in a way that is insightful enough that it's inspiring.

Has your perspective on social and political situations changed since you first began your career as a recording artist?

Very little. I'm still pretty much of a rebel. I think that most of the causes that we espoused when we started were absolutely right on. Human rights, civil rights—we weren't wrong. All people are created equal and everybody has a right to freedom and the pursuit of happiness. The stuff in the Constitution, the Declaration of Independence, and the Bill of Rights is all correct. We believed in that from the get-go. I think we were right that war is a bunch of crap. You know, peace is better than war, there's no question. There are times when you have to defend yourself, yes, and we're in one of those. I think basically, our value systems are the same. God, you know, politics are involved with everything, and it's at a state right now that where it's been very degraded. The win that we just got on campaign finance reform could make a real difference, although the five thousand or so people that control most of the money in the world are already working on ways around it. But I think it was a tremendous win, though I think that as long as the government is for sale, it won't be answerable to the people that elect the officials. I think we have to work towards a more honest government. It's supposed to be a representative democracy. The idea was to have an informed electorate and a representative democracy and not "the guy with the most money and the cleverest TV ads gets the keys to the kingdom." That's not what they had in mind. I think we continue to be politically active, though we don't all agree with each other about things. I'm a liberal about most things, but I personally think we should abolish the welfare system; it stinks. I think if you pay people not to work, you make bad people. I'm sure I'll piss off a lot of people with that, but that's what I believe. But on the other hand, I don't think that we should be giving corporations these huge breaks and making us pay for it. I am particularly enraged by Enron. This blatant "Yeah, we stole hundreds of millions of dollars, and we're keeping it and to hell with you; we're going to stonewall you."

The concept of freak-flag flying: is yours still out there?

Yeah, mine's still flying. I still consider myself outside the mainstream of normal American Squaresville, but that's OK. The strength of this country is that it allows us to have all kinds of different belief systems and different races and religions and ways of living our lives. That's our strength; that's what this is all about. I think it's great that I can live here and be an American and be a staunchly believing Constitutionalist American and have hair down to my shoulders and be a hippie. I think that's good.

After your liver transplant, in 1995 you had a personal rebirth of sorts. Within the course of that year, your wife Jan gave birth to your son Django and you reunited with James Raymond, your biological son who had been placed up for adoption in the early sixties.

Hell of a year, whoo-hoo!

We're talking about a real turnaround here, because the decade or so leading up to then was not so great for you.

Not so great for me. Well, actually, the decade leading up until then I was doing pretty well, because by the time I had the transplant, I was nine years sober. But in terms of misfortunes…my accountant not paying my taxes and telling me that he had and having them come and try to take my house…I had a motorcycle wreck.

And then the earthquake in 1994.

You know, the earthquake knocks the house down, so we call the IRS and say, "OK, you can have it. Ugh." But, the truth is, that which doesn't kill you, makes you stronger, and I'm immensely lucky, man. I'm so fortunate, I can't even start to tell you. I was supposed to be dead seven years ago. I was not even supposed to live long enough to see Django get born. And here I am and I'm getting to do what I love most in the world and Django is in the other room, laughing it up.

He's on tour with you?

Yeah! So, you know, I'm a big ole puddle of gratitude at this point.

Your sobriety must have a lot to do with your realization and understanding of how lucky you are.

After the encores: (left to right) Graham Nash, Stephen Stills, Neil Young, Steve Potts, Donald "Duck" Dunn, David Crosby and Booker T. Jones. San Jose, California. April 5, 2002. Photo: Buzz Person

It certainly did, particularly at first. You know, I was addicted to hard drugs. That's different than just smoking a little pot or something. It's really destructive and it really had me in a very, very bad pocket. I'm very grateful to be free of that. It gave me the chance to get my life started over again. Now, it's not a big concern of mine. Now, my life is focused on all kinds of different stuff—being a good parent, being a good musician, being a good sailor, and being a good pilot. I learned how to fly about six years ago. I'm flying a little twin around. That's the stuff that I do and I'm not wasting a damn minute.

It's wonderful that guys like yourself and Phil Lesh, who also received a successful liver transplant, are so thankful.

Well, you know, everybody reacts to it differently. I can think of one well-known person who got a liver transplant and said, "Oh, man, I got a new one. Now I can go back to drinking," and went right out and did. And it did us all a lot of harm. But I think most people, like Phil and myself, that get a chance, man, we take it and really run with it. Phil hasn't stopped playing for more than about twenty minutes since his. He's just working his butt off and making fantastic music. I admire him immensely for it.

With regard to Phil, let's talk about your 1971 solo effort, *If I Could Only Remember My Name*. You recorded that album with a loose assemblage of San Francisco Bay Area musicians that became known as the "Planet Earth Rock & Roll Orchestra," including members of the Dead, Jefferson Airplane, CSN, and others.

Well, actually, [Paul] Kantner started calling it that after awhile. It was really just an extension of the sessions that produced that solo album. We just stayed in there because we were having a lot of fun. [Jerry] Garcia, myself, and Phil were there almost every night. Garcia was there every night and [Graham] Nash a lot of the nights, and we just were having fun. We'd come up with a song and mess with it. There were no rules and we liked that. [Laughs] It appealed, particularly, to Garcia and me. We loved screwing around.

Just to think about everyone involved with those sessions—Joni Mitchell, Neil Young, Grace Slick, Jack Casady, Jorma Kaukonen—it seems that every one of them is in the Rock and Roll Hall of Fame or will be.

[Laughs] I guess I really don't take the Hall of Fame that seriously. It was just a bunch of really good people. Good folks, really fine people and fine players. And the other guys, [Billy] Kruetzmann and Mickey [Hart], both played drums on it. They were wonderful to me, everyone was.

Tell us about your son James and CPR, the band you play in with him. Let's start when you first met in '95.

Well, he was kind of like a lightning bolt hitting my life. I knew that there was a kid out there, but they don't let you track from the parent down, only from the kid up—then, only if the file has been opened; but his mom had opened it. When he went to look and see who his birth parents were and saw my name on there...he had been a musician for twenty years already, without knowing who I was. So it was a shock to him, and when I heard him play, it was a shock to me! He's brilliant. He's a better musician than I'll ever be. He's an astounding musician and he and I gel very well. We write really good songs together. He's a wonderful cat, too, man. He's an immensely sensitive and intelligent guy. He's more grown up than I am. He's more like my little brother than he is my son, because we both have six-year-old kids and we're raising them at an arms length away from each other. It's been good and hopefully it's only getting better.

Let's bring it back to CSNY. Any future plans after the tour?

You got me, chief. I'm so concerned with doing well right now, that I don't try to figure out what's going to come down the road. And, of course, a lot of it is largely up to Neil. CSNY is largely up to Neil. Neil, in popular terms, in terms of his draw, is bigger by himself than the three of us are. And we know that. But, CSNY is bigger than either, and he knows that. You know, he'll do it, only when he wants to do it. He really only does what he wants to do, and you can't make Neil do anything he doesn't want to. I'm pretty much the same way [laughs]. Because it's music, man, and you have to want to do it well. If you just want to do a mediocre level and crank out your hits exactly like the record, anybody can do that. But, if you want to go for peaks and moments where you electrify people—which is what we're after—you got to want to. It'll happen again, if we all want it to. If it's very good this time, I think it'll happen again.

Your ever evolving relationship with Graham [Nash] and Stephen [Stills]: How does it stand today?

It's working wonderfully. I can't tell you how grateful I am for it. It's a great relationship. Nash is certainly the best male friend I've ever had in my life—my wife being my best female friend. It couldn't be better. Stephen has been absolutely wonderful and working his butt off to do the very best he can. I think all of us are bringing that to this.

One last thing. What is the cost of freedom, and do you think we're ever going to find it?

Yes. I think we know what the cost of freedom is. It's commitment, sacrifice, and hard work. Sometimes, the tree of liberty has to get watered with the blood of patriots. That, I think, is Alexander Hamilton's line, but it's absolutely the truth. I think that freedom doesn't come for free. It requires the hard work and dedication and sacrifice of the people who want to earn it. Freedom has to be earned and it takes courage and it takes work and it takes the willingness to keep working at it. I think, overall in America, we're doing the very best we can. We definitely have some problems, in terms of the government being up for sale—and we need to work on that—but I think we're doing pretty well.

ACKNOWLEDGMENTS

This book would not exist without the writers of the pieces in these pages. I thank each of them with the utmost sincerity and respect: Roy Carr, Lowell Cauffiel, Chuck Crisafulli, David Crosby, Cameron Crowe, Bill DeYoung, Ian D'Giff, Ben Fong-Torres, Todd Gold, Gary Graff, Dennis Hunt, Lenny Kaye, Peter Knobler, Allan McDougall, Parke Puterbaugh, Steve Rush, Ellen Sander, Joel Selvin, Jaan Uhelszki, Penny Valentine, Vicki Wickham and Ritchie Yorke.

Heartfelt thanks to David Crosby, Stephen Stills, Graham Nash and Neil Young for coming together to form CSNY and for sharing your artistry. You've affected the course and quality of my life and countless others in so many special ways. I sincerely hope that the writings in this book bring back good memories and remind you of the impact CSNY has had and continues to have on countless people around the world.

Personal thanks to my dear friend Henry Diltz, who generously allowed me to use so many of his classic, definitive photographs of the CSNY gang—some of which also appear in *Crosby, Stills & Nash: The Biography*. The full scope of Henry's photography talent can be explored at his web site, www.henrysgallery.com.

Special thanks, also, to the other photographers whose excellent images are featured: Roger Barone, Joel Bernstein, Tony Bittick, John Gavrilis, Bruce Hock, Dave Patrick and Buzz Person. All of the photographs included add a fifth dimension to the words in this book.

Deep thanks to Scott Oxman, for generously opening up his CSNY Archives as this book got rolling in earnest, and Paul Higham, with whom I shared this project early on. Paul was an invaluable source and sounding board, tracking down hard-to-find articles from the U.K. and the writers who wrote them.

A small army of friends have been there all along the CSNY trail that has wound through the years. Personal thanks to: Ric Boyd, for introducing me to the music of Stephen Stills in 1972; Tom Lachmar, for patiently teaching me all of those Neil Young songs on acoustic guitar; Tom Stientsra, for reminding me about the importance of following your dreams and that the spirit of *Lonesome Dove* still rings true today; Tod Bottari, for helping me take the ball over the fence and for launching the words; Richard Leimbach, for deepening my love of wooden music and Martin guitars; Debbie Lauriano, for giving me an early appreciation of David Crosby and playing "Triad" so beautifully; John Einarson, for being a loyal colleague and for writing such great books on Buffalo Springfield and Neil's Canadian years; Dan Doyle, for enduring friendship and that front room on Rimpau when I really needed it; Ken Weiss, for always returning my calls, answering my e-mails and being there with the right stuff; Crazy Horse (Frank "Poncho" Sampedro, Billy Talbot and Ralph Molina), for reminding me about the power of being real; and, finally, Cameron Crowe, an ongoing creative inspiration and a guiding light to the heart of my favorite approach to music journalism. A line from Cameron's autobiographical film, *Almost Famous*, says it all: "I will quote you warmly and accurately."

Sincere thanks to: Jimmy McDonough, who may not be a fan of CSNY, but who introduced me to Da Capo Press, the publishing home for my CSN and CSNY projects; Pete Long, for his ongoing musical and archival support and his excellent book, *Ghosts On the Road*, an indispensable guide to all of Neil Young's live performances; Francesco Lucarelli and friends, for their music-driven spirit and *CSN and Sometimes Y* books; Johnny Rogan for his enlightening books on CSNY and Young; and Scott Sandie, for reviving *Broken Arrow* magazine and keeping the NYAS (Neil Young Appreciation Society) alive.

Sincere thanks, also, to the keepers of the CSNY flame on the Web and beyond, particularly: the Lee Shore (Dean "Doc" Dunn, Mick Anderson and everyone who belongs to this resilient online tribe); Dolf van Stijgeren's dynamic www.4waysite.com; Lorraine Kaczorowski and Ramiro Agredo's www.suitelorraine.com; and the official CSN site, www.crosbystillsnash .com, kept fresh and alive by producer/engineer Stephen Barncard, who also makes www.crosbycpr.com rock.

Major thanks to Jann Wenner for kind permission to reprint the classic pieces originally published in *Rolling Stone* and for trusting in my understanding of the special place that these works hold in the history of rock journalism and this band. Special thanks also: to Elizabeth Gorzelany at *Rolling Stone* for her help along the way and to David Crosby for a personal assist at the eleventh hour; to Joel Selvin and Judy Canter at the *San Francisco Chronicle* for kind permissions and sincere support of the project; to Cameron Crowe, Ben Fong-Torres, Ellen Sander, Roy Carr, Parke Puterbaugh, Jaan Uhelszki and Vicki Wickham for generous personal permissions; and to

Dennis Erokan, for creating *BAM: The California Music Magazine* (www
.bamforever.com) and for giving me my first rock writing home—where I
was lucky to work and grow with him and my other friends at the magazine,
Chuck Stanley, Blair Jackson, Regan McMahon, Steve Gellman, Joe Amadeo
and Miles Hurwitz.

The Da Capo Press team continues to be solidly behind my every move.
Special thanks to my friend and editor, Ben Schafer, who believed in this
project from the beginning and helped guide it home. Thanks also to Da
Capo's Kevin Hanover, Lissa Warren, Alex Van Buren and John
Radziewicz.

Loving thanks to my mother Jane for her lifelong support and for the
collector's gene that I inherited from her, and to my father Edgar for his
understanding and generosity. My heartfelt thanks and love always to my
wife Claudia and my son Casey. They deserve special awards for putting up
with my crankiness and stacks of papers/articles/photos during the final
phase of this project. I'm so happy that I'm your Yosemite Man and you're
my Jersey Girl, Claudia. And Casey, keep on learning and growing, buddy.
As David Crosby sings in the final measures of "Wooden Ships," "…set a
course and go."

—Dave Zimmer

CREDITS

Excerpt from *Trips: Rock Life in the Sixties* by Ellen Sander. New York: Charles Scribner's Sons. Copyright ©1973 Ellen Sander. Reprinted by permission of the author.

"Crosby, Stills, Nash, Young, Taylor and Reeves" by Ben Fong-Torres. From *Rolling Stone*, December 27, 1969. ©1969 Rolling Stone LLC. All rights reserved. Reprinted by permission.

"Crosby, Stills, Nash & Young: Flying Freely" by Lenny Kaye. From *Circus*, March 1970.

"David Crosby: The *Rolling Stone* Interview" by Ben Fong-Torres. From *Rolling Stone*, July 23, 1970. ©1970 Rolling Stone LLC. All rights reserved. Reprinted by permission.

"Graham Nash: 'We May Fight, But the Music Wins'" by Vicki Wickham. From *Melody Maker*, June 1970. Reprinted by permission of the author.

"At Home with Steve Stills" by Ritchie Yorke. From *Hit Parader*, August 1971.

"The *Sounds* Talk-In: Stephen Stills and Neil Young" by Allan McDougall and Penny Valentine. From *Sounds*, November 21, 1970.

"Will CSNY Ever Re-Unite and Find True Happiness?: This Is David Geffen, by Gentleman's Agreement, Manager to the Superstars" by Roy Carr. From *New Musical Express*, July 29, 1972. Reprinted by permission of Roy Carr and *New Musical Express* (IPC Media Ltd. An AOL Time-Warner Company).

"Crosby, Stills, Nash & Young Carry On" by Cameron Crowe. From *Crawdaddy*, October 1974. Reprinted by permission of the author.

"Crosby, Stills, Nash, Young and Bert" by Roy Carr. From *New Musical Express*, August 31, 1974. Reprinted by permission of Roy Carr and *New Musical Express* (IPC Media Ltd. An AOL Time-Warner Company).

"Crosby Plays His Heart" by Joel Selvin. From the *San Francisco Chronicle*, August 29, 1997. Reprinted by permission of the *San Francisco Chronicle*.

"Talk Talk: Graham Nash" by Bill DeYoung. From *Goldmine*, June 19, 1998. Reprinted by permission of the author.

"CSNY: Déjà Vu All Over Again" by Joel Selvin. From the *San Francisco Chronicle*, October 9, 1999. Reprinted by permission of the *San Francisco Chronicle*.

"Four Play: Crosby, Stills, Nash & Young" by Gary Graff. From *Guitar World*, February 2000. Reprinted by permission of the author.

"Band of Brothers" by Gary Graff. From *The Oakland Press*, February 3, 2002. Reprinted by permission of the author.

"Déjà Vu for CSNY: Neil Young leads veteran supergroup on hard-rocking tour heading for Bay Area" by Joel Selvin. From the *San Francisco Chronicle*, April 2, 2002. Reprinted by permission of the *San Francisco Chronicle*.

"Looking Forward: David Crosby Muses on Politics, Life and Music" by Ian D'Giff. From Musictoday.com, March 2002. Reprinted by permission of the author.

INDEX

Italicized page numbers indicate photographs.

ABOUT THE EDITOR

Dave Zimmer has been closely following the musical careers of David Crosby, Stephen Stills, Graham Nash and Neil Young—collectively and individually—since 1972. During his freshman year at the University of California, Davis, a friend first introduced him to the music of Stephen Stills. Dave was moved deeply by Stills' combination of sensitivity and strength that was conveyed in the songs on his first two solo albums and *Manassas*. Stills opened a door that led Dave into the world of CSNY. The group's 1971 live album, *4 Way Street*, was in constant rotation on the turntable in his room back home in Palo Alto over the summer of '72, followed closely by CSNY's *Déjà Vu*, the first CSN album, and solo albums by Stills, Crosby, Nash and Young. CSNY's music and lyrics, according to Dave, provided a kind of road map toward a state of greater self-awareness and also helped him find his own voice as a writer.

The first time Dave saw Crosby, Stills, Nash & Young together on stage was at the Oakland Coliseum in 1974. Afterwards, he was moved to scrawl out the beginnings of a song/poem: "Four men walk beside me/I know them not all/I listen to their music/Try to understand their call." He never added to those words, but Dave would eventually get to know and gain a greater understanding of each of the artists and their music after he became a journalist in the late 1970s. Inspired most powerfully by the rock writings of Cameron Crowe and Ben Fong-Torres, Dave found his calling as a chronicler of people's lives. In the early 1980s, he spent a lot of time delving into the lives of David Crosby, Stephen Stills and Graham Nash and wrote a book, *Crosby, Stills & Nash: The Authorized Biography* (first published by St. Martin's Press in 1984, with an updated edition published by Da Capo Press in 2000), featuring more than 275 photographs by Henry Diltz—whose stunning images also grace a number of the pages in this book.

Dave Zimmer and Stephen Stills at Graham Nash's 40th birthday party (white whisker and sideburn "aging powder" courtesy of Susan Nash). The Continental Club. Hollywood, California. February 1982. Photo: Henry Diltz

Dave was as an editor at *BAM: The California Music Magazine* from 1979 to 1990, not only penning cover stories on Crosby, Stills & Nash, Stephen Stills, Graham Nash and Neil Young, but also Tom Petty, Jefferson Starship, Chrissie Hynde, Randy Newman, Robbie Robertson, Todd Rundgren, Tom Waits and many other artists. Since that time, he has worked primarily as a writer and corporate communications executive in the entertainment industry—most extensively for MCA and Universal Studios.

Dave currently lives with his wife and son in West Orange, New Jersey.